Undergraduate Education

Goals and Means

Rudolph H. Weingartner

AMERICAN COUNCIL
ON EDUCATION
Series on Higher Education
ORYX PRESS
1993

In memory of Joseph Katz
a friend for almost four decades
his influence is unmistakable

Copyright © 1992 by American Council on Education/Macmillan Publishing Company

Copyright © 1993 by American Council on Education and The Oryx Press

Published by The Oryx Press
4041 North Central at Indian School Road
Phoenix, AZ 85012-3397

Printed in the United States of America

Library of Congress Cataloging in Publication Data
Weingartner, Rudolph H. (Rudolph Herbert)
    Undergraduate education: goals and means / Rudolph H. Weingartner.
    p. cm.—(American Council on Education/Oryx series on higher education)
    Includes bibliographical references and index.
    ISBN 0-89774-807-7
    1. Education, Higher—United States—Aims and objectives.
I. Title.   II. Series.
LA227.4.W45   1993
378'.01'0973—dc20   92-42399
                                                         CIP

CONTENTS

iii

PREFACE

My professional life has been spent teaching philosophy at colleges and universities and in service as an academic administrator. This book about undergraduate education is the product of both aspects of this background. From the pursuit of philosophy, it derives the reflective attitude that doesn't let one just *do* something but insists on one's thinking and commenting about it. From administrative experience, it draws the need to be practical, together with a certain impatience with any general principles that cannot be linked to activities that make a difference in the real world.

Although the last few years have seen the publication of several significant books on undergraduate education in America, this one differs from all of them. Both culture and literacy are important topics here, among other themes, but not cultural literacy as such, the subject to which E. D. Hirsch's [1988] volume of that title is devoted. Moreover, while the focus in *Undergraduate Education* is always on higher—postsecondary—education, Hirsch is concerned with education much more broadly, and *primarily* with schooling that comes before college.

The focus is not so clearly understood in a slim book that also takes as its starting point what people, nowadays, don't know: *50 Hours*, by Lynne V. Cheney, the chair of the National Endowment for the Humanities [1989]. That book's aim is to combat this ignorance by putting forward, quite specifically and with startling brevity, what should be known by all—a kind of catechism—and it supplements its recommendations with information about what is taught in a selection of American institutions.

Ernest Boyer's *College* [1987], by contrast, paints on a very broad canvas. It is rich in historical and empirical detail; specific episodes or practices at ninety-seven different U.S. colleges and universities are referred to in its text. Every facet of the institution of college is touched on; suggestions and recommendations abound, from those concerning admissions practices to others about job placement for graduates. Although *Undergraduate Education* takes a lesser risk of losing its vision of the forest among the trees, it, like Boyer's work, aims at educational reform and emphatically shares the conviction that our huge educational establishment exists for the betterment of American students.

Not so, really, for Allan Bloom. Our students are as much the target of his critique as of his solicitude. To be sure, in *The Closing of the American Mind* [1987], his larger target is all of modern American civilization, of which those students are the product. As cultural critic, Bloom thus joins two other best-selling twentieth-century prophets of doom, Spengler and Solzhenitsyn. The astonishing sales of their books undoubtedly speak to a widespread need to regret and perhaps even repent—feelings much better expressed in the ritual of buying a book than in the labor of reading it. In any case, reading Bloom would be of small avail for those intent on improving higher education in this country, since neither map nor vehicle is provided for the road that goes from here back to the good old days.

Parts of *Undergraduate Education* resemble most the curricular component of the Association of American Colleges report, *Integrity in the College Curriculum* [1985], in that both set out central curricular goals and share such leading theses as the need for faculties to take corporate responsibility for the education of their students. Unlike that report, however, the book now before you is not rooted in the diagnosis of an educational ailment; it is distinguished from the AAC's, from Bloom's, and from others' in that it bashes neither our institutions of higher education nor our students. However, its expositions do not by any means assume that all is well. Their analytic–hortatory form takes for granted that there often is a wide gap between what is advocated and what is actually the case—that there is much to change and improve.

Indeed, these discussions rest on the belief that it is immensely difficult to do well at the job of undergraduate education, both in getting clear about what goals to pursue and in identifying and enacting suitable means to attain them. They take cognizance, as well, of the manifest truth that success or failure in this complex undertaking depends on decisions made and actions taken in individual colleges and universities—and by each student going through those years of undergraduate education. So that my discussion might guide the thinking about these educational issues, much attention is paid to the *reasons* one might give for proceeding in a certain way, and efforts are made to determine what is *central* to recommended practices. But the price of clarity along these abstract lines is the absence of the kind of detail and example that would inevitably interrupt the exposition of a policy's rationale. This somewhat ahistorical expository strategy is not meant to imply, however, that different proposals here put forward may not already have been acted on, to a greater or lesser degree, at various institutions around the country. I beg such models to forgive this nonempirical lack of acknowledgement in the interest of readability and succinctness.

Undergraduate Education, like most other books, puts forward what its author believes to be true. It would, therefore, please me very much if some of its readers were persuaded of a few of my ideas and, even more, if they set about carrying them out. Yet this volume has a loftier goal still. It is my hope that these pages will contribute to better thinking about undergraduate education and to more fruitful discussions about matters of curriculum and teaching, whatever conclusions might then be reached. I would be immensely gratified if this book helped readers to become clearer about their own goals for undergraduate education and more self-conscious about the fact that practices of every kind must be chosen and measured by the ends they are intended to bring about.

"Property is theft," Proudhon declared, because all of one's possessions are significantly the product of the work of others. While I believe that some of the views expressed in this book originated in my own mind—including those that were at the same time also created in other minds—I know too that I derived many of the thoughts I now hold from others, without remembering whence they came. To all of these authors I am indebted, as well as, I suppose, to the *Zeitgeist*. While I can thus acknowledge by name only the writers whose works are cited in the book, all contributors deserve my gratitude.

It is far simpler, thankfully, to express my indebtedness to those who have more directly assisted my efforts to bring out this book—all of them helpers who share no responsibility for its faults and errors. My colleagues at Northwestern—in the dean's office, the faculty, and the administration—gave me much opportunity and stimulus to think about the issues here taken up. Two institutions deserve my thanks for the year off that enabled me to write a large portion of this book. Originally awarded by Northwestern University at the conclusion of a long term as dean, the University of Pittsburgh agreed to grant that leave when I stepped down after a short period as provost there.

I am particularly grateful to Robert Dunkelman in the University of Pittsburgh provost's office for facilitating my transition to faculty status in numerous ways, and to my colleagues in the University of Pittsburgh Department of Philosophy for their friendly and supportive reception. The fact that from the sidelines my son Mark and daughter Eleanor cheered my move back from administrator to faculty helped a lot.

More specific assistance came from Peter Machamer, University of Pittsburgh, who made available to me his extensive collection of material on science education. Lawrence Lipking, Northwestern University, read an earlier version of the chapter on the humanities and made very helpful suggestions. Joseph Johnston, Jr., Association of American Colleges, Kenneth Seeskin, Northwestern University, and Nicholas Rescher, University of Pittsburgh, read all or most of the book in earlier drafts and offered not only useful suggestions but welcome encouragement.

The help of Anne Gates was invaluable. She took off much time from completing her dissertation in higher education to give me the benefit of her bibliographical knowledge and cheerful willingness to pursue the hunt for needed information and material. I am thankful for her help and for Marie Gardner's, who wielded PC and laser printer with much skill to provide me with a hard copy of numerous drafts of chapters, in the course of writing and rewriting.

My wife Fannia applied her editorial expertise to every line of the final version and deserves much credit for improvements in economy and clarity of formulation. Where infelicities remain, I am likely to have stubbornly rejected her advice. Yet vastly more important—for this book and the experience that made it possible—are the many years of her support and companionship.

CHAPTER 1

PRELIMINARIES

BEGINNING WITH GOALS

Since the days of Plato and Protagoras, someone has always written about and prescribed how the young should be educated. But for more than a decade now the topic of undergraduate education has received particularly lively attention, certainly in America. There is no single reason for that. Some have become unhappy with the status quo; some feel that the difficulty of the task has escalated intellectually, institutionally, and economically; and some speak out of a heightened belief in the social importance of the cluster of issues belonging to the topic of undergraduate education.

These discussions have not been without their effect; they have stimulated or influenced pedagogic reform on campuses throughout the land. Complacency has been reduced in the world of undergraduate education, though much groping certainly remains. The variety of that literature is great. Some pieces preach on single issues, either complaining, proposing, or both; others are concerned with broad aspects of general education; others still deal with many different specialized areas. Numerous books and papers are reports about sectors of the educational arena, though usually they also draw or imply normative conclusions. Others explicitly hold out standards to be met and goals to be achieved.

Educators who attend with care and concern to these exhortations might be compared with health-conscious citizens who keep abreast of the latest reports and advice on food and exercise: what to partake, what to shun. Most pieces, as they come out, strike one as sensible, grounded in research and reflection. Nevertheless, it turns out to be impossible to shape a coherent life from their totality. Worse, decisions in education, unlike those made about what to eat or how long to jog, are made by institutions, by groups of individuals, thus augmenting the difficulty of weighing the significance of different proposals and alternatives.

If the aim is to improve baccalaureate education, one must try to keep the entire mission in front of oneself and make particular decisions with an awareness of the larger context. This book aims to help retain clarity about what undergraduate education seeks to accomplish. Its focus is the student: what is undergraduate education attempting to do for him and her? In what

1

way should those four years (more or less) transform the person who devotes much time, effort, and money to that venture?

Four years, more or less, because the principal subject of this book is the education that leads to a baccalaureate degree, together with the institutional setting in which this complex enterprise takes place. Yet it is important to recognize that a larger number of undergraduates are enrolled in community and junior colleges, with many aiming to complete a two-year postsecondary program, and others planning to continue with subsequent work toward the bachelor's degree. The numerous and complex educational issues that are specific to these two-year programs and their institutions will not be taken up in this book; nevertheless, many of its discussions are to varying degrees relevant to the educational tasks of community colleges.

There are, in any case, immense individual and institutional differences, but there is merit in beginning by ignoring just about all of them. Much tends to be made of a distinction between general and specialized education, but its formulation is usually confined to the college catalogue. What that document says about the pedagogical career of students, however, characterizes that reality only in the way advertising prose is related to the product. If, then, this *de jure* view of undergraduate education is supplemented by attention to what happens *de facto*, general education may simply amount to the sum total of whatever the student did not specialize in—including retrospective conferrals of that title, since the choice to specialize may come quite late in a college career.

Further, when looking at the goals of undergraduate education, there is merit in not distinguishing, from the start, between liberal education and undergraduate professional education.[1] Except for extremists, no undergraduate educators in the professions object to having their students be familiar with literature, with American history, not to mention having them know how to write; except for fanatics, liberal educators do not object to having their students obtain jobs upon graduation by virtue of the fact that they learned something useful as undergraduates. The issue is less ideology (although that enters in) than a belief as to what limitations of time and energy make possible.

---

1. While simplicity requires the use of the expression "undergraduate professional education," I want to register my discomfort with it. Some undergraduate programs bearing that title certainly prepare students (other things being equal) for certain specialized jobs. Engineering schools tend to do that (though seldom within the statutory four years); schools of nursing and library science are further examples. For other undergraduate degree programs with professional labels—such as in music or journalism—correlation of degree and specialized job is the exception rather than the norm, and for a variety of reasons. But in *all* areas, the professional character of the position normally attainable after a baccalaureate education is much attenuated; not only must time pass, but more education is required, before the student becomes a *real* engineer or a *real* accountant. In more than one sense, then, these undergraduate programs are in effect *pre*professional education. But because just about all education is that to some degree, the use of this label is confusing in other ways.

But educational institutions differ, often markedly, in what they stress and ignore, sometimes as a matter of unexamined course and often as the outcome of extensive faculty debates. Much of such curricular discussion might be called atomistic, in that it focuses on a single need, perhaps recently perceived, and takes place within a framework in which educational ends not at that moment under consideration are ignored or, at best, taken for granted. Enthusiasms (or politics, real or academic) easily blind one to the complex interrelationships among educational goals. The way in which such debates are framed often prevents the disputants from thinking imaginatively about a diversity of pedagogic means that might bring about the desired ends. An account of a large range of goals, accordingly, can serve as a context that helps to convert pedagogic decisions more self-consciously into choices.

And so as to remain focused on a variety of goals and stay open to a multiplicity of pedagogical means, there will here be little talk of requirements, since, in two ways, such discourse has a tendency to be reductive. First, requirements are too often thought of as courses, with debates raging as to whether some course should or should not be required. It is difficult in such discussions not to confuse means and ends, and thus to consider the course in question to *be* the educational goal. Yet, if one's goal is to have students learn to think critically, say, or be capable of thinking about values, it should be a second, serious question as to ways in which such goals might be brought about and what role a course in critical thinking or in values might play. Only *after* such reflections is a question about requirements properly raised.

A second trap embedded in the language of requirements is the temptation to substitute part for whole. We require what we believe students *need*, what they cannot do without; fulfilling requirements, however, soon becomes the whole of education. Faculties typically require students to take a certain set of courses (either specifically denoted or permitting some choices); these constitute "general education." Then, through their departments, they direct students to enroll in yet another group: the major or professional program. More likely than not, the remaining "electives" are regarded by both faculty and students as a kind of peripheral play; they are icing, at best, on what is considered the real education. If one adds to this constriction that the language of requirements tends to shrink the conception of a course to its syllabus, the *way* in which courses are taught is left out of consideration, not to mention any learning that is not tied to the classroom.

The practice of requiring courses is an important, probably indispensable, component in the management of a curriculum; I am most certainly not opposed to it. My objection here is to the practice of permitting the decision about requirements to preempt prior discussions and decisions. What should be required is properly determined only in a context in which the particular mission of the institution and the characteristics of its student body have been formulated with some specificity and, above all, in the light of an explicit consideration of a full range of educational goals.

This volume attempts to exhibit something of that range of goals, with the focus kept on what is possible and desirable. We can here abstain, therefore, from elaborate arguments for the inclusion of a particular goal or, for that matter, from noisy declarations in behalf of some political faction, since the desirability (in general) of an educational goal is vastly less controversial than that its pursuit be required. At the same time, making pedagogical achievements the subject matter permits a formulation that does not take means for granted but facilitates reflection on how these goals might be achieved. Five chapters (chapters 2 through 6) are directly concerned with educational goals, with the attempt made throughout to discuss these ends in ways that help one to become clearer about the pedagogical means that might be employed to bring them about. To be sure, except for suggestions put forward by way of examples, no specific courses are recommended in these pages. Instead, some broad implications are drawn from the fact that the only curriculum that counts is the curriculum that changes students.

This last consideration leads the discussion beyond a concern with curriculum abstractly considered. Chapter 7 is devoted to concerns that arise out of the need to close the gap between what is delivered and what is received. It thus takes up some issues about teaching and its relationship to learning, and about ways in which students might be helped to make effective educational choices, given the possibilities provided by their undergraduate institutions. Because that institution's impact on a student's education does not end with formal classes, however, chapter 8 takes a look at student life more generally and at the environment within which students spend their undergraduate years. A final chapter looks broadly at some ways in which institutions can effectively support efforts designed to achieve the goals of undergraduate education, followed by a brief postscript on two topics to which much attention has been given in recent years, the coherence of the curriculum and the campus as a community.

Every baccalaureate institution provides an opportunity for its students to work toward the educational goals to be sketched out here. Each institution, however, must itself determine what to stress, to what degree, and in what manner, while important further decisions are deferred to particular students and their careers. Rather than telling one and all just what an undergraduate education should consist of, these reflections about the goals of undergraduate education stress the issues that must be considered when making decisions about undergraduate education. Accordingly, while the following contains many small sermons, it does not preach a single, overarching educational gospel. But because such self-restraint calls for an explanation, we turn now to a brief account of the conception of higher education that underlies this volume.

A CONCEPTION OF HIGHER EDUCATION

The logical starting point of several recently published lectures telling educators what they should be doing is a conception of the educated person. This is certainly true of the efforts by Bloom, Cheney, and Hirsch, mentioned in the preface. Sometimes good reasons are given as to why the educated person should know this and be able to do that; at other times it is taken for granted that everyone knows why a given set of accomplishments are the mark of someone who is educated. Once the meaning of what it is to be educated is on the table, however, much of importance follows. Higher education—or, more specifically, undergraduate education—"simply" becomes that complex activity designed to bring students to that educated state. The end is given in the conception; the means are that process of education. Call this position the *a priori* view of undergraduate education.

The end controls the means, but the means must encompass more than undergraduate education itself. If the pedagogical activities of the undergraduate years are to be effective, students who embark on that path must, at the start, have the knowledge and abilities that enable them to march successfully toward the educated state that merits a culminating degree. Inevitably, then, the a priori view of undergraduate education is socially elitist, since the specification of the outcome determines who is in a position to embark on this educational journey in the first place. Not surprisingly, we are brought close to a European system of education, where a quite uniform secondary system leads to a certification such as the leaving certificate, the *bachot,* or the *Abitur,* signaling that a student has reached a specific level of competency in a variety of subjects. That certification, in turn, serves as the chief criterion for admission to higher education.

Even if some of the educational sermons delivered of late to the American public are rooted in this a priori view, the position that underlies much of educational theory and just about all of practice in the United States should rather be labeled *a posteriori*. Its logical starting point is the conception of a student as possessing a complex capacity to learn; education is regarded as the process that actualizes this potentiality. Progress is made along a plurality of dimensions and is measured, above all, by what has been added to what existed before—by what has been learned.

On the a posteriori view, there is no single conception of the educated person, though of course not any kind of change constitutes educational value added, nor is every degree of learning sufficient to reach above a threshold. Indeed, one might think of the account of educational goals as constituting a road map of a large land of varied topography. Traveling on every part of every road—certainly during the four years allotted to the task—must be taken to be an unattainable ideal; different individuals will therefore traverse different portions of the territory, with perhaps no two making identical journeys. Thus, if the a priori view of undergraduate education ideally aims at bringing about a population of educated people—all of whom share a certain set of characteristics—the a posteriori position rests content with a class of educated persons who belong to that category by virtue of a family resemblance.[2]

At its root, the a posteriori view of education is populist. The result sought by higher education constitutes a broad range of achievements; it does not have a unitary design. As a consequence, greater diversity in ability and preparation also qualifies for admission to undergraduate education than holds for the a priori view. A plurality of results is open to a plurality of beginnings. In more than one way, this educational philosophy is appropriate to the United States. It is hospitable to a heterogeneous population that is the product of huge waves of immigration from all parts of the world, as well as of the systematic oppression of a native population and the enslavement of an uprooted one. An a posteriori view does not make the facile assumption that all those who are to be educated are essentially of one kind. Moreover, social progress might be seen to depend on an educational philosophy that stresses above all the knowledge and skill that have been *acquired*, rather than simply the condition that has been achieved. The elitist view, to state it in its most extreme form, considers the student of college-entering age to be fully formed and autonomous, to be assessed for the capacity for becoming an educated person. The populist view makes its goal *improvement*, doing *better*. And when that better is not as good as one might wish, it remains open that the better will become truly good in a subsequent generation. Nor does an uncertain floor imply that there need be a ceiling to ambition or to accomplishment.

If the heterogeneity of the American people makes an a posteriori view of undergraduate education appropriate, the localism of American elementary and secondary education virtually make it necessary. Almost sixteen thousand public school districts—under more or less loose guidance from fifty different states—determine in various ways how the children of their communities should be educated. The range from rural to urban, from impoverished to affluent, from concerned to uncaring, from sophisticated to naive is immense. So much do these institutions differ from each other that even if one imagined all children to be starting out with identical capabilities, the accomplishments of American high school graduates would be drastically dissimilar.

2. Wittgenstein observed that not every common noun denotes individuals, all of whom have at least some characteristics in common, the way all tables are to some degree flat and rigid. Instead, such terms may also refer to individuals who belong together because, like members of the same family, each of them has a number of characteristics of some larger set (so we can recognize them as belonging to the same family), though perhaps no two of them have an identical set in common—shape of nose, color of hair, eyes, skin, build, and so on. Undoubtedly that makes it hard to judge in some cases whether they do or don't belong. Thus, if a priorists tend to quarrel about what characteristics belong to the *conception* of the educated person, the a posteriori view gives rise to arguments as to which *persons* are educated.

All children, of course, are not like all others. Thus, if one adds to differing natural endowments the effect of this most variegated system of schooling, uniformity at the undergraduate level would not be achievable either. The very pluralistic world of three thousand or so postsecondary institutions constitutes one adaptation, but the admissions policies of virtually each individual one of them are another. Even the most selective American colleges, accordingly, find themselves constrained to admit students who are inadequately prepared in some relevant areas (according to their own criteria!) because they are both talented and well prepared in others.

Throughout this discussion of the a posteriori position, care has been taken to speak always about *undergraduate* education. Clearly, most graduate and (postbaccalaureate) professional education must be regarded quite differently. In one sense, all education above the level of the bachelor's degree is professional, in that it either prepares students to enter such professions as medicine or law or it aims at certifying, so to speak, that its graduates meet the standards of such titles as "chemist" or "economist." In all of such cases, the demands of a profession (in this broadened sense) significantly determine what knowledge and skills a practitioner must have. In the language we have been using, it is the a priori view that underlies graduate and professional education, since its starting point is a conception of the (professionally) educated person.

The corollary for an admissions policy cannot be evaded. Populism at the level of undergraduate education must give way to elitism at the postbaccalaureate one, since the issue is no longer improvement but the achievement of externally determined goals. Indeed, one might think of our way of conducting undergraduate education in the United States as both a bridge and a screen standing between secondary schooling that is varied to the point of chaos, and graduate and professional education that is called upon to live up to professionwide standards.

Before turning to a closer consideration of the goals of undergraduate education, it is worth commenting on one aspect of recent discussions about undergraduate education. While I believe that I am correct in holding that the philosophy that underlies the *practice* of American undergraduate education is a posteriori and populist, we noted earlier that by no means does everyone who discusses that topic hold this view. One way to understand some of the contrary opinions that are frequently expressed within and outside the academy is to see them as the result of inferences to undergraduate education from thinking that is appropriate to professional education. We have notions of the competent physician, lawyer, chemist, or economist, and seek to "produce" the like in our educational establishments. This way of thinking leads one to make the analogy that undergraduate education should have a comparable "product"—the educated person. But such reasoning ignores that even where there are vigorous disagreements about what a physician, lawyer, chemist, or economist should know, formidable institutions provide a setting for debates about the nature of the competent professional: guilds, licensing agencies, professional societies. Moreover, important criteria for conceptions of such professions are derived from their functions: healing the sick, defending the accused, building bridges, and so on.

But being an educated person is not a profession; society does not delegate the job of defining that state to some expert organization. Nor is the function of an educated person limited to practicing a metier during working hours; instead, to echo Aristotle's formulation, it consists of living well for a whole life. Of such stuff philosophy is made, and different philosophies will generate different accounts of living well and, therefore, different views of what the educated person is. Only in a society that is vastly more homogeneous than contemporary America could one expect to achieve a consensus or an overarching, unitary view on so fundamental a set of issues. Only in a society that is considerably less free than ours would one expect to find coercion sufficient to achieve conformity.

On the one hand, therefore, no shared set of principles exists to which one can appeal in the explication of the position that would replace the a posteriori, pluralistic educational philosophy that underlies this discussion of the goals of undergraduate education. These goals, on the other hand, are put forward as components of conceptions that differ from one educational institution to another; they serve to facilitate educational decisions by institutions, as well as help individual students make choices regarding their own undergraduate careers.

TYPES OF EDUCATIONAL GOALS

Before moving on to an account of a number of substantive educational goals of undergraduate education, two preliminary tasks are worth undertaking. Even a brief glance at the array of educational accomplishments sought by students—and for them, by their parents, teachers, and society, as expressed by spokespersons from its various sectors—makes clear that these aims are not at all of the same sort. Some order is achieved to the extent to which these aims can be grouped according to type. But, more important, a broad characterization of types of educational goals can provide an insight into the nature of the means appropriate to bringing them about. An informal sketch of the quite different categories into which they fall will heighten our awareness that colleges are not just course-giving institutions; effectiveness in education, rather, requires one to be open to a complex set of pedagogic means that are or can be available in institutions of undergraduate education.

A second useful preliminary is the reminder that we are, above all, considering the education of adolescents. To be sure, the number of students in our colleges who have been ambiguously labeled "nontraditional" has become formidable, and means as well as ends for that diverse population will differ variously from those appropriate for recent graduates from secondary schools. However, the largest proportion of baccalaureate students is composed of cohorts of eighteen year olds who leave each spring from thirty thousand or so American high schools to begin college after a summer's respite from study. Not only is the education of this continuous stream of students the largest undergraduate mission, but the goals of their education make up a useful norm from which one deviates in as many ways and for as many reasons as nontraditional students are nontraditional. Those traditional students, however, are adolescents, and their special characteristics must play a role in the formulation of pedagogic goals and in considering the ways in which these goals are brought about.[3]

It cannot be assumed, to begin with, that students entering college are *motivated* to act in ways that will make them good students in whatever sense one might posit. If aptness and strength of motivation were made central conditions for access to undergraduate study—beyond the consideration of past performance in school—the ranks of undergraduates would be radically thinned. On the other hand, since this characterological and developmental criterion does not play a serious role in the decision that admits a student to college, one is left with a need to be concerned with the motivation of students in the pedagogy of undergraduate education.[4]

The fact that motivation is relevant to baccalaureate education—and, more generally, that undergraduates are by no means as yet fully formed adults—implies that undergraduate institutions are engaged in the business of shaping character. They *are*, in the sense that growth and maturation continue during those years of study and that what happens in college influences the direction of these developments. They *should be*, in the sense that institutions of higher education have an obligation to try to give shape to this direction, in consonance with their educational goals.

That even higher education should aim at fostering in its students those qualities of mind that were classically known as "intellectual virtues" has never been controversial. But by using this somewhat archaic term, we are reminded that in effect we are speaking of qualities of mind when we refer to the ability to suspend judgment in the face of inadequate evidence or to the capacity to remain open to the views of others. These are not skills, like the ability to solve quadratic equations, nor are they knowledge, like an under-

---

3. If we take a traditional student to be twenty-four years old or younger, about three and a half times as many of them as nontraditional students were enrolled in four-year institutions in 1987. No significant change in that ratio is projected for the next decade.

4. The professor who believes that the motivation of students is solely the students' concern would undoubtedly be pleased with the smaller, "better" classes that would result if motivation were rigorously used as an admissions criterion. The fly in that ointment, however, is the fact that far fewer professors would be needed to teach a reduced cadre of undergraduates, possibly leaving that very instructor without a job.

standing of Bohr's atom. But since we include fostering such capacities among our pedagogic aims, we have identified one type of goal: the cultivation of certain character traits.

A century ago, when the model of Oxbridge was still a powerful exemplar of undergraduate education in America, there would have been broad, if not unanimous, agreement that moral education is a central function of college. Today there is much dissent, certainly among educators, from the proposition that education during the undergraduate years should include the shaping of character in the conventional, moral, sense of the term. At the same time, this is precisely what is presupposed by the widespread call for education for citizenship and leadership. Many of those for whom character development is irrelevant to higher education can be regarded as deriving their view from a continental intellectualism that is a corollary of a "purist" a priori position of baccalaureate education, while the English tradition that sees the building of character as central makes the development of the country's leaders the single most important role of undergraduate education. The debate between these two sides, however, is made moot by an argument that rests on certain unassailable facts.

If we look at undergraduates, we will surely find that the character of young people between the ages of eighteen and twenty-two is subject to influence by their activities, experiences, and associations during that period of their lives, a fact that is contained in the very notion of adolescence. What they do and what happens to them during these years makes a difference to what they will be in the future. On the other side, the institutions that educate these students exercise considerable control—with self-consciousness or without it—over the activities, experiences, and associations of those enrolled in them. If one then appeals to the premise that *educational* institutions should exercise their powers in ways that are beneficial, it follows that undergraduate institutions should be self-conscious in how they exercise the power they have, and should use their influence constructively and in support of educational goals.

Since at this juncture we are concerned only with the identification of types of educational goals, these observations suffice to have us add moral character traits to the goal of cultivating intellectual qualities.

Much must be sorted out when we take up character traits more specifically. Nevertheless, it is helpful for determining effective pedagogic means to know that their fostering is one type of goal of undergraduate education. Similar assistance can be derived from an understanding of the more familiar aims of higher education. Much education, higher education included, aims at the inculcation of proficiencies or skills. Indeed, in one sense, *all* of education aims at the acquisition of skills, in that the evidence for any educational achievement is behavioral: to have learned is to be able to *do* something, whether that "doing" is walking a tightrope, playing the violin, making a type of calculation, responding to a question by writing or saying something, making a certain kind of sensory or conceptual discrimination, or even making a decision. To have learned x is to be able to say truly, "can do x."[5]

And yet, if education is our concern, this general truth also masks a distinction of importance. We can devise unerring examinations to see whether someone knows how to multiply whole numbers. We can, and do, design trustworthy tests for finding out whether someone has acquired the skill of writing coherent expository prose—mostly by asking the examinee to provide samples of his or her work. Similarly, instructors of mathematics have no difficulty in discerning quite clearly the degree of mastery their students have gained over analytic geometry. However, when we want to ascertain the depth of understanding a student has attained of religion in nineteenth-century Russia as depicted in *The Brothers Karamazov*, our tests—though we give them—are far less reliable. If, then, we move to such questions as to whether a student has learned to think critically or whether he or she is imaginative, any manageable tests we might devise are likely to be inadequate. For many reasons, we have no feasible way of examining for the capacity to make courageous moral decisions.

These differences are not hard and fast and, with the possible exception of the most elementary end of this range—for which simple multiplication was the example—legitimate disagreements are always possible as to where a particular ability is to be placed. There is merit, nevertheless, in making a further typological distinction and in thus limiting the scope of the concept of skill or proficiency to those abilities a person might have or acquire for which manageable, reasonably reliable test procedures can be devised. What is conveniently called "college algebra" (but not all of algebra, if "all" has any meaning in that phrase), the writing of clear expository prose, the attainment of a level of ability in the reading, understanding, and speaking of a foreign language are then examples of the second type of pedagogic goal, to be referred to as the acquisition of proficiencies.

No traditional label quite fits the type of goal that lies "above" the level of proficiency. What we are talking about includes the possession of skills or proficiencies but also calls for the possession of extensive information in quite different categories and the ability to use it, as well as what we call "understanding" of a sort that is not reducible to a formula, even a complicated one.[6] I will call these educational goals "conversancies," thinking by way of example of a certain grasp of Russian literature, as distinguished from

5. Another formulation is "*empowerment*—having the resources, skills, and personal qualities necessary to control one's own fate and to make a difference in the world" (Gamson and Associates, *Liberating Education* [1984, pp. 67–68]).
6. I don't want to take a stand on what might be "ultimately" possible as our use of computers becomes ever more proficient. Right now, grand masters are still beating the best computer chess programs, and no one has even tried to put together software and hardware that could write an essay on Dostoyevsky's conception of God. For the category I want to isolate, it is sufficient that we have no formulae and don't expect to have any in the foreseeable future.

being proficient in the use of the Russian language. The term "conversancy," moreover, like "proficiency," carries in its meaning a certain level of attainment. In the language I propose to use here, that level will be surpassed by "competency" as a kind of comparative, and by "mastery" as the analogue to the superlative.[7]

Before concluding this most general account of some types of educational goals, it will be worthwhile to derive a pedagogically relevant consequence from the difference between proficiencies and conversancies, in abstraction from specific substantive goals. Since there is considerable agreement as to the kind of performance that constitutes various levels of accomplishment of proficiencies, that level can be ascertained without much attention to the genesis of its acquisition. Thus, where it is a goal of undergraduate education that a student possess a certain degree of such a skill, an educator can afford to be indifferent—other things being equal—as to how the student might have acquired that skill, assuming that it has been acquired. Tests, in short, rather than accounts of course work, best determine whether a desired goal has been reached. In such cases as the ability to use a foreign language, for example, or to handle certain branches of mathematics, the educational goal is most effectively formulated in terms of success on an examination, rather than in terms of a series of pedagogical experiences.

When we speak of conversancy with literature, by contrast, we are unable to devise practical, reliable tests for the presence of the characteristics we want our students to come to possess. It is doubtful that a manageable examination on *The Brothers Karamazov* can distinguish between two reasonably intelligent students, one of whom has read a pony on Dostoyevsky's work, while the other has read the book and spent two weeks in class discussions on its substance and themes. The acquisition of the ability to judge, to discriminate, and to understand does not readily reveal itself in a single performance. To grant all that, however, does not require one to abjure reading or discussing good books. It means, rather, that one must think somewhat differently about such educational goals, and indeed about a good part of advanced education.

In the absence of that convenient proficiency examination, we must acknowledge that, in much of higher education, important components of the

---

7. In his *Philosophy of Teaching*, John Passmore [1980, pp. 37–55] distinguishes between closed capacities that can be completely mastered, though they can be more or less complex (e.g., multiplication or solving quadratic equations) and those that are open, in that further mastery is always possible, with these latter varying greatly in degree of openness. He further distinguishes between narrow and broad capacities, where the difference resides in the range of circumstances to which the capacities apply—from the ability to play chess on the narrow side, for example, to the capacity to learn at the broad extreme. He asserts that there are no sharp dividing lines here and that there will be disagreements about what is narrow and what is broad. While no college subject amounts to the acquisition of a closed capacity (though it will contain such capacities as components), there is a congruence between the move from proficiency to conversancy, and the change from a less to a more open capacity, and an analogy certainly holds between capacities of the broadest sort and what I have identified as character traits.

goal one attempts to achieve reveal themselves only in the course of longer and future stretches of time. An observer—a teacher—can have glimpses and samples of a student's progress or lack of it through conversation, specific pieces of data such as specimens of writing, and, of course, examinations. Solid evidence for the kind of intellectual growth that is sought is not routinely available at the conclusion of every semester.[8]

On the other side, considerable knowledge has been accumulated to the effect that the acquisition of desired qualities of mind—in all domains of knowledge—is achieved by having students undergo complex experiences, often, over long periods of time.[9] It is probably true that the "higher" the education, the less reliably we can count on similar causes having similar effects. But we do have evidence that what happens to students matters, so that we must attend to the genesis of the goals we want to achieve. Thus, reading, discussing, writing, engaging in supervised and collaborative research, attending to demonstrations, and participating in simulations— usually in combinations—are among the means that provide a basis, even if not totally reliable, for a prediction of success.

It is, above all, the complex business of having students gain conversancy and even competency in a large number of areas that calls upon so considerable a part of the resources of colleges and universities. At the same time, for students to attain an education of this nature, few, if any, substitutes are likely to be available for participation in the pedagogical experiences devised in institutions of higher education. Aiming at the goal of conversancy is, therefore, a more distinctive activity of undergraduate education than is the teaching of proficiencies. It does not, however, follow that the attainment of certain proficiencies, to which we now turn, is of less than the highest importance.[10]

8. Of course we want students to acquire certain proficiencies for use during a lifetime. That (obvious) long-range goal is not stressed, because we are entitled to say that where there is a satisfactory performance on an examination that tests for a proficiency, the student "has" it for life. The fact that one must also add "other things being equal" (that the proficiency is used, by way of the single most important example) has no direct bearing on the pedagogy that led up to its acquisition.

9. While at this point the discussion focuses primarily on the issue of evidence of success, there are clearly significant differences in what it means to teach in the complex realm of conversancies. When Passmore [1980, p. 49] says that "instruction is of more limited usefulness in teaching open capacities," he can be regarded as making a related point.

10. The distinction sketched between proficiencies and conversancies suggests that certain academic practices deserve rethinking. The discussion in the following chapter will show that formulating certain requirements in terms of a set of courses to be taken—two years of a language, basic composition, calculus—rather than having it be some minimum score on a proficiency examination is indicative of something less than full clarity about the educational goal being pursued. On the other side, the regulations of the University of Chicago's Hutchins College—if only infrequently its actual practice—evince another kind of confusion. The rules of that college exempted a student from any course for which he or she could pass a "proficiency examination." In principle, a youngster could be handed a bachelor's degree upon arrival, suggesting that everything that was to be learned in college was reducible to a skill and that the experience of participation was in no case of sufficient value for it to be insisted upon.

CHAPTER 2

PROFICIENCIES

LITERACY

Literacy, both the most ancient and most prominent proficiency declared to be a goal of education, must be our first topic. But because both the meaning and application of the term are laden with history and beset with ambiguities, a brief account of what we are talking about will improve our grasp of this goal before we plunge into a discussion of pedagogical issues.

The term comes from the Latin for "letter": to be literate is to be lettered, with three broad strains of meaning distinguishable, all three of them still in use.[1] First, a literate person may be someone who is educated, especially in literature, making the person who does not know that Othello strangled Desdemona illiterate. Literacy in this broadest sense is an important theme of this book, but not our topic here.

Second, to be literate is to be able to read, the narrowest sense of "having letters." This is the meaning usually intended when international organizations compare literacy statistics of different countries. At home, many have regarded this lack of literacy to be a national problem and joined Rudolf Flesch in expressing exasperation because Johnny couldn't read [1955]; many are appalled today at the large number of American adults who are in this sense illiterate.[2]

The third meaning of literacy might be thought of as an extension of the second and calls both for an ability to read and write. This is the sense in which the positive noun "literacy"—as distinguished from the much older adjective "literate" and the negative noun "illiteracy"—made its first appear-

---

1. With assistance from the *Compact Oxford English Dictionary*, I, p. 1638. Also helpful is the entry for "illiteracy," I, p. 1374.
2. Rudolf Flesch's *Why Johnny Can't Read* [1955], an attack on progressive education, was neither the first nor the last public expression of dismay about such illiteracy. For an excellent historical perspective on literacy considered as the ability to *read*, see Resnick and Resnick, "The Nature of Literacy" [1977]. Here are a few contemporary samples: "Twenty-five million American adults cannot read the poison warnings on a can of pesticide, a letter from their child's teacher, or the front page of a daily paper.... Fifteen percent of recent graduates of urban high schools read at less than sixth grade level.... Half the heads of households classified below the poverty line by federal standards cannot read an eight grade book.... The United States ranks forty-ninth among 158 member nations of the U.N. in its literacy levels." From Kozol, *Illiterate America* [1985, pp. 4–5].

14

ance in educational circles a hundred years ago.³ Complaints about illiteracy in this broader sense also go back almost to the beginning of writing. In a relatively recent expression of national concern—by way of a December 8, 1975, *Newsweek* cover story—the very phrasing of two decades earlier was picked up in the plaintive question, "Why Can't Johnny Write?"

Not only this complaining but the *object* of the grumbling has an instructive history. Looking at the standards posited for literacy as reading from seventeenth-century England on, a survey of the history of literacy shows that in earlier periods (through the middle of the nineteenth century), religious leaders (first) and civic leaders (later) asked that a large proportion of the population have the modest skill of reading simple, and usually familiar, religious or civic texts. By 1900 in the United States, however, a much more ambitious standard was set—though for the much smaller fraction of the population that completed eight grades of schooling—while a very high standard was expected to be met by a technical-managerial elite. In our own day, that demand for an accomplished elite continues, but in our national goals it is now coupled with a call for a notably more sophisticated reading ability than was asked of those eighth-graders, *and* it is expected to be spread virtually through our entire population.⁴

Though this brief history attended only to the ability to read, the general picture it offers also holds for literacy that includes the ability to write— certainly for the more recent period. This parallelism shouldn't surprise us, since the goals set correspond to the perceived needs for coping with the demands of work and citizenship and, in a highly technological economy, those of being a rational consumer. If for a brief moment the coming of electronic means of communication suggested that the need for writing would wane,⁵ it soon became evident that the pictures purveyed by TV and VCR have not eliminated the need to read the complicated instructions that accompany them. Moreover, even E-MAIL via BITNET and FAX via SPRINT must be formulated in coherent prose to be intelligible.

A recent report attempts a brief formulation of what literacy means in this late-twentieth-century context. For both reading and writing, it distinguishes between surface understanding and the ability to reason effectively about one's reading and writing. Such surface understanding and expression vary both in character and in difficulty with the material to be understood or written—from shopping list to letter to a report of an experiment.⁶ But in any case,

---

3. In 1883, in the *New England Journal of Education*. See *Compact Oxford English Dictionary* [1971, I, p. 1638].
4. Resnick and Resnick [1977], particularly the summary Figure 1, p. 384. For a recent statement of a very high standard of reading ability from a civic point of view, see "a Definition of Literacy for a Democratic Society," in Berlak, "Literacy in a Democracy" [1987, p. 114].
5. The prophet was Marshall McLuhan, in the *Medium Is the Massage* [1967].
6. Applebee et al., *Learning to Be Literate in America* [1987, p. 8].

Although surface understanding is important, it is not enough. In school and in society, we expect a reader to be able to analyze, evaluate, and extend the ideas that are presented. . . . For example, readers must learn to relate what they are reading to their personal experience in order to integrate new ideas with what they know. . . . Similar thinking abilities are important in writing. To develop their surface understanding and convey their ideas to others, writers must learn to draw upon their personal experiences, to incorporate information from other sources, and to evaluate the internal consistency and organization of their ideas and arguments.[7]

This level of "mastery of the written world [is] required by more and more activities in today's society." Analysis of test statistics, however, show us to be very far from that goal. Only 5 percent of eleventh graders were at an "advanced" reading level that enabled them to synthesize and learn from specialized reading material, while only 21 percent of young adults could be so characterized. Even the statistics for the next lower level (referred to as "adept") were unimpressive: 40 percent at grade 11 and 54 percent of the young adults.

While the information was not available to produce completely analogous statistics for writing, it will surprise no one that for eleventh graders, "performance at the adequate level was distressingly rare," with only 65 percent capable of writing "an adequate paragraph on a job application describing the kind of job they would like" and only 22 percent able to write a letter persuading the school principal to drop an unnecessary school rule. And this is merely the *adequate* level, one that does not suppose the writing to have grace or polish, or to convey a logical and effective development of the writer's thought.

Several implications follow from this summary history-brought-up-to-date, even if we begin by attending only to that minority of first-year college students who, at the eleventh grade, had achieved an advanced level of literacy both in reading and in writing. In two senses, literacy is a moving target. First, the demands made on the abilities to read and write are related to the complexity of society and the roles of individuals within it, especially as workers. What is adequate in one era is insufficient in a subsequent one. There is every reason to suppose that more and different demands for linguistic mastery will continue to be made in the future. Second, even this brief account reveals—much supported by entire bibliographies of research and reflection—that the ability to read and write is inextricably tied to the subject matter that is read and written about. Writing clearly is not possible where there is no clear thinking: the development of these twin abilities must be tied ever more closely to the concepts and discourse of different subject fields.

The needed pedagogy, then, is not so much "writing across the curricu-

---

7. Applebee et al., *Learning to Be Literate in America* [1987, p. 9], with the following quotations from pp. 9, 15, and 17 respectively.

lum," as simply writing *in* the curriculum. The former is a special device designed to solve a problem, and we shall return to it. The latter is an abiding curricular necessity. Even an "advanced" reading and writing level of a young adult must continue to be developed during the undergraduate years. The extension of familiar subjects, not to mention the introduction of new ones, requires the adaptation and stretching of existing skills—*both* in reading and in writing—into those new areas. In an ideal world, we would take it for granted that there is substantial writing *everywhere* in the curriculum.

Two further considerations support the claim that virtually all undergraduate teaching must require the integration of reading and, especially, writing. First, there is the familiar necessity that acquired skills must be practiced, in particular when they were learned recently and are as yet held precariously. Students abandoned to passive listening and to multiple-choice quizzes not only fail to further their ability to write but risk deterioration from the level they had attained.

Second, as more is being understood about learning, the importance of the learner being active in that process becomes ever clearer, with writing among the most important of relevant activities. It is simply the case that "students learn their subject matter better in a variety of disciplines if they write about it."[8] Earlier it was stated that writing must be incorporated into the teaching of a large range of subjects for the sake of fostering the ability to write; we must now add that this practice is desirable, as well, for the sake of the subject matter to be learned. We are again led to the necessity of writing *in* the curriculum.

By addressing issues that pertain to students who have come to college after achieving an acceptable literacy standard, we have uncovered relationships that of course hold for all students. On the other hand, we have not yet addressed the issue of proficiency, as here intended, though it will not be difficult to find the starting point. When we look at the entering college population, we see a large gap between actual accomplishments achieved in high school and the level of competency deemed satisfactory for an American citizen near the end of the twentieth century. It becomes the task of undergraduate education to help students close the gap.

The teaching of writing has been widely and deeply studied during the last decade. While continued delving into the process of writing will no doubt lead to the revision of beliefs now held, two are likely to survive. The first, already stressed, sees writing and thinking and what is thought and written about to be inseparable, so that the skill of writing must be acquired within the context of a subject matter. The second tenet has been formulated as a "paradigm shift" in the teaching of writing, from an emphasis on the composed *product* to the process that *composes* it.[9]

8. Walvoord and Smith, "Coaching the Process of Writing" [1982, p. 6].
9. What Thomas Kuhn hath wrought! See Hairston, "Winds of Change" [1982].

Together, these precepts are the foundation of the practice referred to as "writing across the curriculum," reinforced, of course, by the imperative of practicing a skill. We are now not simply referring to making writing daily fare in numerous college courses but to the *teaching* of writing in ways that require ability and training not likely to be possessed by a significant proportion of a college faculty—not even within an English department.

Perhaps the Copernican Revolution is most aptly seen in Mina Shaughnessy's discoveries, stemming from her work, in the 1970s, with open enrollment students at New York's City College. Her insight was

> utterly simple and vitally important: we cannot teach students to write by looking only at what they have written. We must also understand *how* that product came into being, and *why* it assumed the form that it did. We have to try to intervene during the act of writing if we want to affect its outcome. We have to do the hard thing, examine the intangible process, rather than the easy thing, evaluate the tangible product.[10]

Teaching writing is no longer a matter of taking a student's composition and putting in the commas where they *really* belong, circling ill-chosen or misspelled words ("SP"), scrawling arrows and loops to correct word order, or writing "AWK" or just "W" to mark infelicitous expressions. Training is needed in the performance of this task, even beyond the ability—by no means assured—to write well. Writing must be *taught* across the curriculum, where that teaching is done or assisted by denizens of the paradigm that regards writing pedagogy to be concerned with the *process* of writing and *about* some specific subject matter.

While this approach raises organizational issues that will be touched on in chapter 9, where the focus is on institutional support, we must conclude this discussion by noting that neither writing *in* nor *across* the curriculum will in the foreseeable future fully replace courses in composition as the most direct aid to writing proficiency. The logic of current thinking about writing pedagogy would limit writing courses to such special forms as journalistic writing, fiction, or poetry, leaving just plain writing as everybody's business. This logic can be fully implemented, however, only when the *teaching* of writing is *every* teacher's business, so that what is begun in elementary school—before pervasive specialization in teaching—continues through secondary and higher schooling as a regular *part* of most specialized teaching.

Utopia may not be around the corner, but individual instructors can be aided in various ways to integrate writing into their courses. Using special writing assistants (specially trained undergraduates as well more traditional graduate teaching assistants have been successful); creating a center for writ-

---

10. Hairston, "Winds of Change" [1982, p. 84]. The essay discusses many other contributors to the "shift" and (p. 86) characterizes the new paradigm by means of twelve propositions. For Shaughnessy's own account, see her *Errors and Expectations* [1977].

ing where both students and faculty can get *ad hoc* assistance with problems in writing and writing pedagogy; and correlating the use of computer programs that assist in the instruction of writing with courses in different areas are among the ways to support writing in and across the curriculum. But all instruction in the undergraduate writing courses that will long remain with us must be informed by the principle that sees writing as inseparable from thinking and that insists on the ability, on the part of writing instructors, to intervene in the writing process of their students, so as to help them achieve the proficiency we call literacy.

An addendum is in order: the importance of speaking must not be ignored in undergraduate education, even though it stretches the meaning of "literacy" beyond good sense. Electronic wizardry does not eliminate the need for effective written communication; neither does it replace articulate speech. Cellular telephones, radio communication networks, video conferences, added to face-to-face encounters with individuals and groups require the formulation and expression of thoughts in ways that make the speaker readily understood, where what is understood is what is intended.

Colleges have mostly abandoned the cultivation of the skill of "public speaking," and perhaps the formal oratory implied by the phrase is not what is so pervasively needed. Yet there is no doubt that in all kinds of endeavor, public and private, important decisions are made on the basis of verbal exchanges between co-workers, between supervisors and subordinates, and among members of committees, boards, teams, and task forces. The ability to be succinct and persuasive, the capacity to respond to questions and objections raised—and, therefore, the ability to listen—thus function significantly in vocational, governmental, and avocational activities.[11]

It should be a goal of undergraduate education to equip students with the ability to present their thoughts ably in speech. Formal speaking, too, can be an active component of the pedagogy of most undergraduate subjects, whether mathematics or literature, accounting or library science. If effective oral discourse is not literacy because it does not require being lettered, it does call for a command of one's language that is more like the mastery needed in writing, and therefore tutored, than it is like the speaking all children learn at home and in the street.

FOREIGN LANGUAGES

One may surely assume that it would be desirable if more Americans knew a language other than English; supporting arguments for this have been made

---

11. It was Robert Payton who, when he was president of the Exxon Education Foundation, alerted me to the pervasive relationship between verbal communication and decision making.

again and again. The metaphor of the "global village" conveys well how distances among human habitations have shrunk, but it misleads if it also suggests their homogeneity. The hope that before long we would all communicate with each other in Esperanto stemmed from the belief that World War I had been fought to end all wars. The expectation, some twenty-five years later, that English would be the universal language arose out of post-World War II confidence in a Pax Americana. Both, now, seem quaint trappings of the past. People around the world may make themselves understood to us in English, but if that is the only way we hear them, we only hear what they want to tell us. Both commerce and an understanding of the world's cultures rest on an ability to communicate in languages other than English.

But to say "languages other than English" is not enough: there are a great many of those. Before turning to issues of language pedagogy, it is worth pointing out that national need, as reflected in the demand by business and government for individuals with linguistic ability, is not necessarily matched by the distribution of language teaching in the academy. The *supply* of language teaching (in high schools as well as in postsecondary institutions) is a function of the source of language teachers—above all, the large graduate departments in the main Western European literatures: French, German, Spanish, Italian. National *need*, however, is importantly related to the fact that "the less commonly taught languages include those spoken by over eighty percent of the world's population, e.g., Chinese, Hindi-Urdu, Japanese, Portuguese, or Russian,"[12] to which Arabic should be added as well. But on the whole, students are not pressing for the teaching of languages unavailable to them: instead, what students want is also shaped by the configuration of language instruction in secondary schools and colleges rather than by national needs. Cognizance must be taken of this disparity when we comment on the organization of language instruction.

Faculty discussions about languages most commonly ask whether students should be *required* to study a foreign language. The focus on *whether* there should be a requirement deflects from a concern with *what* might be required. "Should students be 'exposed' to a foreign language and, if so, for one year or two?" is extensively debated, and where a requirement is instituted, it tends to be satisfied by the achievement of a passing grade in the last term of the one- or two-year sequence. But when one realizes that in order to avoid failing, little more may be asked of students than that they be present during a certain fraction of language classes, we see that what is required truly is "exposure."

A significant result of this attitude is widespread cynicism among students, since they are asked to invest considerable time and effort, mostly without reaping the reward of acquiring a usable skill. (Most students who have discharged their language duties would be shocked if they had to put their

12. *Language Study for the 1980s* [1980, pp. 15–16].

abilities to actual use, and in trouble if something depended on it.) The waste of time and effort is damaging, and so is the opinion it reinforces that requirements are merely bureaucratic hurdles to be gotten out of the way.

No one, of course, is happy with the relative failure of so much language study,[13] but a clearer vision of its purposes is obscured by additional claims, often put forward as if by way of compensation. In two ways, students are said to benefit from the experience of language study, even if they don't actually learn to use the language. First, such study is said to provide a perspective on one's mother tongue, and thus help to increase one's mastery over it. Second, even the elementary study of a foreign language provides students with a desirable acquaintance with a culture different from their own.

Both of these goals are laudable, but in neither case are the means—one or two years of foreign language study—appropriate. Native speakers of English might become more aware of their own tongue through a study of the history and structure of the language or by way of a study of linguistics that stresses both comparative and basic structural features. Either approach explicitly aims at the kind of overview sought and does so at a level of abstractness and complexity appropriate to postsecondary education. By contrast, the linguistic perspective gained from the beginning study of a foreign language is likely to be inadvertent and episodic, more often than not under the tutelage of an instructor with little training and less interest in this linguistic dimension of language teaching. *That* end surely doesn't justify *those* means!

The study of culture as a byproduct of language instruction brings about equally flimsy results. If what is normally conveyed in this way about a region's history and civilization were the material of a course given in English, it would not even pass muster in high school. Providing information about France or Spain or Russia is of course a necessary aid to language instruction, but as a means of imparting knowledge about the culture and history of a people, it is trivial. Moreover, not even when instructors are carefully selected for their ability to teach a language need they be suitable and informed teachers of a culture. Surely there are more effective ways of introducing students to a culture different from their own than as an accompaniment to the conjugation of French irregular verbs or by way of learning the vocabulary needed to order food in a German restaurant.[14]

---

13. It is helpful, but not sufficient, that the profession of language teachers has said to itself that "much language study consists of a set of exercises designed merely to help a student pass a course (and obtain credit) rather than acquire a useful skill," *Language Study for the 1980s* [1980, p. 12].

14. On this topic, the director of an elaborate empirical study reports the following: "Exhaustive analysis of the . . . data revealed that there is no appreciable relationship between global knowledge as tested and either foreign language proficiency or extent of formal study, or informal study. On the other hand, the affective component of global understanding is associated with foreign language proficiency and language learning history to a moderate degree, though neither its necessity nor direction is assured. The language proficiency results also indicated that although language study is quite widespread, very

The mediocre achievement—at best—of several educational goals is not preferable to a satisfactory accomplishment of one of them. Where the goals are linguistic and cultural sophistication, appropriate pedagogies should be devised on the basis of a clear vision of those purposes. But where the aim is learning a foreign language, that goal is adequately formulated only as a proficiency, as a cluster of skills: understanding and speaking the language, reading and writing it—with each of these abilities reaching a certain level of attainment.

At this juncture, there is room for judgment and discretion about a number of possibilities. Each of these linguistic skills can be thought of in quite different ways: understand or read what *kind* of linguistic expressions (poetry, prose, technical, practical, etc.) under what *circumstances* (hearing someone in person or over the phone; speaking with a standard pronunciation or with a dialect). And with respect to each skill, it must be determined just what *degree of competency* should be attained.

There may be local reasons for making different choices of kind and level at different institutions. Every institution, however, will benefit from the valuable work done by the American Council on the Teaching of Foreign Languages in providing guidelines for language proficiency by means of "generic" descriptions, that is, descriptions abstract enough to apply to all languages.[15] Reasonable precision is reached in the description of nine levels—from "novice—low" to "superior"—for the categories of "speaking," "listening" (where the text makes clear that *understanding* is meant), "reading," "writing," and of six levels for "culture"—from "novice" to "native competence." All levels of all categories, including those pertaining to culture,[16] are carefully formulated as abilities to *act* in some specific set of ways with the language in question, making it, in principle, possible to assess a student's achievements by the observation of performances under carefully devised test conditions.[17]

---

few students have acquired a working proficiency in a foreign language. The discrepancy warrants the serious attention of the language teaching profession," Barrows, *College Students' Knowledge and Beliefs* [1981, p. 136].

15. *ACTFL Provisional Proficiency Guidelines* [1985].

16. At the lower end of the competency levels of "culture," the comportment called for is closely related to the language being studied and is likely to be conveyed in normal language courses. (The *vocabulary* needed to order breakfast in France is not separable from the *food* the French eat for breakfast.) As one moves to higher levels of cultural competency, knowledge of current events, literature, history, and so on are required that are not simply a function of language study. In any case, an outstanding virtue of this project is the fact that at no point does it confuse the proficiency to be gained with the means that might be used to gain it.

17. Two examples, cited in full, effectively convey the nature of this enterprise.
1. Speaking, advanced (seventh of nine levels): "Able to satisfy routine social demands and limited work requirements. Can handle with confidence but not with facility most social situations including introductions and casual conversations about current events, as well as work, family, and autobiographical information; can handle limited work require-

A number of far-reaching consequences follow when proficiency in a foreign language is made the goal of undergraduate education. To begin with, the test that measures the nature and level of students' attainments is given an importance that it does not have when an examination is but one of numerous measures of a student's performance. From the student's point of view, this all-or-nothing assessment makes demands that are highly focused, in contrast to the customary piecemeal way of displaying academic progress. The ramifications for the faculty, if not more serious, are more complex.

The language faculty must adopt both a more professional and a more collegial approach to testing than is typical. If all grading is always an implicit mode of certifying, the fact that it is concentrated in an examination requires that those tests display clearly and consistently the nature and level of students' accomplishments. Fairness to students calls for such professionalism, and so does the need to communicate unambiguously to readers of transcripts. But it is also important for the faculty, since their effectiveness is in part measured by their students' success with a common examination. This need for cooperation in the formulation of examinations must, of course, extend to the shaping of the syllabi intended to help students acquire the desired proficiency.

Testing also plays a role at the entrance to undergraduate language study and deserves a level of attention that it does not receive often enough. Given the immense variety of secondary schools in the United States—not to mention the large number of young people who have been brought up in families (or places) in which a language other than English is used—it is vital to assess how much a student has already accomplished and what instruction is still needed for an attainment of the desired proficiency. Where inaccurate placement overestimates a student's attainments the result is frustration and an inability to cope. Yet underestimating those attainments also has serious, if less obvious, pedagogic consequences. Students who find themselves in a language class that starts out at a level more elementary than they had already reached are frequently tempted to pay insufficient heed to their work. But without continuing to practice a language that has by no means been mastered, students often find it difficult to discern when the material reached in

---

ments, needing help in handling any complications or difficulties. Has a speaking vocabulary sufficient to respond simply with some circumlocutions; accent, though often quite faulty, is intelligible; can usually handle elementary constructions quite accurately but does not have thorough or confident control of the grammar."

2. Reading, novice—high (third of nine levels): "Sufficient comprehension of the written language to interpret set expressions in areas of immediate need. Can recognize all the letters in the printed version of an alphabetic system and high-frequency elements of a syllabary or a character system. Where vocabulary has been mastered, can read for instruction and directional purposes standardized messages, phrases, or expressions such as some items on menus, schedules, timetables, maps, and signs indicating hours of operation, social codes, and traffic regulations. This material is read only for essential information. Detail is overlooked or misunderstood."

the course *does* need their full attention and preparation. They may thus fail to shift into gear when that becomes necessary, with the outcome that *un-der*placement has led the student into academic trouble.

Accuracy in placement, finally, plays a juridical role as well, at least where an institution follows the logic of proficiency into the assigning of credits. One coherent way of handling this issue is to refrain from awarding credit for language competency that was attained prior to coming to college but to give credit for what is accomplished during the undergraduate year. The placement examination would determine the "floor," while proficiency examinations—not the courses taken—would determine what credit should subsequently be awarded.[18]

The conceptualization of this goal as proficiency, rather than as a series of experiences in a language other than English, has additional consequences. By directing attention to an objective, and not simply a process, one is led most naturally to the exploration of pedagogic alternatives to conventional courses as avenues for attaining the desired competency. Not that intensive summer sessions need to be invented anew, nor computer-aided, self-paced language instruction nor programs of residence abroad. There is a large gap, however, between having a general knowledge of these means and the adoption of their, and other, techniques in specific local situations, a gap that requires the solution of both pedagogic and managerial problems. These and other methods for helping to bring about language proficiency become institutional concerns when an institutional commitment is made to languages as proficiencies.[19]

The most conspicuous mark of language instructors is their knowledge of the languages they can teach, a characteristic that then distinguishes them from each other. Normally, what distinguishes them also divides them, since the most common departmental organization is derived from graduate education, where concern with specific languages is ancillary to the study of litera-

18. The MLA-ACLS report recommends that "As an incentive to language study and achievement at the secondary school level, colleges should award credit to students who meet their institutional language proficiency requirement upon entrance, provided that such students continue their study of the foreign language and culture in the next, more advanced college course," *Language Study for the 1980s* [1980, p. 11]. Since my comments on credit policy do not address the issue of a language *requirement*, it can be made compatible with this recommendation. While the latter may indeed serve the desirable purposes intended, it also has the disadvantageous effect of stressing the licensing, rather than the educational, functions of undergraduate institutions.

19. A further implication of an institutional commitment to language proficiency is so millennial that we must confine its appearance to a footnote. Language ability is acquired and retained *in use*. At an institution that takes language proficiency seriously, the use of languages other than English should be encouraged or even required in courses dealing with every kind of subject matter. The French, the Germans, the Burmese, or the Japanese do not believe that an advanced or scholarly use of their language is confined to a study of their literature, any more than Americans think that a knowledge of English is good only for Shakespeare and Hemingway. It would take deep and difficult changes for college curricula actually to reflect this pervasive use of language—and not just English!

ture. On the other hand, placement tests, proficiency examinations, the preparation of material for language laboratories, and broader concerns with language pedagogy are among the complex enterprises that constitute daily fare for *all* language instructors, regardless of the tongue purveyed.

If there is tension between the conventional departmental organization and what all language teaching has in common, it is heightened where language instruction is regarded, above all, as providing means for the attainment of language proficiency. Not only do instructors of different languages share knowledge and experience, but, within any given institution, they must collaborate closely on many of the activities here mentioned—from the calibration of proficiency examinations to the management of language laboratories.

There is no simple solution. As will be further discussed in chapter 9, the familiar departmental organization cannot just be brushed aside, given the strength of that tradition. It may be possible to do justice both to centrifugal and centripetal pulls by superimposing on language departments a functional organization centered on the management of language pedagogy and supporting facilities. Certain faculty members would thus have a dual affiliation, following the pattern of area studies and similar interdisciplinary programs. To such a unit devoted to language pedagogy one could also attach faculty members teaching needed "exotic" languages for which whole departments are not justified. Serious reflection on the means needed to bring about the goal of language proficiency thus has broad organizational consequences for the undergraduate institution.

MATHEMATICS

Johnny can't write; Johnny can't speak a foreign language; Johnny can barely count. As is true for the previous topics of this chapter, the inadequacy of the mathematical skills of our citizenry has, in recent years, been frequently observed and bemoaned. And for two complementary reasons, rightly so. First, it is broadly conceded that the level of mathematical sophistication of American high school and college graduates is shockingly low. And, since proving theorems in plane geometry or solving equations cannot be expected to be learned at one's mother's knee, this deficiency points to a failure of education.[20]

---

20. See Dossey et al., *Mathematics Report Card* [1988]. In 1986, for example, only 51.1 percent of high school students at age seventeen had reached a proficiency level at which they could "compute with . . . commonly encountered percents. . . . calculate areas of rectangles . . . . solve simple linear equations . . . . make decisions on information drawn from graphs" (pp. 31, 32). Only a "few students (6%) in their latter years of high school have mastered the fundamentals needed to perform more advanced mathematical operations" (p. 43). But "because a large proportion of U.S. high-school students elect to avoid mathematics courses, our nation is far from the international forefront in enrollment" (p. 114).

Second, it matters that we have a mathematically competent population. Since the seventeenth century, mathematics has been an indispensable language of the natural sciences. More recently, it has also come to play an increasingly significant role in the social sciences—and not only in economics. Further, "because of its abstractness, [mathematics] finds useful applications in business, industry, music, historical scholarship, politics, sports, medicine, agriculture, engineering [as well as in] the social and natural sciences."[21] The curricular report issued by the Association of American Colleges, *Integrity in the College Curriculum*, makes the point most broadly: understanding numerical data must be part of a required curriculum because "we have become a society bombarded by numbers."[22]

This pervasive relevance of mathematics—not to mention its abstract and aesthetic properties—stems from the fact that it is a formal enterprise. This truth, however, is often ignored, an omission that has pedagogic and institutional implications. In the ancient world, mathematics was associated in equal measure with astronomy and its spheres and with music and the proportions of its harmony, while the modern world has linked mathematics primarily to science and such science-related activities as engineering. Mathematics departments, for example, are usually listed among science departments, both in secondary and in postsecondary institutions, and where distributional curricular requirements are in force, mathematics is frequently counted as a science.

Classifications, to be sure, are merely matters of convenience. Those just mentioned seem plausible enough, even to someone who is aware of the applicability of mathematics outside the sciences and who is cognizant that mathematics is not an empirical science. But many students do *not* know what these classifiers know; to them these conventional practices convey a powerful message: don't pursue mathematics if your interest and bent is not in science. Just as "math anxiety" is a barrier to the pursuit of science—as well as to mathematics, of course—so the institutional assimilation of mathematics to the category "science" turns others away from mathematics. Both negative

---

21. *Science for All Americans: A Project 2061 Report on Literacy Goals in Science, Mathematics, and Technology* [1989, p. 34]. Besides this summary report of the American Association for the Advancement of Science, panel reports on mathematics, the biological and health sciences, the physical and information sciences and engineering, social, and behavioral sciences, and technology have been published. The title, "Project 2061," refers to the year of the next return of Comet Halley, chosen because the children who will observe that appearance will soon be starting their schooling. Phase 1, now accomplished, aimed at specifying goals: "the knowledge, skills, and attitudes all students should acquire . . . from kindergarten through high school" (p. 3). Phase 2 will be concerned with the formulation of curricula and phase 3 with implementation.
22. *Integrity* [1985, p. 17]. The prose verges on the rhapsodic: "We are threatened by [numbers]. We are intimidated by them. We are lied to with their help. We are comforted by them and seduced by them." Et cetera.

effects are deeply rooted in the habits of educational establishments, and both deserve combating.[23]

Precisely because of the impressive ubiquity of mathematics, its concepts, operations, and branches are relevant to undergraduate education in a variety of ways. Some undergraduates might want to specialize in mathematics. This book will take up issues pertaining to such a concentration only by way of a general discussion of the undergraduate major in chapter 5; but the mathematics major is not our subject here. Second, competency in some branches of mathematics—most frequently in the calculus or in statistics—is needed for the study of various branches of the natural and social sciences. Such prerequisites and corequisites must be considered goals of undergraduate education whenever knowledge of these sciences is a goal. But again, this place for mathematics in undergraduate education is not the proficiency now under discussion.

We are here concerned with mathematical literacy as a goal of undergraduate education, analogous to the literacy that consists of the ability to write clear, expository English prose.[24] Not surprisingly, there are both similarities and differences in the way in which these proficiencies must be regarded from an educational point of view.

Mathematical and English literacy are similar in that, for both, the desired minimal proficiencies could, in principle, be attained in secondary school. Where such goals are achieved prior to arrival in colleges, they become the basis for development during the undergraduate years. In both cases, the deepening and enlarging of these abilities involves specializing, though that branching is much more formal in the pursuit of higher levels of competency in mathematics than it is in writing.

But we will see that far-reaching pedagogical complications arise from the difference noted in this last sentence. With the publication of the results of phase 1 discussions of the American Association for the Advancement of Science (AAAS), all deliberations on literacy in science and mathematics have been given a fruitful new starting point. For mathematics, this thoughtful report defines a typical adult as "a person over 18 with no math beyond high school" and addresses the question, "[W]hat are the important ideas of mathematics that people should know and understand by the age of 18?"[25]

---

23. A section, "Emotions and Mathematics," of the American Association for the Advancement of Science's mathematics report deals sensitively with some of the aspects of this issue. By including mathematics as a "science for all Americans," however, the AAAS inevitably, if understandably, perpetuates the confusion of mathematics as a science. See Blackwell and Henkin, *Mathematics Panel Report* [1989, pp. 37–38].

24. The neologism "numeracy" is neither attractive nor entirely accurate, since mathematics is so much more than numbers. "Mathematical literacy" is awkward, since it is difficult to avoid hearing the word "letter" as the origin of the latter term. However, in the choice between the ugly and the awkward, one might consider the die to have been cast by the application of "literacy" to science and mathematics in *Science for All Americans*.

25. Blackwell and Henkin, *Mathematics Panel Report* [1989, pp. 1, 3].

The panel of experts, using numerous consultants, has provided an account of the mathematics that everyone who completes secondary education should know. At the same time, the group believes that just about the entire secondary school population (and not just those headed for college) is, in fact, capable of learning what it prescribes. Its normative proposals are made within the constraint of what it holds to be possible for the vast majority of children who will complete secondary school, although this claim must be supplemented by two further observations. The report itself stresses the first: that to advance from "can learn" to actual achievement is dependent on a radical reform of schooling, a reform that would have to go well beyond classes in mathematics. The second observation, not in the report itself, is of particular relevance here. The goal put forward for typical adults at the age of eighteen, prior to any higher education, is substantially more ambitious than the level of mathematical competency achieved by most adults who have graduated from college.

One conclusion follows plausibly from this unhappy state of affairs: what is today regarded as an appropriate, though not yet attainable, level of mathematical literacy for eighteen year olds must at least serve as the literacy goal for college graduates. If in future years our school systems come closer to meeting criteria of mathematical literacy of the kind put forward by the AAAS, it will become appropriate to consider raising the sights for mathematics literacy at the postsecondary level. For the foreseeable future, however, the application of *future* high school standards to *present* undergraduate institutions creates a sufficiently formidable task. Present colleges, in other words, might be thought of as being obligated to engage in a kind of anticipatory remediation.

We will see shortly that this second formulation, if harsh, highlights a troublesome pedagogic aspect of the achievement of mathematical literacy. The AAAS panel formulates its goals by pointing to levels of competency in three "processes of mathematics" and seven "subject areas of mathematics." The former are abstraction/representation, symbolic transformation, and application/comparison, and the latter are arithmetic, algebra, geometry, analysis, discrete mathematics, logic and set theory, and probability and statistics.[26] The goals that are posited under these headings are selected for what they are—for their fundamentality and broad applicability—not because they are reached after a certain period of study in what are now standard courses in these areas. Clearly, if the attainment of these goals is to become normal for anyone completing high school, powerful changes must be effected in the teaching of mathematics from kindergarten through secondary school.

Given such an incommensurability between preparation and pedagogic goals, the achievement of mathematical literacy poses a very special curricular task for undergraduate institutions. If the line of reasoning suggested by the

---

26. Blackwell and Henkin, *Mathematics Panel Report* [1989, pp. 5–13, 15–28].

Mathematics Panel Report is pursued, there is no way for colleges simply to offer a version of a mathematics course that a certain number of students happen not to have taken in high school. What those students missed in secondary school and before was a *sequence* of courses or, at the very least, a distinctly different *approach* taken in the courses that were given. Anticipatory remediation is not simply a matter of catching up but calls for the devising of fresh pedagogic strategies.

Panels other than the one put together by the AAAS would no doubt single out different mathematical skills and ideas as components of mathematical literacy. Even now complete agreement is unlikely on the list of mathematical areas to be included, not to mention on the future of an ever-evolving field. What we should not expect, however, is a recommendation that confines the conception of mathematical literacy to abilities and concepts drawn from a distinctly smaller set of areas and ideas of mathematics. An exaggerated view of a past sees the necessity of Latin for mastery of English coupled to a grasp of Euclid's *Elements* as the crux of mathematical literacy. Today, no one would make an analogous proposal; the sharpest disagreements with this panel's recommendations could nevertheless be expected to remain within this pluralistic framework of mathematical literacy. Thus the broad point, that pedagogic approaches must meet the needs of what I have called *anticipatory* remediation, is inescapable and does not simply depend on the specific recommendations of the AAAS.

Mathematical literacy, then, poses difficult pedagogical problems with which each undergraduate institution must struggle. Here we will confine ourselves to a brief indication of three general approaches that might be explored. Not surprisingly, each requires moving across some traditional institutional boundary and is difficult to achieve. None is sufficient by itself.

The first consists "simply" of devising a course that tackles anticipatory remediation head on. Such a course would need to select material from different mathematical areas that are generally assigned to different college courses and would clearly not pursue these themes to the level that they are taken there. At the same time, such a course cannot just be a set of lectures on selected fundamental ideas in mathematics, since it is imperative for students actually to acquire manipulative skills in the domains selected. A course of this kind, in other words, must be complete with textbook and problem sets, *as if* it proposed to teach a traditional field of mathematics but with the complication of having to survey a number of mathematical fields, from algebra and analysis to set theory and statistics. Its usefulness as a solution to the problem of literacy—assuming it to be an excellent course for *someone*—will be further dependent on the degree to which the course meshes with the level of preparation of the students enrolled in it and on the degree to which the preparation of enrolled students is similar. Difficult issues, all of these.

Second, much more can be done to build into beginning college-level social science and natural science curricula the actual use of mathematical ideas and techniques appropriate to the given area. Since so large a number of students is underprepared for the use of mathematics, most such introductory natural and social science courses simply do without. The alternative to this practice is as obvious as it is difficult: it accepts these deficiencies as a given and sets out to incorporate, right then and there, some of the pedagogy that would alleviate them—with the additional virtue of providing an immediate context for learning the *application* of mathematical ideas.

The obstacles to such steps are legion, from crowding still further already crowded courses to the availability of appropriate textbooks, not to mention the availability of instructors prepared to carry out such teaching missions. But the necessity for broadly increasing the routine use of mathematics in the undergraduate curriculum goes well beyond the present problem of mathematical literacy. Even if we envisage long-term measures that deal effectively with mathematical literacy, and assume that AAAS standards are achieved by most graduates from secondary schools, the abilities brought to college would wither if they were not put to use.

But progress toward the attainment of standards so distant from our present accomplishments will not be achieved by some small number of giant steps that begin with the new approaches to preschoolers and work their way up from K to twelve. If there is to be progress at all, changes will be both sporadic and gradual, and will certainly need to take place at numbers of levels at once. Of course, wherever earlier schooling improves the mathematical preparation of students, higher levels must then promptly incorporate into their curricula the new levels of competency achieved. But unlike the erection of a house, the curricular building is not subject to gravitational forces that compel one to build strictly from the bottom up; the lower row of curricular bricks need not always be the earlier. Rather, by making new demands in courses that come later in time, new standards are set to influence earlier preparation. The short-run scramble to close the gap between preparation and need for one generation of students is a necessary ingredient in educational progress, which never marches forward in orderly fashion from earlier to later. Means and ends have reciprocal effects on each other.

A third method that can contribute toward the spread of mathematical literacy is an increased use of self-paced, computer-aided instruction. This technique is particularly effective where the antecedent preparation of the learners is variable and where extensive practice is needed. In principle, it is possible to devise self-paced, computer-aided course modules that could cover all areas thought to be important components of mathematical literacy.

A number of obstacles stand in the way of widespread institutional use of this method. The deepest of them is the organization and supervision of such learning in a way that helps students to persist outside the social context created by the familiar class with its teacher. The formation of collaborative learning communities in mathematics is one approach that has shown itself to be most fruitful.[27] Further, the availability of hardware and software constitute budgetary and intellectual hurdles, while the awarding of credit toward graduation for students and credit in the teaching load for faculty are administrative puzzles. None of these issues is trivial, and together they can be formidable. But they are concerned with the means by which undergraduate institutions carry out the goals they set for themselves. Here, in this difficult and important case of mathematical literacy, a clearer formulation of goals might contribute to greater effort to secure the means.

COMPUTER LITERACY

This entire chapter might be called "Literacies," since for the goals taken up in two of the three preceding sections, the term is in general use, while in the case of foreign languages, the analogies are there, even if the importance of speaking and understanding the spoken word makes becoming "lettered" an inept expression. We turn, now, to this chapter's final topic, computer literacy, where the term is used, even though the analogy to those *Oxford English Dictionary* meanings is somewhat more remote.

In the not-so-distant past, knowing how to use a computer did indeed involve a form of literacy, since that instrument remained essentially inert unless programmed to life by means of FORTRAN or another language created for the purpose. Since then, things have become both easier and more complicated. Expert computer use, of course, requires the ability to program—and in a larger array of languages—but, thanks to several different lines of development, much is possible without this literal literacy. Accordingly, those who today advocate computer literacy as a goal of education want to see students have a broad familiarity with computers and their uses, with programming playing only a subsidiary part. Literacy, here, has been stretched to refer to an ability to use a tool that is, at once, immensely versatile and complex. It is versatile in that it can perform numerous kinds of tasks that differ radically from each other, and it is complex in that the many different "attachments"—mostly in the form of programs—that can do all these different things call for different capabilities in addition to the ability to operate the basic tool. So versatile is the tool, moreover, that every time you turn around, someone has significantly improved (and thus changed) one of those attachments or invented a totally new one. And, finally, a clever tool owner can modify attachments, or devise entirely novel ones, to suit his or her own purposes.

Given this complexity, the kind of literacy that is desirable enables the computer user to operate the basic instrument and to approach with confi-

---

27. Attend, particularly, to the work of Philip Uri Treisman at the University of California, Berkeley. For a useful overview, see *Dana Report* [1988].

dence a certain range of commercially available attachments to learn how to use them without formal training. While one may or may not want to insist that "literacy" should include the ability to make uncomplicated modifications in the way tool or attachment works, real tool making is a specialty that goes well beyond the kind of familiarity under discussion. No one is properly schooled in the use of a tool, however, without having a sense of when it is appropriate to use it and, given an envisaged task, how. If, as a tool, a computer is a means, to be familiar with it is to know what ends it can serve, and in what way.

If this account is a bit cumbersome—especially since, today, familiarity with the language of hardware and software is more prevalent than with that of machine tools and their attachments—the analogy of the computer as a versatile tool does provide a helpful perspective. One learns to use a tool properly—and practices that use so as to build up and sustain a skill—in the course of learning the craft in which the tool is customarily used. If the tool is versatile, there may be numerous such crafts.

Since we are not talking here about tool making and design nor about computer science—this logic of computer as tool points to a pedagogy of computing across and in the curriculum. The computer has a place in the pursuit of scholarly topics in numerous arts and sciences subjects and, of course, in many professional subject areas. In the form of word processing, it plays an increasingly significant role in all writing, whether in specific courses devoted to it or in the writing that is itself in or across the curriculum. To the extent to which the teaching of relevant subjects is up to date, the techniques utilizing computers are appropriately a part of the syllabus.

The rapidity with which the world of computers moves brings a number of special problems; when we turn to these in a moment, we will also be brought back to the issue of computer "literacy." But first we must take up an aspect of the computer's versatility that gives it a very special role in the context of education. The extensive introduction of computers in the curriculum is justified by their use in diverse fields for research and in the management of the substance of those fields—to solve equations, analyze financial data, or calculate the tensile strength of some alloy. Computers, however, are also useful for *learning* many aspects of different subjects; they are a versatile educational tool, as well. Their introduction into the curriculum is also justified by the *pedagogic* roles computers can play.

Recently, these computer applications in teaching and learning have been most helpfully classified: "The computer can help an instructor deliver instructional content and develop student skills in a number of ways. It can act as a teaching machine, a simulator, a resource, or a tool."[28]

---

28. Heermann, *Teaching and Learning with Computers* [1988, p. 4]. For an overview, see pp. 4–12; for extensive discussions, see chapters 3–6, pp. 46–102.

1.   The computer as teaching machine, usually referred to as computer-aided instruction, is particularly useful where drilling is a normal mode of learning; we have already referred to it in connection with language instruction and mathematics.

2.   When the computer is used to simulate, it models physical or social phenomena, usually in a way that permits the manipulation of parts, so that interrelationships can be better understood.

3.   As resource, the computer supplies information, either because it stores data or because it is used to communicate to external sources, such as a library.

4.   Finally, as a tool, the computer can perform a great variety of tasks, by means of such instrumentalities as word processing, spreadsheet, accounting, graphing, statistical packages, and other familiar and unfamiliar kinds of software.

Only the first of these computer uses, as is implied by its name, is specifically pedagogical. But while all the others are (primarily) tools for investigation and problem solving in various fields, they most definitely have their applications in teaching. The pedagogic use of computer simulation, its employment as a source of data, or its use as a tool may be identical to the way in which a practitioner in the field would use the computer, or it may be very different. But in either case, computers are introduced into the curriculum so as to achieve the secondary result of increasing students' ability to use them. In short, two overlapping ways bring computers into the curriculum: the actual roles they play in the subjects being studied, and the pedagogical assistance they give in the study of those subjects.

This pervasive applicability of computers in undergraduate education, together with the rapidity with which that situation has developed and continues to change, has created a challenge for faculty as well as for students. At a not-so-distant future, we can envisage a time when most students and most faculty will walk into a college classroom as already quite sophisticated users of computers. Both groups will have attained the level of the homeowner as repairman—that is, the equivalent of ability with hammer, screwdriver, and saw—with the latter group additionally versed in computer uses appropriate to the subjects they profess. Schooling, from early on, will have brought them to this point.

At this time, however, students vary greatly in their readiness for participation in a computer-using portion of a syllabus, while faculty members are most unequally prepared to make use of computers in their teaching. In a sense, the problem of computer literacy amounts "simply" to finding ways for bringing about that twofold preparedness at this time, even in the absence of pervasive schooling from childhood on. We are again speaking of anticipatory remediation, this time for faculty as well as students.

If the analogy of computer as versatile tool is sound, the pedagogic issues, nevertheless, are not of the same order as those associated with mathematical literacy. What is here needed is a familiarization with computers that is fostered by access, encouragement, and assistance: availability of hardware and software, incentives for using them, and help in working with them.

Of course, such threefold support can be packaged into "computer literacy" courses, with modules touching on different topics that are likely to be of use to many who are needful of assistance. Given the practicality of the needs, moreover, the more efficiently such a course aims at serving the workaday needs of novice students or faculty, the less likely will it be of a kind that should yield credit toward graduation.[29]

But with or without such courses, the computer literacy problem cannot be solved short of the creation of a computer-friendly campus atmosphere, manifested in easy access to computers and software, and in the availability of knowledgeable people standing ready to help with advice and workshops. Such an institution is capable of accommodating to the needs of very differently prepared arrivals on campus and ready to be helpful with a large variety of uses of computers, while creating a setting that encourages their utilization.

Such a campus is, in any case, needed for a longer haul. For a foreseeable future, the capabilities of computers and software, as well as the range of their applications, can be expected to grow and change. Accordingly, even for literate, if not specialized, computer users there will be new things to learn and try out. Perhaps the familiarity with computers that has been called computer literacy will spread more rapidly than the ability to meet literacy standards for writing. There will not, however, be a time when, in institutions of higher education, computer users will not need help and support in making use of new developments in their learning and research.

---

29. Clearly, courses can also be devised (indeed, they exist) combining an introductory study of the theory of computing and computers with the practical know-how here under discussion. While no questions need be raised about the creditworthiness of such courses, they would also go well beyond our narrower sense of computer literacy.

CHAPTER 3

CONVERSANCIES

SCIENCE

We do not expect undergraduates to attain expertise in a subject they study in college, if only because most disciplines are deeper and wider than can be fathomed in the time available. *Conversancy* with a number of areas, however, *is* a goal of undergraduate education, with the understanding that this notion is open to considerable variation in the firmness of grasp attained. But to be conversant with an area suggests being familiar with its basic information and with the modes of thinking and investigating that enable one to move around in it. With all of its imprecision and range, conversancy implies an understanding that is a sufficient basis for further learning and a perspective sufficiently broad so as to enable a student to see some of the field's relations to other worlds.

To ask that students become conversant with a number of areas is to posit a number of quite distinct educational goals. But there is a commonality: the very notion of conversancy embodies the futility of separating the acquisition of information in a field from learning its principles of investigation and validation. The "facts" of chemistry or history cannot be learned and understood apart from the way such facts are discovered and related to each other, any more than ways of "doing" chemistry or history can be taught without teaching those chemical and historical facts. No coherent meaning can be given to the notion of methods of chemistry or history, abstracted from their operation in some specific chunk of the world—chemical or historical. And when facts are asked to stand by themselves, the statements that might formulate any of them, however potentially important, amount to no more than answers to trivia questions, or to the recitation of items of information in a language that is unknown to the speaker. For those items to constitute someone's knowledge, they must gain the meaning that is imparted by an understanding of interrelationships, of their place in an exposition, an account.

An important function of the language of conversancy, then, is the insistence on a note of realism that might impede the propagation of myths of quick fixes in higher education. Here, as elsewhere, we are fooling only ourselves when we simplistically see the tasks of education to be "nothing but" the imparting of information or the passing on of methods, as if either were viable in isolation from the other. We will see, instead, even in the general discussions that are appropriate in this context, that quite different pedagogical and institutional problems are faced as one seeks to devise means to assist students to become conversant in a number of different domains of thought.[1]

Of the three broad areas of study, the natural sciences, social sciences, and humanities, college graduates, as a group, have the least conversancy with the first, while there is virtually unanimous agreement on the importance of knowledge of the natural sciences. Unquestionably, natural science is the most elaborate and successful intellectual product of the last five hundred years of human thinking, and, in the course of the last hundred years, the world we live in has been transformed by applications of this sophisticated scientific knowledge. Thus both an abstract understanding of the natural world, as well as informed decision making in many aspects of public affairs and private life, are dependent on a conversancy with science to a degree that could not even have been imagined until recently. Yet while these truths stand essentially unchallenged, students, except for those specializing in a science, devote considerably less time to science than to any other traditional area of undergraduate study. And the time that *is* spent in pursuing knowledge of natural science tends not to achieve the goal of conversancy.[2]

We speak routinely, in discussions of undergraduate education like these, of science courses and of teaching science to nonscientists, while we do not similarly ask for courses in history for nonhistorians, literature for non–

1. There is a tendency for those who are particularly upset by what college (or high school) graduates don't know to respond, with some vehemence, that we must tell them, so that they *will* know. What the implied pedagogy ignores is that those fact-beads on a string do not add up to knowledge, if they are retained at all. It is probably an oversimplification to regard E.D. Hirsch's [1988] "cultural literacy" movement as calling for the *teaching* of the facts he thinks everyone should know, in isolation from the contexts in which they play a role. Followers of his, however, give the impression that they believe that to be possible and desirable. Neither Cheney [1989] nor subsequent interpretations by its author (e.g., "Further Debate" [1990]) make clear that this fundamental point is understood.

2. A study of transcripts of thirty public and private institutions that provide a four-year baccalaureate education—carefully selected to be representative of different sizes, tuition levels, degrees of selectivity, and overall missions—suggested the following summary: "In more than half the institutions, more than one-eighth of the graduates took fewer than three courses in the natural sciences and mathematics. . . . At most institutions, natural sciences and mathematics enrollments accounted for less than 20 percent of the course or credit units earned by the graduates." Zemsky, *Structure and Coherence* [1989, pp. 36–37; also see the revealing bar graph, p. 35].

   That we face a real problem is supported by the report of a survey on "scientific literacy," especially when one considers the modesty of that concept relative to the conversancy here proposed as a goal of undergraduate education. "Scientific literacy can be described as a 'reasonable' vocabulary of scientific and technical terms—for example, the ability to define a molecule—together with a basic understanding of the process of scientific thinking. . . . In 1979 only 7% of American adults met the criteria described above; in 1986 the level dropped to 5%. . . . Of the over 2000 Americans interviewed in the 1985 study, no one with less than a high school diploma qualified as scientifically literate. Only 3% of high school graduates qualified; the proportion rose to 12% among holders of B.A.s and 18% among Ph.D.s." Miller [1988], reporting on his study.

literary critics, or even anthropology or sociology for nonanthropologists or nonsociologists. But even if these omissions are to be faulted—and it is a pervasive thesis of this book that there is a difference between educating undergraduates and initiating them into a profession—there is a deep basis for the distinction thus tacitly made.

Since the latter part of the nineteenth century, and at a sharply accelerating rate, the natural sciences have become increasingly technical, and concomitantly they have become ever more specialized. The long periods needed for initiation and technical study—with certain dispositions and talents presupposed—have created a division between insiders and outsiders that is deeper than in other areas of study. One effect on outsiders is that even intelligent and attentive persons, though uneducated in science, cannot eavesdrop on conversations among members of the clan. To hear is not to understand.[3] The effect on insiders, on the other hand, is to foster the view that the gap can be bridged only if others traverse the same long road that brought them to the status of qualified practitioner. It is not surprising, therefore, that introductory courses in the natural sciences are inevitably composed of the beginning sequences of extensive step-by-step progressions toward mastery. Most frequently, then, the *introduction to a science* is in effect the start of an *induction into the profession* of a particular science, into the field of the professor.

But the conversancy we seek—though so far not much has been said about it—is not likely to be achieved if an introduction consists of the first steps of an induction. It may be an exaggeration to liken course sequences in science to a long dark tunnel, with emergence at the end of the journey rewarded by a panoramic view. But, then, neither does such a sequence resemble a ladder so placed that each new step affords an ever-better view of the total vista. Those first steps do derive most of their significance from their function as preparations for *further* steps, with the fulfillment—the payoff— coming later on the path toward mastery.

The very notion of conversancy, by contrast, introduces desiderata of a quite different kind. Since undergraduate education seeks to have students become conversant with several areas of study, we must understand any one conversancy to be attainable in a reasonably compact way, with considerable differences in time and effort taken for granted. More important still, while the orientation to an entire domain—as is intended by the goal of

---

3. Members of other academic professions might protest at being tacitly accorded a less "professional" status; irritated readers might want to point out that the poststructural discourse of literary theorists is also unintelligible to the uninitiated. A serious response would take us much too far afield; suffice it here to point out that the most technical economists report their findings routinely to noneconomists and that it would take incomparably less long for an interested physicist to get the hang of the lingo of followers of Derrida than for a literary scholar to follow a lecture reporting a recent result of an experiment at a nuclear accelerator.

conversancy—can take quite different forms, it must in all cases attend to principles, concepts, and findings that are of central importance to the field.

If conventional introductions, designed to be the first steps of a long ascent, will not guide toward conversancy, no simple, single substitute will bring about this goal. In effect, we are facing a version of an ancient metaphysical conundrum—that of seeing at once the one and the many. To this point, we have spoken both of natural *science* and of the natural *sciences*, as if singular and plural nouns meant the same. But there *is* a difference, and by looking at what is associated with both, we will become clearer about the achievement of conversancy.

The use of the singular invokes commonalities belonging to each of the natural sciences or to all of them together. There are many different ways to formulate these common traits; for our purposes it is helpful to follow the designation of topics in the important report of the American Association for the Advancement of Science, *The Liberal Art of Science* [1990]. Under the general heading of "The Nature of Scientific Understanding," one group of topics is subsumed: scientific values and ways of knowing; collection, organization, and classification of information; discovering scientific laws, devising models, and developing theories; the limits of scientific knowledge; the vocabulary and terminology of science; and the role of mathematical concepts in understanding science. Under the heading of "Integrative Concepts," the following are put forward: scale and proportion; change and evolution; causality and consequences; and dynamic equilibrium. Under the rubric of "The Context of Science," the following two broad areas are taken up: the historical development and intellectual and cultural contexts of science; and the ethical, social, economic, and political dimensions of science.[4]

An understanding of these themes suggested by the singular noun, because they pertain to all of the natural sciences, is an eminently appropriate goal of conversancy. Conventional introductory courses to particular sciences, as conventionally taught, however, will, at best, touch on only a small number of these topics. Moreover, many of the principles and issues there involved

4. These topics, here quoted in full (spacing, capitalization, and quotation marks omitted), are briefly clarified in a summary statement, *The Liberal Art of Science* [1990, pp. xii–xiv] and discussed more fully in the section, "Aspects of Scientific Understanding" [pp. 15–26]. The AAAS project that addresses precollege education formulates these common topics somewhat differently (spacing, capitalization, and quotation marks again omitted). Under the broad heading of "The Scientific World View," these basic principles are cited: the world is understandable; scientific ideas are subject to change; scientific knowledge is durable; science cannot provide complete answers to all questions. Under the rubric of "Scientific Inquiry," the following is stressed: science demands evidence; science is a blend of logic and imagination; science explains and predicts; scientists try to identify and avoid bias; and science is not authoritarian. Finally, to characterize "The Scientific Enterprise," it puts forward the following: science is a complex social activity; science is organized into content disciplines and is conducted in various institutions; there are generally accepted ethical principles in the conduct of science; and scientists participate in public affairs both as specialists and as citizens. From *Science for All Americans* [1989, pp. 25–31].

are likely to remain implicit as the course goes about its introductory business. Given their importance and complexity, however, justice cannot be done in this way to an understanding of the enterprise of science.

As we turn to the *sciences*, to the plural, prudence suggests that we introduce a further distinction. Particular sciences evolve and are given distinct names, a function both of the problems dealt with and of the social history of the institutions by which scientists are organized—departments, institutes, laboratories, and so on. This history, reflected in the subdivisions of universities and colleges, has curricular consequences. Distribution requirements in natural science are the most obvious result, since students are then typically asked to select one (or more) courses from offerings by *departments* such as astronomy, biochemistry, biology (or, variously, departments of cell biology, evolutionary biology, microbiology, molecular biology), chemistry, geology, and physics, and, occasionally, the physiological branch of psychology. In an important sense, what is studied by such students in the natural sciences is a function of the institutional sociology of scientists.

Without question, where the aim is induction into a field, pedagogy must be most responsive to the way in which its practitioners are organized. An introduction that seeks conversancy, on the other hand, cannot give automatic primacy to such "political" subdivisions of the academy. Its task, instead, is to aim at familiarity with issues and problems, with different aspects of nature that the sciences attempt to understand. Again, a Project 2061 formulation succinctly conveys the kind of distinction intended, with the understanding that numerous alternatives are possible. Under "physical setting," the following subjects are listed: the universe, the earth, forces that shape the earth, the structure of matter, transformations of energy, the motion of things, the forces of nature.[5] What is here a single plausible heading, however, refers to issues that are variously parceled out to such departments as astronomy, chemistry, geology, and physics, with variations that depend, in part, on particular institutional organizations. An analogous list of topics is generated under the heading of "the living environment." Given the recent burgeoning of the life sciences, however, departmental names and boundary lines are far more variable and fluid, so that more local differences can be expected in the way in which issues and topics are distributed.[6]

Whatever list one might adopt, it is fruitful to think about the conversancy with science as a grasp of a set of central topics, discoveries, and problems, rather than as pieces of academic fields—physics, chemistry, astronomy, and so on. Moreover, since an understanding of the nature of scientific inquiry

5. Cited from the table of contents of *Science for All Americans* [1989, p. i]; the discussion on pp. 47–56. The primary goal of the AAAS report, *The Liberal Art of Science* [1990], is to propose a fundamental change in science pedagogy. In concentrating on this goal, it does not posit substantive topics analogous to this one from Project 2061.
6. For the Project 2061 life science formulations, see *Science for All Americans* [1989, pp. 59–64].

and the scientific world view—stressed when we attended to conversancy with science in the singular—cannot effectively be gained in abstraction from scientific content, it suggests course work that aims simultaneously at both aspects of the goal to be attained.

Many specific kinds of courses can be devised to satisfy the broad criteria here put forward, and they can be taught at quite different levels of rigor and technicality. One design calls for a single, sweeping, team-taught course; others make available shorter, more specific units. The framework of one is historical, while another focuses on the most recent formulations feasible. Whichever of such paths is taken, the pedagogic road to conversancy will not much resemble those courses that aim at "exposure" to natural science, sometimes collectively and derisively lumped under the heading of "physics for poets." For even the very general formulation of the educational goal put forward here requires pedagogic reflections of a sort that remain in abeyance when the objective is simply to have the science faculty "do something" for students not destined to pursue the serious study of a science.[7]

It is not surprising that a significant fraction of the science faculty sees the teaching of science to nonscientists to be a futile chore, not to be taken very seriously. Long years of all-absorbing specialization have led many practitioners to see their field almost exclusively from within the complex, technical domain that it is. And since in higher education educators mostly are, and certainly should be, such "insiders," many find it difficult to envisage a conceptual terrain between the step-by-step induction resembling their own education and a contemptuous pearls-before-swine "physics for poets." Serious discussion of central theories of physics without employing the calculus seems absurd; a rigorous account of the nature of DNA without presupposing biochemistry seems a contradiction in terms. Thus precisely what is needed to achieve an important goal of undergraduate education seems most foreign to a significant proportion of the science professoriate.

But the achievement of conversancy with natural science constitutes an enormously important goal of education. The task is intellectually serious, even if it is not technical, and the pedagogy leading to conversancy can be responsible and rigorous, even if it must largely do without the precision, power, and elegance afforded by such devices as mathematical formulations.[8]

---

7. The appendixes of *The Liberal Art of Science* [1990, pp. 73–106] give expositions of a considerable number of sample courses and programs.

8. Since mathematical (or other technical) precision and the coherence that comes from systematically interrelated details are also significant expressions of what natural science is all about, it might be argued that the conventional, "professional" introductory course is just what is wanted for conversancy after all. That this path precludes a breadth that is even more important has been tacit all along, unless a very large portion of undergraduate study is devoted to conversancy with natural science. To be added, however, is the empirical truth that, without subsequent use, not much of what is learned in such meticulous introductory courses adheres to the memory, so that what might be most effectively taught is nevertheless not likely to be retained.

But the difficulty of the task must be acknowledged as well. The issues, problems, discoveries, and theories to be learned are selected for their importance (in several senses) and not for the place they have in the exposition of a discipline. The pedagogic quandary they thus pose is real enough. On the one hand, much of what must be taught is quite removed from ordinary experience or commonsense knowledge. On the other, because the topics to be taught are not properly embedded in a discipline, many of the tested ways of teaching them are unavailable for use. Pedagogically, the teacher who thus assists students to become conversant with natural science sails in relatively uncharted seas. Yet that teacher must be a member of the science faculty; the role we seek cannot be delegated to those who are themselves amateurs. Only someone capable of seeing science from the inside can extend the helping hand that will reduce the gap between insiders and outsiders. The very training, knowledge, and rigor that sometimes make practitioners of science diffident about involvement in a "superficial" conversancy are needed in the pursuit of this significant educational goal. The path toward conversancy with natural science is also a form of initiation; the ritual cannot be performed by anyone who is not a priest of the temple. Perhaps more than in any other area, there is here a disparity between the natural propensities, so to speak, of the faculty and the educational needs of undergraduates. The challenge faced by undergraduate institutions is that of finding ways to assist and support its science faculty to carry out this mission. That charge is as difficult as it is important.

HISTORY

Integrity in the College Curriculum includes "historical consciousness" in its "minimum required curriculum."[9] Its authors do not say so, but one reason for this formulation might be a tendency of Americans to divide the temporal world into two lumps: the present, composed of the period spanned by personal memory, and the past, consisting of all the time that came before. (Perhaps the childhood and youth of the very elderly are an exception and become, for them, a part of the past or at least a transition between past and present.) The reason that *is* advanced by this report is the understanding that such consciousness can bring both to the present and the past. After a brief account of the benefits of possessing a "consciousness of history," the report's authors note further that "if everyone and everything has a history, then the opportunities for nurturing historical consciousness in a baccalaureate program are manifestly unlimited," though they caution, as well, that historical consciousness cannot be expected just to come naturally.

There is a sense in which in an undergraduate curriculum, "history is all

9. *Integrity* [1985, pp. 18–19], the source, as well, of the quotations that follow.

over the course of study—in the languages, art, music, literatures, social studies, the sciences, and in history itself." But a closer look suggests that we have little more than unrealizable opportunities for history. Note is taken, in those courses, of sequences in time: Fielding before Dickens before Hardy; Mozart before Beethoven before Brahms; Galileo before Newton before Einstein; Manet before Cezanne before Picasso. More often than not, the works of such creators are then studied in temporal order. It is much less clear, however, how much of an historical consciousness is or can be nurtured by such familiar courses.

As things are, a plausible, but by no means certain, historical harvest is knowledge of the actual order in which works and makers appeared on the scene; a second, still shakier one is the cognizance of just when. Not just the inattentiveness of students accounts for this minimal cultivation of historical consciousness but, more deeply, the way in which cultural and intellectual products tend to be treated in undergraduate education. Put simply, the works that are studied are mostly looked at, one at a time. Only secondarily is attention paid to relationships to predecessor works, and then the focus is largely on matters of resemblance and dissimilarity. Always granting exceptions, even less time is spent on social, political, economic, or religious conditions (and the like) that might help account for some of the characteristics of the works under scrutiny. *When* something was brought about is thus just another fact, detached from anything else; it is not hard to see why it should often go unnoted and, when remarked, unremembered.

If this is true for most "historical" courses in literature, philosophy, science, or the arts, we should not expect them to be caring nurseries of historical consciousness, in whatever sense. Nor should we demand a significant change. Given what might be called the economy of undergraduate education, it is imperative that most of such courses concentrate on the works themselves, for they are often large, almost always important and complex, and frequently expressed in a language unfamiliar to the student. The job of analyzing and interpreting these objects of study and of fathoming their implications—not to mention becoming versed in the techniques of analysis and interpretation—are so enormous and vital, as rightly to crowd out most other activities. Yes, historical information and perspectives have their place in such courses, but in the undergraduate context they are as subordinate to the main activities as is learning about a foreign culture while pursuing the study of its language.[10]

10. If one ignored the needs of undergraduates, one would still have to pay heed to the capabilities and predilections of professors, shaped by the scholarly fashions prevailing when they were educated. Time appears and disappears in cyclical fashion in the study of the artistic and intellectual products of the human mind, as does the social context of their creation. For the older generation now teaching, the history of philosophy is a great conversation conducted across all barriers, temporal as well as geographical, and great works of literature and art are each unique and to be studied for what they are in them-

The historical consciousness we want to nurture includes an abiding awareness of the fact that time stretches and that "in" that time, changes are ever ongoing. The realms of art, science, and philosophy do provide opportunities for honing such awareness, even if largely unexploited in courses devoted to them. But, in any case, there is more to the historical consciousness than such temporal awareness. We want, in addition, to develop a sense of the *complexity* and, often, complicatedness of these changes, of the richness, so to speak, of the causality by which things happen. Historical naïveté takes historical events to resemble the toppling of a bowling pin in the local alley: the ball was bowled by the player, hit the pin, and the pin fell over. Historical consciousness, by contrast, is aware that causality is multiple and often unclear and that one should count on a play of interactions among the realms of the social, the economic, the political, the psychological, the military, the religious, the scientific, the artistic, and so on. Such sophistication, moreover, includes the capacity to sort out tangled skeins in making progress toward an understanding of how what happened came about. It includes, as well, a sense of the limits of historical understanding, given its dependency on the questions that are actually formulated and the evidence that can be brought to bear on the answers.

For all practical purposes, then, the nurturing of a historical consciousness worthy of that imposing appellation is likely to require the formal study of history.[11] And if the study of history is needed, then there is much merit in positing as a goal knowledge of the history of the civilization of the student's country.[12] Historical consciousness, it has been an assumption all along, is not some abstract form that can be acquired—or even meaningfully described—independently of a study of the histories of institutions and people, actions and events, made specific with names and places and dates.

---

selves. Recent neo-Marxist scholarship, by contrast, is interested in how those works are shaped by the time and place at which they were created. The backgrounds of the professoriate thus determine what is possible and what is likely.

11. To be sure, the authors of the *Integrity* report are likely to be right that historical consciousness cannot just "be delivered on order by the history department in large survey courses or in textbook assignments in narrative histories" [1985, p. 18]. In history, as in other fields, how a topic is taught makes a crucial difference, determining whether the student is converted from passive recipient into active learner. For a discussion of this theme, see chapter 7 of this book.

12. The shock that only 32 percent of the 17 year olds tested not long ago placed the American Civil War in the period between 1850 and 1900 is matched only by the knowledge that those youngsters most certainly did not make up for their lack of fundamental information by the sophistication of their historical consciousness. This is one finding, among other appalling results, of a study that has served as the empirical basis of concern about historical (including geographical) and literary knowledge. The multiple-choice examination tested for knowledge of some 300 facts that eleventh graders might reasonably know. From Ravitch and Finn, *What Do Our 17-Year-Olds Know?* [1987]; items tested for, pp. 263–277. Shocked as we are by these findings, it is worth remembering that they tell us what students don't know; they tell us nothing about how to teach them.

The purpose of nurturing historical consciousness is to cultivate understanding of our world. The purpose of making the study of American history the *way* of fostering that mode of seeing and grasping is that it is the study of *our* world and that of students who live and have their futures here. In one sense this claim is innocuous—after all, we *are* here; in another sense, there have been waves of serious challenges to this position.

America is a new country, populated by people mostly stemming from elsewhere, placed in a continent not discovered (by outsiders, to be sure— the natives knew they were here) until a millennium and a half after Christ, two thousand years since the Greek origins of our civilization, and another half a thousand since its Judaic roots. This line of thinking suggests the educational goal not of American history (or not only) but of the history of the West. And the argument can be taken further. America, today, is not only populated by inhabitants who hail from the European continent but by immigrants and descendants from Africa and the Middle East, Latin America and the Caribbean, as well as all parts of Asia. Further, the globe on which all of humanity resides has shrunk in every way in which parts can be related to each other; little takes place anywhere on its surface that remains irrelevant to our lives. A study of the history of the world thus becomes an appropriate goal of undergraduate education.

The considerations put forward in the two preceding paragraphs are unexceptionable: the Magna Carta is barely less relevant to America's history than the Declaration of Independence; knowledge of eighteenth- and nineteenth-century African culture makes a distinct contribution to the understanding of central components of our own culture—to mention but two examples. Curricular conclusions must nevertheless be drawn with caution. The attempt to crowd into a course all-that-is-important-to-know is not likely to be educationally successful, if success is measured by what students can recall and use a few years later. Still more significantly—given how we began this section—an endeavor of that sort may well scuttle any effort to nurture historical consciousness.

Because it is true that *vita brevis est, ars longa*, with a similar ratio holding between the undergraduate years and the mountains there are to be learned, one is perpetually tempted to try to achieve a plurality of goals by means of a single course. But more often than not, the attempt to kill several birds with one stone succeeds only in frightening away the whole flock. Historical consciousness, it was said earlier, cannot be cultivated where the objects of study are merely looked at in temporal juxtaposition; there must be an exploration of the processes that connect them. Undoubtedly, numerous types of courses can provide the opportunities for the achievement of this goal; it is up to the historians in different institutions to design courses that are suitable in their particular context. I will, however, register here the skeptical view that a history of *everything*, once over lightly, does not teach the history of *anything*, nor what historical processes are like. At the same time, global awareness must indeed be regarded as a goal of undergraduate education and the next section of this chapter will concern itself with that issue.

We have spoken of historical consciousness and of history but not of the social sciences. While history is sometimes classified as a social science, an addendum is in order about those fields conventionally so designated: economics, political science, and sociology, as well as major areas within anthropology, geography, and psychology.

An unkind wit once remarked that one simple move would markedly improve undergraduate education, namely the placing of a strict limit on the number of social science courses a student is permitted to take. One assumption that underlies this crack is, clearly, that the restriction would require students to take more work in the humanities and the natural sciences, rather than professional courses (not a few of which, in such fields as education, social work, library science are, in any case, courses in applied social science). It will be instructive to pursue an explanation as to why this shift in emphasis is supposed to be a Good Thing, as the authors of *1066 and All That* would say.

If it is not assumed, prejudicially, that there is a substantial difference in the quality of teaching across all those fields, the comparisons must be made on the basis of syllabi. The way things go in the real world, the humanities and the natural sciences do possess an edge. The former almost always require the reading of books of substance, so that even if the teaching is poor or inappropriately modish, students are at least brought into contact with significant works. Similarly, the teaching in natural science courses may well be problematic, but one can almost count on the fact that the substance of the course will be mind stretching: the scientific discoveries, theories, or principles taken up are not merely matters of everyday experience expressed more formally in the jargon of a technical language.

In the social sciences, the probability that courses will be in some analogous way "teacher proof" is nowhere near as high. Textbooks, rather than original works, are the rule, and the mode of discourse is often journalistic, veiled to some degree by the special rhetoric each field devises. *Of course* new information is conveyed to students by these means, but far too few social science courses, if not addressed to advanced students, depart from the realm of what might be called expanded everyday experience. And providing a store of information is never a sufficient curricular goal of higher education.

While I would claim that this picture of much of social science teaching is on the mark, it must also be insisted that this world of textbooks—continuous with the "social studies" of precollege schooling—reflects very poorly the central intellectual contributions of the social sciences. This is no place to enter into the century-long controversies about how much the social sciences resemble the natural sciences. We will, instead, build on a point on which there is broad, though certainly not unanimous, agreement. The operative term was coined in the nineteenth century: the social sciences are nomothetic, from the Greek *nomos*, meaning *law*. Their scholarly aim does not end with the description of individual phenomena, actions, events, institutions, but seeks to understand these as components of broader patterns or instances of overarching regularities.

It is in a display of this, the intellectual center of the social sciences, that their contribution to nonspecialist undergraduate education must lie. While such a study can take a number of quite different forms, we will conclude this section by mentioning just two. One pole is occupied by the reading and discussion of a selection of the great, "classical" social science theorists. Some of the founders of modern economics come to mind—Adam Smith, Ricardo, Marx, for example; others are to be found among the "fathers" of modern sociology—Durkheim, Simmel, or Weber. The study of such works will not only acquaint students with important antecedents in our intellectual history—and some are therefore at times included in general education courses concerned with "Western civilization"—but insofar as they propound *theories*, they constitute exemplars of nomothetic thinking about human behavior.

The other end of a continuum that displays the nomothetic character of the social sciences is occupied by the study of social phenomena by methods so rigorous and precise that considerable clarity is achieved in the generalizations arrived at and in the relationships that hold among them. Because economics is capable of formulating virtually all of its theories in mathematical and statistical terms, it is, in this sense, the most mature of the social sciences. An analogous or even identical rigor has been attained in portions of all the others—certainly sufficient to the purpose of exhibiting the nomothetic character of the social sciences to undergraduates.

When such significant intellectual contributions of the social sciences are put at the center of undergraduate teaching, the tacit charge of shallowness contained in that reformer's taunt is undermined, and that domain can also be regarded as a goal of undergraduate education.

GLOBAL AWARENESS

We have already alluded to global awareness as a goal of undergraduate education. More elaborately, the *Integrity* report calls for "international and multicultural experiences," with a view to combating provincialism and producing "citizens of a shrinking world and a changing America."[13] While these goals and the reasons given have been broadly accepted in recent years, efforts to attain them would be helped if a number of issues were sorted out.[14]

---

13. *Integrity* [1985, pp. 22, 33].
14. For evidence that there is considerable room for improvement in global understanding, see the summary chapter of Barrows, *Global Understanding* [1981, pp. 134–137].

The theme that is common to the many things subsumed under "international and multicultural experiences" is the call for a latter-day enlightenment. Traditional perspectives are to be broadened *from* a center that is white, male, and heartland America *to* a world that is not just masculine, includes races other than white, and encompasses lands and cultures of the entire globe. The goal, to repeat the phrase, is to educate citizens fit for a shrinking world and a changing America.

An important part of what is intended here pertains to attitudes. A suitable citizenry is sensitive and responsive to the concerns of women, the poor, African Americans, Hispanics, native Americans, Asians, and all others populating our land who are not white, middle-class males. A fit citizenry does not bifurcate the globe unequally into Americans and (mere!) foreigners but is responsive to the complexity of our world. But note, we are here not referring to some single attitude. The same person might be empathetic regarding race and insensitive to gender; awareness of America as but one neighborhood of a global village does not preclude deep prejudices toward black people, and so on. All such attitudes derive, of course, from experience in early years: parental example and upbringing, childhood environment and youthful schooling. But a postsecondary institution can affect the dispositions students bring to college through its ethos and the ways in which it is expressed, especially in the arrangements of life outside the classroom—always noting, to be sure, that the human spirit is not enlightened by a single lamp, that the shadows of bigotry are cast from a diversity of sources.

But these attitudes are also related to knowledge, since ignorance is more likely to induce disdain or animosity or fear than affection and respect. And as we are thus brought back to the curriculum, the plurality of the assignment has potentially formidable implications. There is much to be known about each of the worlds with which acquaintance is sought. Area studies—for every portion of the globe—have for many years introduced students to the characteristics of the boroughs of the global village. More recently, African American studies, women's studies, and Hispanic studies have been introduced, with their own bodies of information, modes of research and analysis, and growing literature of books and articles. If "producing citizens of a shrinking world and a changing America" requires students to take courses in all relevant domains, such curricular combating of provincialism and ethnocentricity calls for more work than can be fitted into four undergraduate years.

But shouldn't going to college be an enlightening experience as a matter of course? Should it not be inevitable that whoever participates seriously in higher education—whatever specific courses are taken, whatever the major—will truly become a citizen of a shrinking world and a changing America? Should it not be inevitable because the requisite breadth and multiplicity of perspectives are to be found everywhere in the curriculum? Regarded in this way, the curricular doctrine that asks undergraduates to take special courses about women, African Americans, and samples of "international studies" in effect asks students to compensate for omissions by their faculty. Regular courses in history, sociology, psychology, literature, and so on, *could* take adequate cognizance of the role of women, minorities, and of the world outside our borders, though in fact they seldom do so adequately. When does a course in urban sociology study Casablanca or Shanghai as examples, in addition to Detroit and Los Angeles? How serious is a segment on post–Civil War America in looking at the changing role of women? When has a course in Shakespeare considered French and German views of *Hamlet* or the *Tempest*?

Were we, ineptly, to answer these rhetorical questions, we would surely have to say, "very seldom, indeed." Yet, if the themes that are here our concern were part of the stuff of all undergraduate courses in which they could be relevant, the enlightenment we are after would simply follow. To be sure, even an ideal curricular diffusion of these themes would leave students far short of becoming expert about any of them. But since we are not looking for specialized knowledge, such internal modification of important portions of the curriculum would remove the need to raise as a separate issue this provision of "international and multicultural experiences" for undergraduates.

We are far from this point. Thus, when we ask students specifically to take courses that *do* deal with these matters, we in effect seek to overcome a provincialism and ethnocentricity that still characterizes much of their faculty, at least as reflected in the syllabi of many of their courses. We find ourselves in a peculiar time trough, in short. On its front rim we see the demands just articulated: that the undergraduate curriculum attend to certain kinds of broadening of its students. The back rim is characterized by the teaching faculty's graduate education, much of which paid little or no attention to such issues. Students and faculty are both struggling in the hollow and scrambling to emerge from that depression.

Over a longer time span, these pedagogic concerns are likely to influence the development of the disciplines themselves more significantly than they have to date. Put more plausibly, the broader and deeper changes in our society that have generated these undergraduate educational concerns will increasingly effect comparable changes in the disciplines and professions themselves. As that development progresses, faculties in different fields will reach the trough's forward rim and graduate from their postbaccalaureate studies to teaching courses that incorporate, unbidden, these broader perspectives. Students will then emerge out of the trough in the faculty's wake, relieved of the obligation to make a special effort to attain what will then surely be twenty-first-century enlightenment.

During an extended interim period, compensatory measures are in order, of which at least three types can be distinguished. The easiest path is the most conventional and asks students to select one course from a set of alternatives, each of which deals with one of the themes here under discussion. In the light of the numerous *different* concerns that are subsumed under "international and multicultural," the inadequacy of this response is manifest. But to require several courses, in recognition of the multipartite nature of the goal, most certainly risks overburdening students with requirements.

The second solution is to devise a special "international and multicultural" course that treats a cluster of themes within a single framework. Undoubtedly, such a task can be executed more or less well, yielding courses that are more or less coherent, more or less rigorous, with the miscellaneous character of the themes to be included constituting a serious limit as to what can be accomplished. Even at their best, therefore, such courses must also be regarded as pedagogic stopgaps, maintained only until a more permanent—and respectable—solution can be implemented. This "more respectable" is appropriate, even where the special course is well designed. On one side, while such a required course might initially be welcomed by students as filling an acknowledged gap in their education, its *ad hoc* character will almost certainly lead later student generations to greet it with skepticism, if not cynicism or contempt. On the other side, there is the problem of "delivery." Few institutions have a sufficiently large number of faculty who are both willing and able to teach well such a special course. The same conditions that make it difficult for faculty members to incorporate these "international and multicultural" themes into their regular courses stand in the way of adequate teaching of a special course on a scale large enough to reach an entire student body.

The third alternative is for an institution to go to the root of the matter by engaging in what might again be called anticipatory remedial education, but once more for the faculty. Since there is a systemic gap between the educational mission of undergraduate institutions and the preparation of their faculties to implement it, the compensatory measure that tackles this discrepancy most directly is "on-the-job" education of faculty members, analogous to the training corporations give to recent graduates from business or engineering school. In both cases, the employing institution helps its members expand and adapt the learning they have prior to coming to the institution—and on the strength of which they were hired—to the performance of tasks required to carry out the specific mission of the institution. In short, until faculties bring the requisite learning to their teaching positions based on their prior education, undergraduate institutions can achieve their pedagogic goals by assisting the faculty introduce into the regular curriculum the themes that will help students to become "citizens of a shrinking world and a changing America."

ART

The place of art in our society is full of paradoxes; it is therefore not surprising that its position in our educational practices should also be problematic. On one side, no other society has ever been so ubiquitously subjected to man-made visual images and sounds, propagated by methods of ever-increasing sophistication. One can imagine that there might be people who, from birth to death, have never experienced a music-free environment; one can suppose there to be individuals whose eyes, except when closed by sleep, are never out of touch with some depiction or design that is the product of technique. Fictional tales—conveyed in print, on television monitors or cinema screens—by far outnumber accounts, in whatever media, of what actually happened. A huge complex of industries, a sizable fraction of our GNP, is devoted to the production of something resembling art.

What is sometimes called high art plays a large role as well. Many institutions in our land are devoted to bringing its products to the public: art museums and galleries, symphony orchestras, theater, opera, and ballet companies. That public, moreover, is large—if never quite large enough to sustain fully adequately the establishments that purvey these works, since, compared with European practices, relatively little governmental support is provided for them. The media report on activities in the arts and review exhibits and performances, though to a much greater extent in newspapers than on television and, in turn, much more extensively in magazines and journals than in the daily press.

Yet in spite of signal differences between high and popular art, for much of the public there is also a continuity in attitude: in the passivity with which those surrounding images and sounds are received. The objects in art museums and galleries, as well as the activities of performers, are often regarded as diversions, so to speak, where the works of art—the symphonies, the paintings, the ballets—are taken to be the agents that should be doing something to or for the spectator or listener, while that "consumer" has experiences that are pleasant or interesting or thrilling or, alas, none of the above. And when those feelings are not aroused, the most plausible account must refer to characteristics of the works in question that simply fail to "reach" the viewer or listener—a condition that can hold for a given particular work or for an entire style or period. A secondary explanation pleads that the consumer simply lacks the taste for a certain kind of art object, either because of the particular make-up of the receptors of this individual or because the consumer is typical of an entire period.

In principle, then, art has the power to entertain and stimulate, but on this same view—more prevalent than tends to be avowed—it is also taken to be congenitally incapable of enlightening. For we live in a logocentric universe, where to *mean* is to be expressed in *words*. More accurately, that world should be called "prosaic," since, for many, only propositions mean something and anything that might be called an idea is by its very nature conceptual. On that view, expository prose is the sole medium of thinking, so that meaning can be derived from literature—from novels or plays, say—only to the degree to which propositions can be distilled out of them. Meaning is to be derived from works of painting or sculpture only if they are sufficiently representative to permit analogous propositional inferences, relegating much art—lyric poetry, nonobjective painting and sculpture, most architecture, most music—to the realm of the literally meaningless or insignificant. Thus, because books call for activity—they need to be read, one activity, and if they are to be understood, they may need to be thought about, another activity—there are capabilities that must be acquired. Music and the visual arts, on the other hand, are very distant from this realm of propositions and concepts, where the need to learn is taken for granted.

Because these attitudes and beliefs just described—though seldom made so bluntly explicit—are widespread in our culture, they condition the role of art in education, both as to what is actual and what is possible. As long as audiences of art regard themselves essentially as passive receptors, art will at best have a peripheral place in the educational scheme of things. If one adds to all this that art is a somewhat problematic leisure activity—"Arts and Leisure" is the title of the relevant section in the Sunday *New York Times*—it is not surprising that the role of music and art in undergraduate education is like an orphan's.

To begin with, if there is cause for hand wringing about the writing ability high school graduates bring to college or about their knowledge of history, their preparation in music and art is even sparser, since few secondary schools even make a serious effort in the arts. Second, while our conception of a "good student" includes the ability to write and knowledge of history, we are prepared to accept very little knowledge of music and art even from those we consider to be the very best. Thus, to the extent to which knowledge of art and music is made a goal of undergraduate education, one cannot, realistically, speak of "higher" education, if that implies a dependency on some prior, more elementary instruction. Third, most students do not bring to their undergraduate education a desire to learn or learn more about these arts; that is not thought to be important. Fourth, that same view is also quite prevalent in the faculty: the academy may in some ways be a place set apart from the everyday world, but it participates nonetheless in the culture of its surroundings. In sum, the absence of pressure from students, coupled with indifference on the part of a significant portion of the professoriate, is not likely to put (nonspecialist) undergraduate education in the arts on a more solid footing.

To avoid ineffectual utopianism, these pages have focused on the conditions that limit the seriousness with which education in the arts will be taken as a general goal of undergraduate education. But to say the least, the history of music and art suggests that a very different view is possible. Surely, Phidias, Raphael, and Michelangelo or Bach, Mozart, and Beethoven are among the very greatest minds to be found in the history of the West, a truth we do not learn from reading their biographies but from an examination of their works, the *products* of those minds.

Many of these, though not all of them, are capable of making an immediate impression—as attractive, as stimulating of feelings, as interesting—a directness that is precisely the chief source of the attitude we have been talking about. But such experiences by no means exhaust what is there to be grasped; few such objects can be "read" at one sitting, so to speak. Such works of art—and not just masterpieces—are the product of the specific ideas, feelings, and insights of their creator, and they are the embodiment, as well, of the techniques, styles, and cultures of their time and place. Repeated experience of works of art are, in principle, cumulative, because the perceiving mind also contributes to these encounters.

Such reflections require that one leaves behind the passive "receptor's" stance toward works of art and lead, as well, to an abandonment of the prosaic view of the world of ideas. Active noting can bear fruit, and ideas will be discovered that cannot, as such, be formulated as propositions. Increasing familiarity with these "languages" of the arts might lead one to the point at which it does not seem puzzling to have Wagnerian chromaticism and the analytic cubism of Picasso and Braque placed next to Mendel's laws and Nietzsche's conception of the death of God and to have all of these regarded as belonging to the important ideas of those revolutionary one hundred years beginning in the middle of the nineteenth century.

The stresses and tensions between those two sketches—that of the current place of art in our culture and the contrasting view of art as bearing meaning—suggest that the central goal of undergraduate education in art must be the closing of the gap between those two visions. Independently of the curricular setting within which they might be pursued, a number of precepts seem indispensable. First, and above all, such education must foster an active stance on the part of the student vis-à-vis works of art; everything else depends on it. Specifically, students must come to take for granted that one must take *note* of the features of a work of art, *discern* its characteristics, *discriminate* its different properties. The verbs appropriate to an apprehension of music and art are not just "hearing" and "seeing" but also, and crucially, "listening" and "looking"—terms that denote that the mind of the person experiencing a work is active.

Such an attitude is the indispensable foundation for learning to grasp some of the richness of works of art, a complexity that has a multiplicity of dimensions. Thus, as a second goal, attention must be paid to those features of works of art that are relational, with their intelligibility depending in part on contexts that lie outside the work. Learning the histories of several arts is, of course, vastly too ambitious as an object of undergraduate education. This suggests that the goal, above all, must be an introduction to some of the skills needed to search out how the characteristics of works of art are conditioned by their historical and cultural settings—in all probability by means of judiciously selected examples. But a third goal is of equal importance: the attainment of the ability to grasp those features of works of art that are directly observable in the work itself, calling for that ability to note and to make sensory discriminations. In the end, however, it must be recognized that these are not separable activities, for an understanding of a work involves the comprehension of how all these features are related to each other and to the medium in which they are expressed.

It is worth noting, further, that a curriculum that stresses these goals will help dispel another myth about art that is propagated, in part, by practices common during the earliest years of schooling. When art enters the curriculum as an activity for children, youngsters are often encouraged to be imaginative and to liberate themselves symbolically from inhibitions and restrictions in their use of crayons, paint, or clay. Intended or not, this practice can easily convey the view that, when it does not represent, artistic activity is the free exercise of the imagination and an unfettered expression of feelings: art as a kind of play—skillful, but without constraint. By contrast, when the viewer or listener assumes an active, probing stance toward works of art and acquires some of the analytic skills needed to discern their actual features, these works come to be seen in another light. What might once have been taken to be an unencumbered flow in which anything goes is then recognized to be an expression of imagination as constrained by canons of a style, by the characteristics of a medium, and, in various ways, by historicity. At the same time, it becomes manifest that those limitations are also opportunities for artistic exploration and innovation. It must thus be a fourth goal of undergraduate education in art to combat a widespread cultural preconception and have students come to see and understand art as disciplined.

Fifth, the search for an increased capability to discriminate the features expressed in a medium of art may require that one gets one's hands dirty. Unfortunately, a misplaced professionalism leads some musicologists and historians of art to draw a sharp line between the *practice* of art and the scholarly *study* of the works that such practice brings forth. The former are regarded to be the goals of specialized conservatories and art schools, while only the latter are seen to belong into the general undergraduate curriculum. But surely, such a rigidity is counterproductive. The effort to become familiar with the languages and building blocks of art is aided by an acquaintance with the mental and physical processes that create them. After all, the manifestation of works of art as structures of sound, stone, pigment, and so on is not peripheral to them *as* works of art; first-hand acquaintance with the practices and techniques used to put them together can contribute importantly to an understanding of these works.

If, in this way, we were to devote a comparable effort to learning how to make sense out of nonlinguistic works of art as we do to works that have linguistic form, we would become analogously proficient at deciphering the meanings embedded in the culture from which the works of art under study sprang. It is most certainly the case that by converting ourselves from passive receptors into actors who see the need to "read" objects composed not of words but of colors and sounds, we acquire the capacity to become familiar with some of the greatest products of the human mind.

This work, this analyticity, this bringing to bear different kinds of information on an encounter with a work of art, moreover, does not in any way cancel the pleasures derived from works of art when they are taken in passively. On the contrary, the change to an active stance, the knowledge focused on a present experience, the increased propensity and heightened power to make discriminations—all have the potentiality of making those pleasures vastly more complex and more intense. Objects that are often treated as occasions for agreeable diversions become the source of the deepest satisfactions, as well as of a greater understanding of the potentialities of the human mind. To take steps toward the accomplishment of the goals here sketched will hardly lead to conversancy with art. The achievement of these modest goals, however, is a necessary condition for the attainment of genuine conversancy in the course of encounters with art throughout a lifetime.

CHAPTER 4

THE SPECIAL CASE OF THE HUMANITIES

DEBATE ABOUT THE CANON

One way of achieving conversancy with the humanities is to call for some acquaintance with certain academic disciplines, notably literature (usually subdivided into national or linguistic areas), philosophy, the study of religion, the history of art. These fields generate departments, and they, in turn, generate curricula. But conversancy with the humanities must, above all, stand for familiarity with important products of human devising—mostly works of literature, philosophy, and religion broadly conceived—and an ability to use the methods by means of which they are understood and interpreted. Alternatively, then, a discussion of the humanities can quite sensibly center on a consideration of the works with which undergraduates are to become acquainted.

The question as to which works are to be picked is embedded in a cluster of controversies, not all of which can be taken up within the framework of this book. One dispute pertains to a topic that plays a role no matter what is decided about the canon of books to be studied. Disputes about the nature of interpretation in the humanities are being vehemently pursued, making every aspect of reading a literary work problematical. The range of positions that might be labeled objectivist are under attack by theories that can variously be characterized as relativist, historicist, subjectivist, skeptical, or simply nihilist—many of them identified with a political left. Primarily literary criticism and some art criticism are affected by these movements, with philosophy, religion, and more historically oriented studies of literature and art much less influenced. But these subjectivist views are nonetheless of great importance and effect, if only because so large a number of academic humanists are to be found in literary departments, especially English, in which they are prominent.[1]

Another theme among the ongoing controversies in the humanities—though intertwined with the arguments about the meaning of literary

---

1. See Lawrence Lipking's [1989] useful and lucid essay, "Competitive Reading," for an account of how theory affects practice.

works—-is indeed about the books that should be required reading. On closer examination, however, one formulation of the issue is not *which* books should belong to the canon but whether there should be a canon at all. "A course with such readings creates two sets of books," an advocate of this extreme position declared, "those privileged by being on the list and those not worthy of inclusion. Regardless of the good intentions of those who create such lists, the students have not viewed and will not view these separate categories as equal."[2] The canon should thus be abandoned altogether, because "the very ideal of excellence implied in the canon itself is . . . considered 'elitist' and 'hierarchical,' " traits that belong to a Western tradition that is "in large part oppressive, imperialist, patriarchal, hegemonic, and in need of replacement, or at least of transformation."[3] And the main purpose of teaching the humanities is to contribute to that transformation.

While it is important for us to acknowledge the existence of this goal for the teaching of the humanities, it would significantly deflect the purposes of this book to engage in a serious debate with this radical thesis. Instead, a quite conventional goal of undergraduate education will here be taken as starting point, without further justification: that a central aim of the study of the humanities is to make students familiar with some important works and help them acquire the ability to understand and interpret them.

With so minimal a starting point, much room for argument is left— indeed, most of the discussion by the participants in the debate about the canon, with the traditionalists ranked on one side and with most members of the literary left on the other. Even those who remain outside the debate, because they hold that there should be no canon at all, are driven to discuss books when participating in faculty discussions about courses rather than pamphleteering or preaching to the converted in academic conference. Thus, for practical reasons and for the sake of discussions of curriculum, the account of the canon debate now to be presented makes it a common assumption that students should become acquainted with *some* selected list of works.

Given that assumption, the traditionalists say, undergraduates should read specified books that have been acknowledged as significant works in our literary and philosophical tradition, that treat in an exemplary way the deepest issues pertaining to the human condition. Time, acting through generations of thoughtful readers, has been the most reliable mechanism of selection. But common, informed consent has recognized that a few, relatively more recent works are also appropriate candidates for this canon of books, which provide valuable glimpses into the nature of enduring values.

---

2. Mary Louise Pratt, participating in the Stanford debate about its course in Western civilization, as quoted in Searle's review essay, "The Storm over the University," [1990, p. 36]. This timely article very effectively distinguishes the more and less radical positions on the left side of the canon debate, a distinction of which use is made here.
3. Searle, "Storm over the University" [1990, p. 36].

The antitraditionalists, members of the literary left, point out that the works of this traditional canon were produced almost exclusively by white males, most of whom were members of the upper classes. Not surprisingly, the books of the traditional canon exemplify *their* sense of excellence and give expression to the visions of *those* humans, so that their books afford a look at the nature of those values that have endured for a class that has historically been dominant. To rectify this imbalance, the received canon must be revised so as to include works that will reflect the whole of our society and recognize the significance of the role of women, of races other than white, and of classes other than ruling. Appropriate works must, therefore, be added, even though that has to be at the expense of traditional members of the canon, given that a list of books to be studied cannot be indefinitely extended.

This streamlined summary hides a number of confusions on both sides, variously pointed out in the public debate. We turn to exhibit some of them, one side at a time, since such a discussion will make it easier to draw consequences of direct educational relevance. First, the traditionalists, when their case of present inclusion does not simply rest on the fact of past inclusion, often convey the impression that the quality of the works in the canon is outstanding, as measured by the highest aesthetic and philosophical standards. Such a view is then used to argue against having canon members replaced by aesthetically or philosophically inferior works nominated by members of the literary left. Any compromise with the highest standards diminishes the central goal of having students become acquainted with the *best* products of the human mind. A pedagogic corollary claims that because the works of the traditional canon have been tested by many people over long stretches of time, they are more effective than other writings in conveying to students the deepest insights into human values.

But note, to begin with, that even prior to recent critiques from the left, that canon was hardly a definitive, unvarying, agreed-upon list. If the canon is meant to catalogue the very best, time alone is impotent as cataloguer; some individual or group must assess what has withstood the test of time. Since the great canon debate is carried on about some canon as such, without reference to a specific set of works, we need remind ourselves of what life in the real world is like. Thus, there exist large, nonidentical lists—such as *Great Books of the Western World* [1952], among the more recent, and *The World's Greatest Literature* [1900] and *The Harvard Classics* [1909–1910], sometimes known as "Dr Eliot's Five Foot Shelf," from the turn of the century—as well as countless longer and shorter lists created and purveyed for various purposes, including, and especially, for undergraduate courses. No doubt, a number of works appear on most of these lists, while many more will appear only on a limited selection of lists. In our world of means and ends, there is no platonic form of a canon as such. The epithet, canonical, applies to lists that must allow for considerable variation of individual judgment, for differences derived from the purposes for which a particular list was created, and from the era in which it was formulated.[4]

The perusal of actual lists said to be canonical will surely lead one to note violations of that highest aesthetic-philosophical standard. Only sophistry would have the *Communist Manifesto* measure up, not to mention *Das Kapital*; nor is Freud an obvious candidate for inclusion by such lofty criteria. A timid person will mostly raise questions about relatively recent writers, because time hallows membership in the canon. But a brasher, disrespectful critic might also point out that Goethe's *Faust* contains a fair bit of German-Romantic clap trap and that long patches of Fielding's *Tom Jones* are boring. And so on, each according to his or her own prejudices.

These are not meant to be grounds for banning these works from the canon. I merely wish to point out that no aesthetic criterion will account for the entirety of any of the lists actually claimed to be canonical by someone. Instead, more than one work is catapulted into the realm of the nearly uncontroversial by virtue of one or several characteristics that are rooted in *history*: because the work has been influential, because it depicts or represents well some particular historical period, or because it epitomizes an historically or humanly important view, attitude, or emotion. Similar thinking accounts for the fact that there is well-nigh unanimous agreement about the inclusion of certain *authors*—Homer, Plato, Shakespeare, Freud, for example—without an equivalent agreement about the canonization of specific *works*, or about the inclusion of works without analogous consensus on parts, where, as is true of the Old and New Testaments, no course can sensibly assign them in their entirety. But agreement on an author, rather than on a work, confirms that historical thinking influences the process of selection.

A second issue—the pedagogic effectiveness of books that have been admitted into the canon—may not often be made explicit, but it remains a constant undercurrent. Canonical works, it is thought, have been tested by time and a large community of readers for their success in conveying the kind of insights we want our students to gain. The concern that is presupposed by

---

4. Humanities A, a year-long course, has been required of all freshman at Columbia College since 1937. The following summary from an account provided for the celebration of the course's fiftieth anniversary gives an indication of the state of the canon in this most stable of courses. "In all, more than 130 different books have been read . . . a statistic that does not take into account many other texts taught only in individual sections during free-reading periods. . . . [A small] number have persisted on the list since 1937 . . . : the *Iliad*, the *Oresteia*, *Oedipus the King*, Dante's *Inferno*, and *King Lear*. Others have been absent from the roster for only one or two aberrant years: Thucydides' *History*, Plato's *Symposium*, Aristotle's *Ethics*, the *Aeneid*, Augustine's *Confessions*, Rabelais' first three books of *Gargantua and Pantagruel*, Montaigne's *Essays*, and *Crime and Punishment*," Mirollo, "Humanities A"[1987, p. 36]. Since between twenty and twenty-five authors are read each year, with usually more than one work by quite a few of the authors (e.g., Sophocles, Plato, Shakespeare), even within a well-guarded tradition, the group of works that has essentially persisted for fifty years thus comes to distinctly less than half of those studied. No intact canon there.

this belief is certainly laudable, since it is rooted in the educational purpose of devising authoritative lists. Faith in the list's effectiveness, however, is inevitably based on its longevity, rather than on an empirical assessment of which works succeed in conveying what to whom.[5] Moreover, nothing we *do* know about learning suggests that, for *different* students in *different* cultural contexts, the greatest success in conveying a complex set of ideas is always likely to be achieved by the *same* means. Unless, of course, what is to be conveyed is exactly what a particular book conveys. This circular argument reaffirms the goal of having students become familiar with a selection of writings, for the sake of that familiarity—a reasonable goal for some small set of authors or books but certainly a very different one from the aim under discussion.

The literary left is not without its own confusions as it argues for a "political" modification of the canon. First of all, the tendency to discuss lists and canons wholesale, rather than work by work, is particularly misleading in this context. Careless references come to one from the left about *the* tradition of the dominant class, as if every work on those canonical lists presented an aspect or version of the same view. A glance at such lists—by someone who has read the books—is sufficient to reveal that this is patently not the case. Indeed, it is willfully ahistorical to suppose that writings from lands and periods as far apart as biblical times, ancient Greece, nineteenth-century Russia, and twentieth-century Vienna should in this way resemble each other, even granting that what came earlier is in a position to influence what came later.[6] Far from being in accord with each other, many texts selected from canonical writings can serve as the basis for an understanding of the major sides of most of the deepest social and political issues, including those concerning the status and role of women and of races other than white. Alert teachers have undoubtedly been doing that in their classes, long before the eruption of the canon wars.

A related confusion surely underlies some claims to canonical mono-

---

5. As a proponent of acquaintance with the Western tradition via important books, I will confine to this footnote that aspect of my skepticism that might be stretched into cynicism. That a book is canonical, published widely, and frequently assigned to be read in required courses is not conclusive evidence that it is actually read, not to mention understood. A personal anecdote, by way of example. Spinoza's *Ethics* was a required book in the required humanities course I took as a freshman at Columbia College (see note 4). On the day our class of eager veterans of World War II was to begin a discussion of the *Ethics*, our instructor confessed that he did not understand the work and announced that the hour would be used to write an impromptu essay. He went to the blackboard and wrote, "What God Is." He then asked us to write, uttering no further word of explanation. Annoyance was tempered by relief, since we were now permitted to struggle with Spinoza in silence, and we surmised that our essays would not count much in the final grade.

6. For those members of the literary left who also hold a subjectivist theory of interpretation, the argument that the canon authors all purvey essentially the same view is likely to be, at bottom, tautological, and perhaps of political use, but of no intellectual merit. "All these guys of the canon are saying the same thing," goes an informal version of that tautology, "because we read them as saying the same thing."

lithicity: that between the characteristics of the causal agents—the authors—and those of the effects brought about—their works. Most of the works of the canon were indeed written by white males who were members of a dominant or upper class. It is not the case, however, that what they wrote is characterized by a corresponding sameness. No warrant here, any more than elsewhere, underwrites inferences from general characteristics of agents to general characteristics of their actions. White, middle-class males have been murderers, others have been self-sacrificing heroes; some—very few!—have created works that appear on canonical lists, while others have written essays objecting to that fact; some white middle-class males are traditionalists, while others are members of the literary left.[7]

Intellectual historians will of course need to say more about the canon controversy, but enough has been said for a look at its educational implications. From that vantage point, this quarrel seems patently self-indulgent. When it is not airily about a canon-in-the-sky, it is about the books that should be *required* of students, formulations that do not come close to questions about *students* and what they should learn. It remains, rather, with the *professoriate* and what its members stand for. "By what I require ye shall know me," saith the canon gladiator. One believes in the indispensability of the Western intellectual tradition, whereas the creed of the other is to give voice to the hitherto downtrodden and oppressed.

The language that is used by the protagonists sounds as if it intended to communicate what *students* should know; but, in effect, it declares who the protagonists themselves are, what *they* believe should be prescribed. More than one audience outside the faculty guild is encouraged to eavesdrop on this discussion. One side appeals to a governmental and business establishment and the other to a rainbow coalition of students and politicians. Each contingent expresses approval and disapproval in its own characteristic way—dispensing praise and blame on a scale vastly greater than usually encountered in the world of academics.

One can opt out from any discussion and declare that the making of canonical lists is simply a function of power: those who shout the loudest, corral the votes, pay the piper, are the ones who determine the substance of those lists. On the other hand, one might insist, instead, that the formulation

---

7. If like causes brought about like effects, there would never be any point in watching a baseball game, since just about all baseball players resemble each other much more than Homer resembles Dostoyevsky. On the causal principle tacitly assumed by some members of the literary left, pitchers, hitters, fielders, and base runners would all be doing the same thing, and all baseball games would be the same. And if one responds that "in a sense" all baseball games *are* alike, while differing enough to make them worth watching, one should agree to give the books of the canon a similar scrutiny, to see how they do and do not resemble each other. And if another game altogether is to be played: by all means! But let it be the game of education, with means derived from educational goals posited. In any case, contrary to what appears to be held by many a participant in the canon debate, there is no substitute for actually looking at the writings being discussed.

of such catalogues of works is not a matter of force but of the authority that derives from the purpose for which such a list exists. The proper context, then, is education, and the list's purpose is the teaching of undergraduates.

FROM THE PERSPECTIVE OF STUDENTS

The crucial shift in perspective is to replace the topic of what books should be required to be read by all students with a prior consideration of the educational goals to be brought about. What books are to be read or required then becomes a consideration at a second stage, when it becomes time to specify the means that might be used to bring about the envisaged pedagogic purposes. And we take an initial step toward clarity when we see that the canon debate tacitly assumes more than one educational goal, more, even, than a single complex goal.

One multifaceted purpose is embedded in the very idea of establishing a canon with which a younger generation is to become familiar. It rests on the function of education as conservator, which assumes that students should be sent out into the world equipped with a grasp of what their tradition has accomplished to that day—both as an aid to understanding the world as it then is and as a platform from which to change it. At the same time, the tradition should come to be known by its most outstanding works, so that the goal of making Western culture intelligible simultaneously acquaints students with some of the most profound reflections on fundamental issues of human life and some of the most impressive products of the human mind.

In one sense, the goal just described is objectionable only to those holding the radical view that maintains that familiarity with some selected list of works is not a desideratum at all. Where the disputants do not share any aspect of this educational goal, there is no debate about what belongs into the canon but at most an argument as to whether there should be such a thing. On the other hand, where there is general agreement on this end, its complexity is such that the attempt to meet its multiple and incommensurable criteria must give rise to numerous controversies. But such a discussion about which works students should become familiar with—appealing to historical, aesthetic, and philosophical criteria—would not be a version of the current dispute about the canon. Rather, it would resemble a continuation of the old-fashioned debate that led to the likes of the Harvard Classics, the Great Books, and to Humanities and "Western Civ" courses in colleges around the country. No doubt, the debate will at times be made more strident by a structure that requires this conversancy with the tradition to be achieved in the span of a year-long course, at best.[8]

8. The topic here is educational *goals*. Because having students read and discuss important works is a necessary ingredient of all relevant means, the most effective may indeed be the

Clearly, a second educational goal of importance is implied by positions expressed in the canon debate. Undergraduates should become conversant with a world other than white, male, middle class, or Western. The need for such an extension of traditional undergraduate education has been widely recognized in many discussions of undergraduate curricula. The preceding chapter took up the goal of global awareness and showed that it is both important and complex. But we saw there, as well, that no single curricular device will achieve this goal, so that the inclusion, in a required course, of works expressive of attitudes and views of cultures other than those that have been dominant in the West can undoubtedly contribute to it. At the same time, one must recognize that for few goals of undergraduate education is a single pedagogy equally effective in all contexts.

A third educational goal embedded in the canon debate has, to varying degrees, played a curricular role at least since the introduction of black studies in the sixties, as well as in the somewhat later development of other ethnic studies and women's studies. It is conveniently formulated as an answer by a member of the literary left to the earlier accusation that some versions of this position confuse similarity of causes (the authors) with similarity of effects (the works). That response concedes that while inferring from the first to the second would indeed be fallacious, no such argument was intended in the first place. Rather, the proposal being advanced by the literary left is frankly more radical: a new member is proposed for the canon precisely because the *author* is African American or a woman and only secondarily because the *work* deals with issues that pertain particularly to African Americans or women.

The nomination for induction into the canon is not specifically intended to recognize a great book hitherto neglected or, primarily, to provide essential information for student-readers; the object is quite different. Inclusion among required readings in required courses, it is noted, confers prestige not only on the writings selected but also on their creators. An authoritative body, usually a faculty committee, is seen as formally evaluating books and authors. When that body singles out a certain list as required, it declares a group of authors—persons now dead or still alive, male or female, African American or white—to be of importance. And if the authors of many of the required works *all* share significant characteristics, the process of selection inevitably conveys the additional message, however unintentionally, that *only* authors of the kind chosen deserve the highest respect. In order to convey a quite different

---

requiring of a course that takes up an agreed-upon set of books. This conventional academic wisdom to the contrary notwithstanding, such a course cannot be taken to be the *only* means to accomplish an exceedingly complex end.

message, this argument then concludes, works by authors other than white, male, middle class must be included.[9]

That "must" certainly does not follow unaided from what preceded. We have said already that one can't validly infer from certain similarities among authors to similarities among their works. We must now add that it is equally fallacious to argue from the fact that faculty groups have a positive view of a small list of authors that they lack respect for an entirely different category of author. If a given list "conveys" a message that is neither intended nor implied, why not simply explain that fact, rather than modify a curriculum on the basis of a spurious argument? College students (not to mention professors!) should certainly be smart enough to understand this reasoning, or at least be smart enough to learn. Isn't that what critical thinking is all about?

At this point, we can readily imagine that the debate becomes repetitious, so that it reiterates, no doubt with increasing heat, two very different positions. From the literary left: nontraditional authors *must be included*, so as to help bring into the mainstream important segments of the student body and American society, rather than alienate them still further. From the traditionalists: these are students engaged in higher education, *let them understand* the nature and purposes of the traditional canon, that of becoming acquainted with the best that Western culture has produced. Without introducing further considerations, this standoff cannot be resolved. And such further criteria must surely be rooted in the nature and goals of the *education* of undergraduates.

THE CANON AND THE A POSTERIORI VIEW OF EDUCATION

Even a testy "let them understand" coheres with a view of undergraduate education that was characterized as "elitist" and "a priori" in the opening chapter. The logical starting point is a certain conception of the educated person—undoubtedly one that includes familiarity with the traditional canon of the humanistic tradition—as an outcome of undergraduate education. Students recruited into college are assumed to have the level of achievement, competence, understanding, and motivation needed to traverse the road toward the posited goal; they are regarded as capable of coping with the curricula and pedagogic methods that are devised by the faculty for having their students achieve the desired result.

A signal burden for a smooth functioning of educational life is thus placed on the institution's admissions office, since motivation and attitude, in particu-

9. Because St. Augustine and Alexander Pushkin were partially black, even the traditional canon has been said to include authors who were not white. Inclusion by reclassification surely does not accomplish the intended goal.

lar, are not the concern of the educators. It is the students' responsibility to measure up, and where there is a failure to do so, student and admissions office, both, have made a mistake, with transferring or dropping out the unfortunate next step. As regards the issue before us, students will either see immediately the value of what they are studying and that singling out one list of works does not imply disrespect for another list, or they will come to learn it in time, or they will be properly reproved for being incapable of reaching this understanding.

The a posteriori view of undergraduate education provides a quite different perspective on this issue. The conceptual starting point is the student, on the one hand, and a multiplicity of potential goals, on the other—rather than a unitary conception of the educated person. On one side, then, empirical questions must be asked about the students enrolled and the findings must then be brought to bear on the devising of pedagogic programs for those students. On the other side, degrees of priority must be assigned to the potential goals of undergraduate education, partially as rooted in the characteristics of a particular student body and partly derived from the institution's own educational mission. (The a posteriori view is compatible with pluralism in higher education.)

A realistic look at American students would undoubtedly induce us to concede the correctness of the view of the literary left: a good many of them come to college with attitudes toward women and racial minorities that perpetuate long-standing and deep-seated prejudices. On the side of goals, very few are likely to disagree that our society would be well served if these attitudes were modified in the direction of respect and fairness. (In any case, our moral development has reached the point where it is no longer acceptable to *say* otherwise, whatever one's belief.) One would not, however, expect a similar consensus as to what should and what should not be the task of higher education.

That the four undergraduate years should be enlightening and broadening experiences and thus counteract male chauvinism and prejudice toward African Americans and other minorities is not controversial. For most, it will therefore follow that institutions are obligated to maintain an ambience that has relevantly constructive influences on students' character. Further, there is widespread agreement that, in various ways, an undergraduate curriculum should *inform* students about the roles of women and African Americans and teach them to think more clearly about a cluster of related issues. Such a pedagogical goal will justify the inclusion of writings by women and African American writers in a course of required readings—as already asserted—provided, of course, that the chosen works themselves have appropriate characteristics, independently of the sex or color of the authors.

The degree to which one stresses these goals and the practices designed to help achieve them measures the importance one attaches to the need for higher education to contribute to the changing of social and political views and attitudes in our culture. That the decisions that must be made are difficult must be avowed. But it should be equally clear that such assessments can be avoided only by fleeing into an a priori position of undergraduate education, a view that would rule out such a consideration altogether.

Still, we have not yet reached the issue of including books by certain authors in required assignments in order to engender respect for the sex or color of those *authors*, by virtue of the esteem that is accorded to them in being admitted to the canon. A quite different set of considerations from those so far taken up must be brought into play, one that does not as such pertain to women but to American racial minorities, especially to African Americans.

Distinctions need to be made, where both the traditionalists and the members of the literary left prefer to paint with a large brush. The position of the former makes persons nominally irrelevant: only the books of the traditional canon count. The latter see themselves as speaking for a coalition of all those who are not white, male, and middle class. That may be good politics, but it is a poor way to classify. (Plato had it right a long time ago when, in his *Statesman* (262d-e), he has the Stranger teach young Socrates that you can't intelligibly divide human beings into two classes: Greeks and all the rest!) As we now turn to the issue of *participation* in higher education, the fate of women is clearly different from that of racial minorities. And among the latter, the participation of African Americans stands out as being of especial significance, if only because of the size of that minority in American society.

It is indeed a major task for higher education in the United States to achieve a massive improvement in the recruitment, retention, and graduation of African American students. This immense and complex topic encompasses schooling at all levels and certainly constitutes a multifaceted task for postsecondary institutions. While many aspects are not germane to the present discussion, one facet is relevant everywhere: rendering institutions of higher education genuinely hospitable to black students. No part of college and university life is by fiat exempted from scrutiny for the potentiality of contributing to the goal of increasing the number of African American college students and graduates.

That includes the curriculum itself. Again, only an a priori conception of undergraduate education provides a platform that entitles one to rule out, *ab initio*, any curricular proposal that does not aim at the education envisaged, and some specific version might indeed halt any further discussion of the present topic. However, once such a priorism is abandoned, the need to weigh the relative importance of goals, and the appropriateness of the means, cannot be escaped. An a priori view of undergraduate education is explicitly rejected in this essay, supported by the claim—the rhetoric of college catalogues to the contrary notwithstanding—that it is also rejected in the practice of the vast majority of American undergraduate institutions. Moreover, while many traditionalists in the canon debate stress the importance of familiarity with the humanistic tradition in a way that suggests that they begin with a conception of an educated person, there is no reason to think that they can convincingly work out such a view, not to mention depict it as functioning in contemporary American society. Therefore, the relationship between the enrollment and graduation of African American students and the selection of African American authors in a course largely devoted to some version of the traditional canon is an appropriate subject for discussion.

There is good reason to think that self-respect plays a significant role in strengthening the dispositions needed for success as a student. And self-respect, in turn, is bolstered by the respect one is accorded by others, an observation that makes the selection of African American authors relevant to the creation of an institutional atmosphere that is supportive of African American students.[10]

Yet, in spite of the immense importance of the goal and the symbolic significance of the means, two concerns stand in the way of making an unqualified recommendation that a selection of books by African American authors should be included in a course aiming at conversancy with the humanistic tradition. The first is quite specific but useful as an example of what must be taken into consideration when curricula are discussed; the second constitutes an application of the broader view of pedagogic thinking that underlies this essay.

First, on any campus on which a reasonable consensus is not reached about the purposes of a course in which a prescribed set of works are read and discussed, the good that might be accomplished by the inclusion of certain authors could easily be undone and worse by the way in which the course is looked upon by the faculty and by the manner in which it is taught. If a faculty conveys to its students that authors "inferior" to the "greats" are grudgingly included so as to "placate" a minority of students, the self-image of African American students will hardly be improved. No specific conclusion follows from this observation; a given campus must struggle with the truth that if one is concerned with *education*, decisions about syllabi cannot be made in isolation from the way in which they are taught.[11]

The second point pertains to the relationship between educational goals

10. In a book concerned with schooling earlier than college, a look at research results was summarized in this way: "In this chapter we have seen that there is a persistent and significant relationship between the self concept and academic achievement at each grade level, and that change in one seems to be associated with change in the other. . . . Although the data do not provide clear-cut evidence about which comes first—a positive self concept or scholastic success, a negative self concept or scholastic failure—it does stress a strong reciprocal relationship and gives us reason to assume that enhancing the self concept is a vital influence in improving academic performance," Purkey, *Self Concept* [1970, p. 27].

11. When time is taken into consideration, the ingredients in the decision become more complex still: what will be the influence on future faculty members of a present decision to include or exclude? Curricular decisions are often made without sufficient awareness of the institutional effect of the decision over a longer period of time.

and the means selected to accomplish them. Although discussion has shown that conversancy with the humanistic tradition is a more complex pedagogic goal than might appear, its achievement most certainly will call for the reading and understanding of significant works. In spite of the fact that a course in which students take up a selection from an expanded canon of important works is clearly most responsive to these purposes, it cannot be assumed that a required course with a rigidly prescribed reading list is the sole means for their achievement. Long before the current canon debate, such courses were not universally adopted, and it should not be surprising and certainly not shocking that this solution is rejected by some at this time. Gerald Graff's proposal, for example, to "teach the controversy" is a creative way of making students familiar with our cultural tradition in its most recent manifestation.[12]

Similarly, the improvement—quantitative and qualitative—of the education of American minority students, especially African American, is a vital national goal and constitutes a major challenge to undergraduate institutions. But while the implementation of that goal also has curricular implications, no particular, sole means is entailed. Specifically, it does not follow as a matter of course that there should be a required course of prescribed books and that that course should include books by African American authors. Institutions vary considerably along a multiplicity of dimensions, and the goals of undergraduate education are many and complex; all of these considerations must be brought to bear on the development of a specific curriculum for a given school.

12. See, among other papers, Graff, "What Should We Be Teaching When There's No 'We' " [1987]. Aside from the fact that many choices remain to be made even after Graff's solution has been adopted, it will not be found to be suitable in every context. Proponents who are disinclined to compromise are likely to reject it. Strong traditionalists will want no part of these "contemporary manifestations," while voices strongly from the left will want the inclusion in the canon of African American authors, for example, to be unwavering. In any case, the Graff proposal requires a sophistication on the part of a critical mass of faculty and students that is not necessarily found on every campus.

CHAPTER 5

COMPETENCY: THE MAJOR

THE MAJOR AS PREPARATION

The term "major" or "concentration" refers to an institutional practice, not to an educational goal. Nevertheless, its dominant role both in arts and sciences and professional undergraduate education requires that we discuss this curricular feature explicitly. Moreover, even when we talk of competency or study in depth—in the formulation of the *Integrity* report[1]—we are not speaking of a pedagogic goal in the style of those so far discussed. Until now, we have been concerned with a variety of specific substantive achievements—proficiency in writing or mathematics, conversancy with science or American history, and the like. But when the goal is competency without determination as to the area in which competency is to be achieved, or study in depth without specification as to *what* is to be studied deeply, we are in a different realm of discourse. At times, however, the long way around is the more expeditious; we will more readily clarify this educational goal if we begin our reflections not with it but with the practice of the major.

In several ways, the major dominates undergraduate education. First and most important, students spend a good deal of their undergraduate time on the major. A 1976 study shows that the range between 31 percent and 40 percent of all courses taken is the median requirement for majors enrolled for a bachelor of arts, while the range, 41 percent to 50 percent is the median for those graduating with B.S. degrees, with at least the undergraduate professional programs in engineering and the health sciences requiring still more.[2] If these ranges are medians, think of how many students take more courses than that to satisfy major requirements!

Second, the major exercises what might be called ideological domination. Although, for many, the larger portion of undergraduate study lies outside the major, those nonmajor demands are fragmented by their plurality and variety. Because the major confronts students with a relatively unified style, it is by far

---

1. The *Integrity* report makes study in depth a part of its minimum curriculum [1985, pp. 23–24, 27–32].
2. There is hard evidence that between 1967 and 1974 there was little change in these proportions and anecdotal evidence that, if anything, still more time is now taken up by the major. For a succinct account of the major's history and scope, see Levine, *Handbook* [1978, pp. 28–35].

the single largest intellectual influence on them.[3] When one adds that—at least by the middle of their journey through college—students tend to see the major as defining their identity as students, together with the fact that the faculty is most comfortable in teaching their own specialties, one can join a third, social–psychological dimension to the major's dominance.

The major, then, is a powerful force in undergraduate education. It "usually consists of a number of courses in one field or in two or more related fields. . . . [and] is intended to provide students with a body of knowledge, methods of study, and practice appropriate to a subject or subject area."[4] What such specialization comes to, and what its pedagogic purposes are, is the central and difficult issue of this chapter. One aspect, however, is at least conceptually straightforward: specialization can directly prepare students for careers or advanced study, professional or graduate.

The major has been common in American higher education for a century or so, the same century that has seen American college and university faculties organized into departments and has witnessed a phenomenal growth of professional education, undergraduate and graduate. These institutional facts— found, moreover, in a social and economic environment that stresses the preeminence of a career—have, *de facto*, made preparation for the next stage the primary rationale for the undergraduate major. Accordingly, we will first want to consider some of the ways in which the prominence of this justification affects the decisions that are made about majors and then consider some of the limitations of regarding the major as preparation.

That the purpose of the major is so often seen as extrinsic to the educational activity itself is an important, though not the only, impetus for having educational decisions about the major delegated in various ways. To begin with, even though the institution prescribes courses of study and grants degrees corporately, a kind of senatorial courtesy leads the faculty to delegate the determination of the major to departments or analogous program committees. More likely than not, the corporate role is confined to setting limits to the number of credits that may be required by a major and, much less frequently, to prescribing some senior exercise to be carried out in all majors.

But this only begins the chain of delegations. Departments are composed of experts, and senatorial courtesy requires deference at least to those who are senior enough to be enfranchised. The subspecialties of these faculty members must in some way be included in the major; indeed, such inclusion partially justifies their departmental membership in the first place. And a complementary courtesy demands that the specialist alone determine the syllabus for that subject and how to teach it.

3. In the small minority of institutions in which a sizable and distinctive general education program is required, its influence may still intellectually dominate the major for a significant proportion of students.

4. Levine, *Handbook* [1978, p. 28].

Delegation of educational authority, then, is a product of specialization, but it is equally a function of the extrinsicality of an important purpose of the major. The success of a department that regards itself as preparing students for practice or further study is measured by the relevant success of its students, a fact that has an effect on its decisions.[5] One such external influence on the major is informal and often subjective, consisting as it does of the sum total of departmental beliefs about how success is achieved out there in the world, with the evidence fragmentary and anecdotal. The upshot tends to be the principle, *when in doubt, include,* since the failure of even a small number of students to reach their goal is vastly more obvious than the harm of a one-sided education for a much larger number.

The aim of a second influence is more precise and steady. Often, graduate departments, professional schools, employers, and—especially for professional majors—accrediting and licensing agencies are quite explicit in their demands, to the point of specifying courses. Entrance requirements or preferences, personnel officers' guidelines to school placement officers, or conditions for accreditation all leave their mark on the curricula of majors. The prerogatives of expertise and the demands of external agencies thus tend to crowd out the determination of majors by faculties of particular institutions. And because these forces also suppress attention to potentially intrinsic pedagogic values of the major, a closer look at the relationship between the stage that prepares and those it prepares for is important.

For many students, of course, the undergraduate major is followed by related advanced study or by employment that calls for the knowledge and skills acquired. Undoubtedly, this orderly sequence occurs more consistently in job-related undergraduate professional programs, such as engineering, nursing, or education, than for arts and sciences majors, though there will be differences among the latter.[6] That the major prepares is not fiction. Insofar as undergraduate education in America can be regarded as a bridge from variability of talent and schooling to postbaccalaureate education and professional employment (where relatively uniform professionwide standards prevail), majors are the main girders of that bridge.

Accordingly, it is quite appropriate for undergraduate institutions to look outside for guidance in the design of certain of their programs. But for educational institutions with pedagogic goals of their own, some modes of looking are more fitting than others. Even the few broad principles to be

5. This success consists primarily of being *hired* by the right employers or being *admitted* to further study. The feedback mechanism is inadequate to make future *performance* in these roles a measure of the success of the educators. This point should be ignored only by those who believe the gap between personnel and admissions decisions and subsequent performance to be sufficiently small to be overlooked. We shall return to this topic shortly.
6. It would be worth elaborating on this theme and distinguishing between degrees to which different undergraduate majors actually lead to the stages for which they prepare. This exercise, however, would have to depend on casual observation, anecdotal evidence, and plausible guesses; there seems to be no statistical evidence on this important relationship.

suggested here, however, will call for different policies in different professions and fields.

One must distinguish, to begin with, between students making their entrance into that next stage and functioning within it once inside. To the ears of a faculty, the keepers of portals have by far the most audible voices: campus recruiters, personnel officers, deans of admission, licensing agencies. And while these representatives speak for their institutions, they nevertheless bring to their tasks special perspectives of their own. The success of company recruiters and personnel officers, for example, is measured primarily by the degree of satisfaction of the first supervisors of the new employees, whether or not this forecasts a longer-run flourishing of the employee. Admissions officers, given their task of dealing with large numbers of applicants, tend toward the use of indicators that permit decisions to be made efficiently—that is, relatively rapidly, and without too much "subjective" discretion by the decision makers.

Since the accomplishments of students who do not get through the door will not then be further tested, the preparing faculty must, of course, pay heed to such entrance requirements. But, as educators, they must also look beyond that portal to the functioning of their students over a longer career. Just as we expect a law school to prepare students for a career in the law (and not just for the bar exam), so the faculty in charge of an undergraduate program must base its curricular decisions on an understanding of a longer and deeper trajectory. Bluntly put, *faculties* must make the educational decisions, not recruiters and admissions officers.

A bureaucratic point that has considerable pedagogic consequences corroborates this fundamental principle. For the sake of convenience, requirements are often stated in the language of courses. Required: one semester of calculus; one year of accounting; one course in design; a year of organic chemistry; and so on. But what is actually needed on the job or in advanced study is never a *course* but certain substantive *knowledge* and certain broad or specific *skills*, expected to be acquired in those courses.

No doubt they usually are, and no doubt much more is, as well. Courses are packages, with the selection of contents a function of the structure of the field, of habit, history, and convenience. It remains open as to whether, when a course is specified, what is substantively needed includes all that is required. Where a discipline's internal organization does not dictate the package's components, it can easily happen that a broader *educational* decision is made for the sake of a narrower *admissions* need. When a conventional course is required for the sake of a certain ability or quality of mind, an educational decision might suggest a quite different road toward that goal.

This theme—that the faculty responsible for a major must translate external demands into decisions of its own—becomes central when the issue of the major as preparation is placed in the broadest perspective. We are moving in realms in which much more is to be learned in preparation for the next stage than there is time for. As a result, on-the-job training and continuing education within the workplace have become very big business, indeed. Such activities range from informal (but time-consuming) on-the-job training, to instruction in company-specific practices, to technical courses and workshops that closely resemble those of the academy, to instruction that is indistinguishable from that provided in colleges and universities, right up to degree-granting corporate institutions.[7] In short, everywhere the growth of knowledge has been such that students must embark on that next stage before being fully prepared for it.

At best, the undergraduate major can only do part of the job of preparing, even if it had no other goals; the faculty cannot avoid selecting what is to be included and what will be left to be learned later. Three broad principles should govern such choices; the fact that they are virtually self-evident most certainly does not assure that they are observed. First, where learning one thing builds on the prior knowledge of something else, that dependency dictates an order of learning. Because this simple logic has immediate pedagogic consequences, it is in general, though by no means always, adhered to. But since the adverse consequences of violating either of the other two principles do not become manifest until long after the undergraduate years, an equivalent simpleminded logic does not have analogous coercive force.

Institutional setting may make a big difference as to how adequately some material is taught or whether it can be taught at all. Some teaching should take place in colleges and universities, asserts this second principle, because it can only be taught there or can be taught much better there than elsewhere. Other knowledge or skills are more readily acquired in the environment of the postbaccalaureate stage. Where needed as part of preparation, the first of such subjects should be included in the major, in place of subjects that might be acquired elsewhere, while one ought to omit those in the second category, even in the face of pressures from students who want to get there faster.

A recent study of professional education analyzes the notion of professional competence into six components, to take a single example. One, called "contextual competence," "signifies an understanding of the broad social, economic, and cultural setting in which the profession is practiced."[8] Since it

7. See Eurich, *Corporate Classrooms* [1985]. It is not easy to estimate the size of this "booming industry" (p. 1). A mid-1970s estimate by the American Society for Training and Development—thought to be conservative—comes to $40 billion spent annually, *not* including on-the-job training and *not* including what would be an equal cost for wages paid to employees while training (p. 6). As to numbers of people involved, an authority "hazards the guess that in 1978 business firms gave in-house training to about 6.8 million trainees, and the number of courses taken would be somewhat higher—8 million—if one uses the ratio of courses to participants given in the [Bureau of Census Current Population Survey]" (p. 7).
8. Stark et al., *Responsive Professional Education* [1986, p. 30]. On the basis of an extensive review of the journal literature, together with a faculty survey, this study identifies six components of "professional competence" and five of "professional attitudes" as goals of professional education. Indeed, when in doubt, include. For a summary, see Table 3, p. 13.

is unlikely that all six components can be adequately acquired in the course of an undergraduate professional program, it makes sense to include material that takes advantage of the availability, at an institution of higher education, of such departments as economics, sociology, anthropology, say, not to mention broad library holdings. On the other hand, and for a number of reasons, if the intention is indeed to focus history and the social sciences on the profession being studied, such "contextual competence" is much more difficult to acquire "on the job." Suitability of place, absolutely or comparatively, suggests that "contextual competence" be given some priority in the design of a major.

On the other side, the point has been made with some force that schools will never succeed in educating teachers in such a way that they are good teachers when they *start* teaching. Programs that aim at preparing teachers should therefore teach *how to learn to teach* and leave the job of actually becoming good teachers to the years of beginning practice.[9] Wherever such an observation is taken seriously, important *curricular* decisions follow.

Finally, there is the power of time. Some things not learned early are later learned with much greater difficulty at best. The "interpersonal communication competence" called for in that study on professional education[10] is surely best acquired when young. For reasons rooted in psychological, if not biological truths about human development, the cost of postponement can be high. Other studies are best engaged in earlier rather than later for economic or sociological reasons. For what one is free to explore at an earlier stage may later be precluded by increasing pressure to specialize and by economic constraints. Options open in youth that might, in principle, be recaptured later tend, in practice, to remain out of reach.

That these truths have long been known is no assurance that they are incorporated in educational programs. They are, however, of particular relevance to the design of majors, insofar as they are intended to provide an adequate preparation for stages beyond the undergraduate years.

THE PEDAGOGICAL PURPOSES OF THE MAJOR

We have been concerned up to now with the educational effectiveness of the major as preparation for specific future stages, without attending to the educational function of the undergraduate major for those who do not take that road. While there is a paucity of statistical evidence on the careers of students after college, it is widely known that for many of them, the major is not at all followed by related advanced study or employment.

First, quite a few undergraduate majors simply do not prepare for some

9. I owe this point to Professor Willis Hawley, made at a symposium at the meeting of the Association of American Colleges, in January 1990.
10. Stark et al., *Responsive Professional Education* [1986, pp. 36–40].

designated next step. Often this is obvious to students and faculty alike, but at times both groups, especially students, suffer from misapprehensions. Many interdisciplinary majors have no graduate counterparts, nor are there specific jobs for someone who has completed a program in ancient civilizations, say. But, more insidiously, some professional-sounding majors are wrongly believed to qualify the graduate for a position in that profession. Many bachelors in journalism, for example, will be disappointed not to be hired as reporters; the fact that some undergraduate economics majors like to call themselves economists does not make it so when they are on the lookout for jobs. This perspective on the major not only raises questions about effective communication with students but about the very ethos of the major as preparation.

Second, for at least two reasons, numerous students who intend to use the major as a road to relevant advanced study or employment never get there. Even where a *program* prepares, many individual students simply do not do well enough to make it. In some areas, the standards for success are so high that the number who fail to reach the next stage is large. Think of the biology majors who are not admitted into a medical school or a Ph.D. program! On the other hand, a program can be well designed to prepare students for a career, and they might complete it admirably but may find that the number of openings in the world of work is so small that there is no room for them. At different times, this disproportion has held for every profession for which undergraduates prepare: education, engineering, music, library science, pharmacy, and social work, to give a few prominent examples.

Third, many students concentrate in programs without *intending* to prepare for a specific next stage. For some majors—particularly in the humanities and social sciences—this group is in the majority. Some students are in pursuit of a present interest or have a belief in a major's long-range benefits; others are enrolled in their major by default, because they lack a defined interest altogether. And when we add to this group those students who find later that the major they chose at age eighteen or nineteen no longer conforms to their talents or interests, the number for whom the major is *not* preparation for career or advanced study grows larger still.[11]

If a sizable student body fails to benefit from the extrinsic purposes of majors, it becomes doubly important that the major and its components fulfill intrinsic pedagogical purposes as well. This is the topic to which, finally, we now turn.

Although in fields of study that are appropriate to higher education, genuine competency can normally not be attained by the end of undergraduate

---

11. In a liberal arts setting, the major can usually be selected or changed as late as the junior year, while the choice of an undergraduate professional program is often made in the very choice of the institution, such as an engineering school or a nursing school. But in both kinds of cases, there are students who find that they had been mistaken either about themselves or about the program they selected and who desire to change direction subsequent to graduation.

study, positing it as an educational goal certainly takes one beyond mere conversancy with a subject area. Similarly, more than conversancy is asked for when the aim is said be the study of a field in depth. But whereas competency and depth are simple words, they are not the easiest of concepts; we will be helped in characterizing this goal and in seeing it as educationally valuable (whether or not it serves a preparatory function), if we take note of some of the characteristics of *what* is to be studied in depth or in *what* that competence is sought.[12]

In the language of undergraduate bulletins, what is studied as a major is, most frequently, a discipline or field; but at times, it is more than one field, or an interdisciplinary area, or even a domain that is devised *ad hoc* by a particular student. While these conventional terms refer to a large range of intellectual structures that differ greatly from each other, there is general agreement that, to be suitable for concentration, the subject matter must have a reasonably broad significance in the economy of what-there-is-to-be-known and that its central methods of inquiry should be above a certain threshold of sophistication. In addition to such widely acknowledged principles—an acceptance that certainly does not guarantee unanimity in their application—intellectual structures must share at least two further traits if they are to be appropriate for the kind of studying envisaged.

First, the subject matter being studied must possess a certain coherence that is more than nominal. No single principle of coherence, to be sure, will "govern" any subject, although some are likely to predominate over others. Methodologies of investigation, modes of argumentation, and categories of evidence sought in support of claims will at times tend to account for a subject's coherence. In other instances, cohesion is more dependent on an overarching cluster of theories. A very different principle of relatedness is that of historicity, which can play a crucial role both in human and nonhuman worlds. But for all of such unifying themes, the notion of coherence must not be understood in a mechanical or simplistic way. Few disciplines, for example, are actually organized in strict hierarchical fashion, if any are at all—certainly not the realm of mathematics, which is often represented as being so. Indeed, even some academic disciplines of long standing are divided into subdisciplines that are in many ways quite remote from each other. Nevertheless, the relationship of the parts to each other is never merely additive—like beads on a string—nor are they related merely externally or "politically," as being of concern to scholars to be found in the same department. Instead, the relationships that make for coherence are internal and cumulative, where the next or the new rests in some way on the preceding and the old.

The second fundamental principle of a field fit to be studied in depth is

---

12. The two formulations, the attainment of competency and studying in depth, express different aspects of the pedagogical goal of the major and are both helpful in the effort to clarify it.

that it must in principle be inexhaustible. For such a field, no future time can be envisaged when all there is to be learned will have been learned, so that "completed" can be stamped on the volume. Moreover, such a domain is not merely additively inexhaustible—like an infinitely large heap of sand where there is always one more grain to pick up and examine. The inexhaustibility, instead, must be essential or structural: whenever something new has been learned, whenever a question has been answered, that new knowledge, that answer, must give rise to new questions in turn.

Given the large range of subjects in which a student might concentrate, the formulation of characteristics meant to fit all of them is of necessity so abstract as to risk vacuousness. Still, if one pays heed even to this sketchy account, some quite common practices are ruled out—and not just certain frivolous *ad hoc* majors devised by and for individual students. Premedical and prelaw majors are widely offered in undergraduate institutions, and yet these are not "fields" in which one can become competent or that one can study in depth. What unifies such would-be majors is the external goal of preparing a student for professional study, without possessing internal connectedness as well. Moreover, the subject matter of these putative majors had better be quite finite, or nobody would ever qualify for medical or law school. Such presumptive majors, in other words, preclude genuine study in depth or the achievement of competency in a domain and are thus not majors at all.

More relevantly for our immediate purposes, these abstract traits of subjects in which one might concentrate help to characterize the nature of the study itself. Thus, if the field in which a student majors is in principle inexhaustible, competency simply cannot involve knowing everything about it; plumbing its depth in study cannot mean trying to reach bottom. But this lesson must be taken further. Where the road to be traveled is a long one, it may make good sense to get as far as possible every day, so as to shorten the time until the goal is reached. One must think very differently, however, when the voyage takes place on a road of infinite length, since the purpose of the trip cannot be to reach the road's end. Attention is directed to the *way* one travels, to bypaths and byways that make detours from the main thoroughfare, to the scenery along the way, and to the opportunities that are provided by the regions one passes through. It is irrational to march, head down, purposefully forward toward the goal, if there simply is no such goal. We will return to this theme and not just to the metaphor.

Competency in a field or subject matter can be characterized as knowing how to get around in it so as to get on top of it. Since our topic seems to dispose one to spatial images and to metaphors of journeying, surely the foundation of such a competency is learning to be a good traveler. The needed equipment is the basic information of a field, the information that is presupposed or shared by many of its branches. It calls, further, for gaining the ability to use the basic methodologies of a field in both a narrower and broader sense of the term. The first may entail learning a language, a technical vocabulary, such methods as a set of laboratory techniques, of styles of inter-pretation, of iconographic research—to name just a few categories of the many and constantly growing methods by which knowledge in different fields is grasped and accumulated. But also needed is a comprehension of the field's method in a broader sense, constituted of knowing how a problem in a given field is formulated, having a sense of what counts as a response to a question, and being sufficiently oriented to know where one must begin to look for an answer. A good traveler is a competent inquirer.

To be on top of a subject area also implies seeing that subject in perspec-tive. No one who lives always inside a building can be said to be genuinely familiar with it, even if acquainted with every nook and cranny. A view of the larger whole includes a grasp of a field's presupposition and that subject area's relationship to other fields, as well as to the world in which we live. The perspective that comes from seeing a subject area in a broader context is a necessary ingredient of competency, even of the attenuated kind that is possi-ble within the confines of undergraduate education.

Needless to say, these broad characteristics of a major designed to guide toward competency have curricular consequences. Most obvious is the need for leading students toward a command of "their" field's basic information and methods, and to do so on a schedule that permits other study within the major to build on that foundation. That this calls for making distinctions between the fundamental and the peripheral, as well as for temporal order-ing, is more evident in principle than is realized in practice. Particularly in the humanities, the "softer" social sciences, and some of the professions, there is a tendency not to make the requisite distinctions in the first place. Such reticence may correctly reflect the fact that problems of fields like sociology, business administration, or the works studied in English literature, say, do not stand in a hierarchical relation to each other. But for someone who is newly coming to a field, the order in which methods and material are learned may be of pedagogic significance, even where the implied scheme of priorities disappears when the field is looked at from the vantage point of someone who is already competent.

The most formidable enemy of competency as a central goal of the major is the drive toward coverage. Nor does all the pressure to crowd in more and more come from outside, in behalf of the major's preparatory function. Be-cause it is much easier to learn—and teach—a little about a lot than it is to achieve a deeper grasp of less, a kind of intellectual laziness on both sides of the lectern reinforces the tendencies earlier discussed. But if the major is not designed to delve more deeply into a subject area, but merely to cover ground, any real distinction between conversancy and competency will be lost, and with it a significant dimension of undergraduate education.[13]

13. The pedagogy of a little about a lot is subject, moreover, to the vagaries of easy come, easy go. Large amounts of detail are not remembered much beyond the conclusion of a

The objection, here, is to having the major survey every corner of a field; it must not be regarded as opposition to a certain amount of specialization. While the number of such highly specialized courses should be kept down,[14] they are of great value when properly placed in a student's career. They provide opportunities for building on the attainment of more fundamental knowledge, and they become the occasion for students to work with greater independence than tends to be the case in the central courses of a field. Real specialization presupposes the prior or simultaneous acquisition of numbers of skills of inquiry that are then brought to bear on more narrowly focused problems. The experience to be sought is the allegorical digging that is suggested by the metaphor of studying in depth, an activity that competes for the student's time and energy with the surveying of a large part of a subject area.

With this mention of "digging," we touch on a feature of the major that is as important as it is difficult to implement. Earlier we insisted that a subject matter appropriate for study as a major must be held together, so to speak, by principles of coherence, substantive and methodological. Assuming, then, that these relationships do obtain, it should be clear that they hold among the components of the field; they are a part of the logic, so to speak, of the domain in question. Yet in a successful *study* of a major, those relationships, that logic, must be shifted from its abstract place "in" the subject matter to the minds of living students. They must be seen (by someone!) and understood. Accordingly, the major must be designed and taught in such a way as to *display* its field as characterized by those principles of coherence.

One might call this the problem of translating the objective into the biographical or of making the abstract manifest. Some of the work must be done within particular courses offered as the major, in particular in those courses devoted to the fundamentals of a field. The more difficult aspect of

---

course (unless kept alive by continuing use), while the basic ability to find one's way in an intellectual realm, if properly acquired, can become the property of a lifetime. For twenty dollars, the humorist, Don Novello, who appears in the character of Father Sarducci will grant diplomas for completing his Five-Minute University, in which one learns only what one would have remembered from the more familiar university five years after graduation. In economics, for example, he hammers in, "Supply and demand; supply and demand."

14. Not only should the number of highly specialized courses that students take be kept small, but so should the number of such courses that a department offers. First, freedom of choice is not increased when the number of alternatives becomes bewilderingly large—coupled with inadequate information about them and inadequate skill to make discriminatory judgments. (We return to different aspects of this topic in chapters 7 and 9.) Second, the fact that an instructor specializes in an area and would like to teach a course in that specialty does not make the course suitable for an undergraduate major. However much scholarly issues are appropriately decided by those having the requisite specialized knowledge and skill, the composition of a major is a corporate educational responsibility of the faculty, and the pedagogic issues that govern it are not the "property" of any scholarly subgroup.

this translation, however, consists in the relationship that courses have to each other, both in the way the content of one is made to point to the content of others and in the way students are guided, as they move from course to course within the major.

If the achievement of such biographical coherence for students requires collaborative pedagogic action on the part of the faculty that governs the major, a last characteristic to be taken up here calls for their collective self-restraint. A field is seen in some perspective when it is looked at from diverse vantage points outside it. It must thus become a part of the major to have its students enrolled in courses that place their subject area into a larger intellectual and social context. While interdisciplinary majors often incorporate such related material into their requirements, the more conventional, departmental major is likely to need co-requisite courses from outside the major department, if the field is to be placed into a broader setting.

The study of a major possessing, to a reasonable degree, the characteristics here outlined constitutes a distinctive component of an undergraduate education. Its benefits, aside from those dependent on its preparatory function, are abstract but nevertheless of great value. The deeper study of a particular area of knowledge reveals something of the structure of all knowledge, as that is reflected in a sample. The sustained activity of the studying itself depicts, in a way that unfolds through time, the relationship between inquiry and knowledge. Indeed, while one might speak of knowledge as being contained in books shelved in a library, one cannot speak of knowledge as contained in a mind as long as it remains unconnected to an understanding of the inquiry that led to it.

The successful pursuit of a major should, in addition, give rise to two kinds of experiences for which no amount of discourse can serve as a substitute. One is the sense of what it is like to discover something. When small children play hide and seek, one can hear from quite far the squeals of delight as the seeker finds a hidden friend. The jubilant sounds express the exhilaration of discovering the concealed playmate—not quite expected just then—as a consequence of having searched behind many a tree and bush. The pleasure comes from having one's concerted searching crowned by success. The game of inquiry is a most sophisticated adult analogue, both in the nature of the pursuit and in the complexity of the pleasure of discovery. Scholars and scientists evolve from individuals who have become addicted to the gratifications of exploring and discovering.

A second kind of experience is both opposite and complementary. Life is short, but art is long, I quoted earlier in Seneca's Latin, a truism for which there is frequent application. The saying, though, however pithy its formulation, is no substitute for the realization—in the very course of study and inquiry—that the process cannot end, that there is ever more to be learned. The very path one traverses in order to learn more teaches how much more there is yet to be learned; the pleasures of discovery are thus both mitigated and heightened by a recognition of the magnitude of this adult version of the game.

As long as one prescinds from a major's benefits as preparation, its most important pedagogic value may well lie in experiences of this kind and in the contributions it can make to fostering habits of mind that are likely to outlive the acquisition of the major's particulars: independence of mind, respect for evidence and argument, and so on. This matter of intellectual virtues as a goal of undergraduate education will be the subject of the next chapter. Here we must conclude with some remarks on the tension between the major as preparation and its direct pedagogic benefits just discussed.

That there is tension follows readily from all that has been put forward in this chapter. There is the issue of sheer magnitude: the achievement of both the intrinsic and extrinsic goals requires more of a major than can be crowded into it. But there is direct conflict as well, since many of the demands for coverage are actually antithetical to sound pedagogy. Yet this tension is all too seldom felt in actuality. The composition of a major, after all, is usually the vector resultant of all the forces that operate within the responsible department or group. And missing from that group, more often than not, are articulate protagonists of the educational goals that are intrinsic to this special course of study.

A first step toward a resolution, accordingly, is the thoughtful discussion of every major in every institution, so that the demands for preparation and the needs of the major's immediate educational goals are articulated and weighed vis-à-vis each other. Such weighing, moreover, must be done within an institutional framework that takes into consideration the nature and ambitions of its students (and not simply those of its faculty). The degree to which a reconciliation is possible will never be known until a certain thought experiment has been conducted in all those places. What courses and course sequences *would be* required, it must be asked, what choices *should be* permitted, what pedagogic methods *ought to be* used, if one designed a major that is regarded as *ideal from a pedagogic point of view*. With the help of a sketch of such a model, one might then carefully determine just what changes—that is, what compromises—need be made, what flexibilities might be introduced so that the demands of the major-as-preparation are also met sufficiently not to jeopardize the futures of the institution's students. But without becoming clear as to what one would do if *un*fettered, it will not be possible to know what can be done under the more usual circumstances that include constraints.

Another source of resolution is the extension, in different ways, of professional programs, so that there is more room to satisfy two masters. Recent years have seen much stretching of this kind, from undergraduate engineering programs that have remained four years only nominally while actually requiring considerably longer, to Holmes Group teacher training programs that have formally been extended to five years. Increased longevity, as well as the growth of knowledge, justify such changes, but stretching the time does not in itself guarantee that both functions of the major will be fulfilled. Unless a faculty retains a firm grip on its own pedagogic goals for undergraduates, all the time that may newly be made available might well be claimed by the ever-growing demands of that next stage.[15]

The importance of achieving some competency in a curricular area, the importance of having the experience of studying in depth, the need to prepare for a subsequent stage in life, all make the major an essential part of undergraduate education. However, if one puts the demands of a major into the broader perspective that includes, on the one hand, all the proper goals of undergraduate education and sees undergraduate education, on the other, from the perspective of an entire lifespan, one is inevitably led to limit specialization during the four years or so of college study.

One might liken a person's educational progression through time to an upward climb inside a pyramid made of transparent walls, with the early years of life and learning spent near the floor of the pyramid. As one moves upward, two things happen simultaneously. The higher one gets, the closer one comes to the outside walls of the pyramid, so that one's scope for action is progressively reduced. But that same increased elevation from the pyramid's floor provides one with an ever-better view of what lies outside the pyramid to which one is confined. More mundanely, it is inevitable—whatever may come right after a college education—that the range of subsequent learning will be more narrowly focused than during prior years. Whatever one's intentions, many forces push toward progressive restriction, in the manner of a natural law that is rarely defied, and then only with great effort. Yet increased experience of the world offers an improved vision of possibilities. More often than not, that better view of the world outside the pyramid from higher up leads one to wish that one might still have the room for alternative actions that was available lower down.

Education cannot protect students from the realities of life, but one might think of the entire enterprise as a form of mitigation. An older, more experienced generation imparts some of its knowledge to the members of a younger one, so as to help them to act rather than be passive recipients of whatever might impinge on them. That is what we do when we teach children to read or young adults to perform experiments in organic chemistry. No instructors, however, are assigned the job of teaching how to choose between greater and lesser specialization at certain stages of life, even though there is something important to be known, something that the experienced might impart to the unseasoned. Instead, the scheme of requirements of an institution that spells

---

15. Extending the period of undergraduate education clearly does not automatically contribute to the achievement of the two goals of a major, aside from the important fact that it makes undergraduate education more expensive. See a thoughtful discussion of this issue in connection with the education of teachers in Johnston et al., *Those Who Can* [1989, pp. 43–51].

out what undergraduate education is at that college—what is permitted, what is prohibited, what is encouraged, what is frowned upon—teaches that lesson. Although it is taught outside the classroom, *what* is taught nevertheless deserves to be the result of the thoughtful application of the knowledge of the teachers, just as that is taken for granted in what happens in the lecture hall. The determination of the place, the nature, and the scope of the major in undergraduate education is just such an important lesson provided by the faculty of an undergraduate institution.[16]

16. A recent study of the major contains helpful material. See *Liberal Learning and the Arts and Sciences Major* [1991].

CHAPTER 6

CHARACTER TRAITS

CHARACTER TRAITS AS GOALS OF UNDERGRADUATE EDUCATION

In chapter 1, we briefly brought up character traits as educational goals, divided them into intellectual and moral virtues, and went on to other things. But in order to understand how and to what degree undergraduate education might foster such goals, we must do more sorting out. To begin with, we need to look at the kind of characteristics we are talking about. Next, we turn to a critical consideration of some of the arguments that dismiss the relevance of any such character traits for higher education. Finally, we move to our prime purpose of clarifying the goal of fostering certain character traits in a way so as to facilitate the exploration of pedagogical approaches.[1]

It will fix our ideas to have before us the following two somewhat miscellaneous lists of characteristics widely regarded as desirable traits of college graduates and other fellow citizens. Though attributes are classified as *moral virtues* or *intellectual virtues*, the distinction is not sharp and several traits might plausibly appear in either list.[2]

Moral virtues: Honesty, integrity, emotional stability, generosity, sense of fairness, ability to cooperate, ability to take risks, awareness of and concern for the interests of others, capacity to make commitments and participate in a community, ability to make moral discriminations and judgments.

Intellectual virtues: Appetite for learning, imaginativeness/creativity, respect for viewpoints of others, tolerance for ambiguity, respect for facts and the ability to suspend judgment in their absence, ability to reason/think critically, and solve problems.

Most everyone is likely to agree that it would be a fine world if most college graduates possessed these attributes. Some would no doubt list addi-

---

1. The professions of psychology and philosophy have developed technical literatures on the cluster of issues raised in this chapter. Given its practical orientation, this discussion will not satisfy the standards of rigor of either of these fields. The use of nontechnical labels, such as "character traits," "intellectual virtue," and "moral virtue" should serve as a reminder of that fact.
2. Though drawn from many sources, these lists are particularly indebted to Bok, "Purposes of Undergraduate Education" [1974].

tional traits, including a number pertaining to sexual behavior, sobriety, and religion. Others would reduce the list, claiming that some items are none of higher education's business. The discussion must begin, however, with a response to the challenge that undergraduate education is simply not in any way capable of contributing to the furthering of such virtues.

One objection asserts that by the time students reach college age, it is too late to acquire most or all of these characteristics. If, by the late teens, a person is not habitually honest or imaginative, for example, no later educative measures can be expected to change that fact. While it *is* most desirable to have an honest and imaginative citizenry, the attainment of this goal, unfortunately, has no bearing on undergraduate education.[3]

Although most or all of the traits on these lists certainly do manifest themselves at a much earlier stage than late adolescence—if they appear at all—this does not make college irrelevant. What was acquired earlier can later be reinforced or undermined, encouraged or squelched. College life—its curriculum and experiences outside the classroom—can strengthen or weaken characteristics that undergraduates had previously acquired.

Far less abstract are considerations deriving from the change of context from secondary school to undergraduate study, often accompanied by a departure from home for college. This move transforms the environment in which previously acquired characteristrics are brought into play. Indeed, the change is likely to generate entirely new arenas for the expression of many of the listed attributes. Even if imaginativeness is a gift conferred at birth, much must be learned about exercising that imagination in worlds newly opened in college. Honesty may be a deeply rooted disposition; yet there may be much to learn about acting honestly in novel and more complex contexts. What was earlier acquired can thus be developed in new directions, with many aspects of undergraduate education potentially effective.

Characteristics that can be regarded as developing in stages should be looked upon as special cases of this commonsense account of development. On Kohlberg's view, for example, most people reach a conventional level in their moral development, where morality consists of living up to the expectations of others, of fulfilling agreed upon duties, and of contributing to society. Only a fraction of the population moves beyond this level to a principled one, he holds, where moral action conforms to moral principles that are understood by the actor and accepted as the actor's own. Whoever reaches this principled stage tends to do so in late adolescence—precisely, that is, during the normal college years. Undergraduate institutions can surely play a role in this transition to more self-conscious, autonomous behavior, by constituting a

3. This is essentially the view taken by Bok [1974].

setting in which challenges to routine thinking and demands for reasons for one's views are daily fare.[4]

Before further exploring these relationships, we turn to a final and most powerful basis for supposing college to be irrelevant to many of the traits on our list. Long ago, Socrates raised the question whether virtue can be taught at all and never reached an affirmative answer. It is by no means foolish to follow him into such skepticism with respect to significant characteristics on both of our lists. However such traits as integrity, creativeness, generosity, or tolerance for ambiguity may have been acquired—assuming they are not simply the product of genetic endowment—the Socratic skeptic will maintain that it was not with the help of a teacher or as a consequence of lessons.

Whether or not virtue can be taught is, in the end, an empirical question— or, rather, several of them pretending to be one, since the many attributes that are called "virtue" may very well differ with respect to their teachability. Unfortunately, there is little adequate evidence on this cluster of issues, nor is evidence easy to come by. On the contrary, illegitimate inferences are here particularly tempting. One must abstain from arguing, for example, that because *my* teaching fails to accomplish its goal, it is not possible to accomplish it. One must resist, as well, the more important version of this inference, which appears to be free of the subjective, because it is rooted in a widely accepted conception of college teaching, consisting of lecturing, assigning readings, class discussions, and the like. Even if one were to grant that such teaching actually fails to bring about the desired results, we are not yet entitled to conclude that this or that character trait cannot be engendered by teaching at all, perhaps teaching of a quite different sort. Even parents sometimes come to realize that virtues tend not to be instilled by lecturing at one's children. Not only more and better evidence is thus needed, if we are to get a better purchase on this issue, but we must take a harder look at how we go about teaching.[5]

---

4. For a useful summary, see Kohlberg, "Moral Stages" [1976]. For an account that diverges from Kohlberg by differentiating significantly between the development of women and men, see Gilligan, *In a Different Voice* [1982]. Nothing about the differences in developmental accounts contravenes the modest point here put forward: that it is possible and desirable to become more sophisticated in judgment and behavior than might have been learned at one's mother's knee or from one's school teacher and that higher education might be instrumental in increasing that sophistication.

5. In *Education and Learning to Think* Resnick [1987], comments on the periodical shift from emphasis on basic subject matter to "various forms of process- or skill-oriented teaching" and then urges that we not "allow these pendulum swings to continue" (p. 49). While this concern (and her entire volume) pertains to primary and secondary education, the pendulum swings similarly in undergraduate education between skill and process at one pole and substance at the other. If, in the language of psychology, such higher order dispositions (which are certainly represented on our list of virtues) are closely related to subject matter knowledge, then we simply do not *know* what teaching can do, if that teaching is limited primarily *either* to subject matter *or* to process. We will return to this theme.

We must avoid a still more serious form of reduction. Suppose we adopt a Socratic skepticism and maintain that virtue cannot be taught. It would nevertheless be a grave error to conclude that it cannot be acquired by learning, for one must not assume there to be an automatic connection between teaching and learning. If it is deplorable that the former need not be accompanied by the latter, there is compensation in the fact that there is much learning without teaching. We are back to an earlier conclusion. If at least some of the characteristics with which we are concerned can be acquired by learning, the circumstances under which such learning takes place become relevant. And even where the activities of a teacher are not among them, it becomes pertinent to inquire how and whether such learning can appropriately be fostered by undergraduate institutions.

Socrates' ancient views notwithstanding, the need for a reply to skeptics who hold undergraduate education to be irrelevant to most of the traits listed is, in many ways, a product of our time. The professionalization of *undergraduate* education, emulating the Johns Hopkins or German model of *graduate* education, has obscured a long tradition that took for granted that character development should continue as part of the education that follows secondary school. The modern roots of this view can be found in Locke and Rousseau, and more recently were expressed in some of the nineteenth-century rhetoric about Oxford and Cambridge. In twentieth-century America, this attitude has also made sporadic appearances, most notably in the influential 1946 *Harvard Report,* actually containing two sections entitled "Traits of Mind" and "The Good Man and the Citizen." There, the objective of a central portion of undergraduate education is the characteristics of mind to which it leads:

> By characteristics we mean aims so important as to prescribe how general education should be carried out and which abilities ought to be sought above all others in every part of it. These abilities in our opinion are: to think effectively, to communicate thought, to make relevant judgments, to discriminate among values.[6]

But if neither philosophy nor tradition are sufficient to overcome the professionalized view of undergraduate education, very mundane truths also serve as the basis for a reconsideration. Everyone for whom some time has elapsed since graduation from college is painfully aware that even material that had there been learned well tends to be forgotten, unless it was subsequently in active use. What has been learned is recovered with increasing difficulty and in more fragmented form as the college years recede further in time. This fact,

---

6. *General Education in a Free Society* [1966, pp. 64–65].

experientially known to all college graduates, is confirmed, as well, by various empirical studies of alumni.[7]

Nevertheless, we are not tempted to argue that a college education is futile. For most people, in spite of all they have forgotten, college has made an enormous difference: there *is* a significant residue.[8] Central among these lasting effects of undergraduate education is the development and strengthening of some of the traits on our list, including such exceedingly broad attributes as the capacity to deal critically with issues and problems, including moral and political ones. To the degree to which they are developed, these powers tend to have considerably greater endurance than the specific substance—the literature, the experiments, the exercises—that are among the means employed to cause their growth. We cannot, it is safe to conclude, ignore intellectual and moral virtues, when considering the goals of undergraduate education.

CHARACTER TRAITS ANALYZED

In the course of claiming that it is neither too late nor futile to aim at fostering character traits at the college level, it was suggested that activities beyond the classroom play a role, that the entire institution of higher education is implicated. While this extension of the sphere of relevance to learning will be pursued in later discussions, we must note here that there are also limits to the function of undergraduate institutions in the advancement of virtues.

Fostering must not be confused with therapy, nor college with a hospital—even though the line between the curative and the remedial is wobbly, and in spite of the fact that no undergraduate institution can remain wholly aloof from functioning in the therapeutic realm. Nevertheless, our concern is limited to the *normal* development of traits during a phase of life capable of building on the acquisitions of childhood and early youth. It is appropriate, for example, for undergraduates to come to learn how principles of honesty apply to a more complex intellectual domain than they had

---

7. An extreme formulation has it that "most studies show that 50 to 80 percent of what is learned in courses is lost within one year," though the author goes on to qualify in various ways. From Bowen, *Investment in Learning* [1977, p. 88]. Another summary states, "One can assume that much specific knowledge gained from college courses will be forgotten, particularly by the majority of college graduates who go into fields that do not require such knowledge," Astin, *Four Critical Years* [1977, p. 200]. Both discussions make use of a formidable study, Hyman *et al.*, *The Enduring Effects of Education* [1975]. But without benefit of empirical research, the Harvard Committee raises this rhetorical question, "At the time of his examination the average student hardly remembers more than 75 per cent of what he was taught. If he were a sophomore when he took the course, how much does he recall by the time of his graduation, how much five years later, how much or how little, when he returns on his twenty-fifth reunion?" *General Education in a Free Society* [1966, p. 64].
8. Bowen's useful term, *Investment in Learning* [1977, p. 64].

hitherto known. College, then, is normally the place at which students become familiar with the intricacies of plagiarism, and it is appropriate that their learning be supported by teaching, as well as by disciplining practices. It is not, however, the function of undergraduate education to attempt to cure an intellectual kleptomaniac; expulsion may be appropriate, instead.

But much leeway remains. The range of concerns of each undergraduate institution is to some degree a function of its particular mission, also informed by knowledge of the nature and needs of its students. The pluralism of American institutions of higher education is not limited, after all, to differences in size, cost, difficulty of admission, or even of curricular and extracurricular programs. That array also includes single-sex and denominational institutions, for example, with goals for the development of character traits that may be quite distinct from the missions of most other colleges. This range must be acknowledged but cannot be taken up here. In the remainder of this chapter, accordingly, the discussion of a few clusters of character traits that are often held to be central among the goals of undergraduate education will be made to stand for a consideration of many others.

Among intellectual virtues, we will attend to imaginativeness (or creativity) and, above all, to the complex of attributes generally discussed under such headings as critical thinking, reasoning, or problem solving. Among moral virtues, we will consider the interrelated characteristics of concern for the interests of others and the propensity to make moral commitments and to participate in different communities. A third complex attribute of importance is not readily subsumed under either of these categories, the ability to make moral discriminations and judgments.

A closer look at all of these traits reveals them to be attributes that *enable* or *empower*, a fact that is often reflected in the explicit use of such terms as "capacity" and "ability." Such traits make certain modes of behavior possible for their possessor that would not be readily available for someone lacking those capacities. Skill and knowledge thus play a role in the very make-up of at least most of the characteristics under scrutiny, clearly with educational implications that need to be explored. Before turning to these issues of pedagogy, however, we must become aware of the fact that skill and knowledge cannot provide a complete account of these attributes. Where such terms are used as "concern," "respect," "awareness," "tolerance," or "appetite" (as in "appetite for learning"), we are given an explicit signal that something else besides either knowledge or skill is called for, however much those may in some way be involved.

To become clear that something is added, we need only compare these special traits with a capacity that is simply a skill or proficiency. If I am proficient in French, presumably I *can* speak the language, but it certainly does not follow that I *will*. I may just not make use of my ability on a visit to France, either because I want to dissemble, or because I am ashamed of my accent, or merely because I am lazy. A proficiency is quite like a tool or an instrument: its owner can decide to use it or to keep it stored away. That someone has the ability to play the piano is no more a guarantee that there will be piano music at any given time than is the fact that he or she owns a piano. Both piano and pianistic ability are needed, but even together they are insufficient to produce music without the pianist's resolve to sit down and play.

Concern, respect, awareness, tolerance, and appetite are not, in this same way, possibilities. Their expression or actualization are not dependent on an analogous decision to use the characteristics possessed. When we know of people that they have a concern for the interests of others or a respect for persons, we don't merely know that they *can* act in certain ways but that they are likely to *do* so. If additional conditions need to be fulfilled for the likely behavior to occur in actuality—and in the real world that is always the case — making a *decision* to use an ability is not among those conditions. For a concerned or respectful person, there is no room for a further explicit *resolve* to behave in a concerned or respectful way.

This unconditional component is conveyed by the old-fashioned term "virtue." When we recommend someone as honest, temperate, or coopera- tive, we mean much more than that he or she *knows how* to tell the truth, exercise self-restraint, or work smoothly with others. We mean to convey, rather, that the person can actually be expected to behave in an honest or temperate or cooperative way; and when we seek to engender or develop such traits, we expect to foster a propensity that permits us to count on honest, temperate, or cooperative behavior.

That morally virtuous behavior should not be dependent on a decision is commonly taken for granted. That intellectual virtues have a similar nature may not always be equally obvious. A creative or imaginative person is some- one whose thoughts and actions can usually be so characterized, not someone possessing the skill of imagination, to be used when he or she decides to do so. When we hope that our students will become careful and critical thinkers, we are not just looking forward to the day when they *know how* to be meticulous and analytical in their thinking, investigating, and arguing but when their thinking is actually characterized in this way as a matter of course.

Just as a person is not honest simply because he or she knows how to refrain from taking other people's belongings, so a student does not become a critical thinker when he or she has learned to make certain intellectual moves. Merely knowing how is quite compatible with not getting around to using those abilities, except perhaps when asked to do so on a class examina- tion. Reflection about the entire list of character traits will reveal that in each of the ones mentioned, this element of actuality plays a role. We have not grasped the nature of moral or intellectual virtues as goals of education, if we have not understood that their possession is more than the possession of skills or knowledge.

THE COMPONENTS OF KNOWLEDGE AND SKILL

With this complexity before us, we are ready to return to the theme of skill and knowledge. It should not surprise us, in this context of higher education, that the virtues of special interest to us have such abilities as a component, even if their nature is not exhausted by them.[9] To begin with, conversancies can play a significant role in the development of a number of the character traits with which we are concerned. If the *Bildungsroman*—a genre to be found in all literatures—gives expression to the theme that an expanded range of experience fosters the growth of the protagonist, these forms of higher education can have a similar effect. Where conversancy with science, history, or literature is achieved, it is like travel away from home, from one's province, into worlds hitherto unknown. Such learning can serve as a way station—constructed of ideas, models, or facsimiles—that stands between the relatively confined and closed world of childhood at home and the open expanse of adult life. Another metaphor has this learning serve as a partial map of a large world that is as yet beyond the student's acquaintance.

Considered as protoexperiences, then, certain conversancies are directly relevant to some of the character traits that have been singled out. Concern for the interests of others is dependent on an awareness of such interests. Such a grasp must be broadened from youthful experience if that virtue is to function in a larger realm. Respect for the viewpoints of others—perhaps misleadingly classified as an intellectual virtue—is similarly dependent on a comprehension of an enlarged range of beliefs. If imaginativeness entails the ability to go beyond present experience, its power, in any given case, is to a degree dependent on the scope of actual experience in the domain in which imagination is being exercised.

The general point is clear: conversancies function in the cultivation of important traits of character, with a number of areas capable of extending a student's familiarity with what nineteenth-century German philosophy has unilluminatingly baptized "values." Studying literature (and not only "great" literature), history, religion, some anthropology, some philosophy expands one's knowledge of what has been or is being held to be good or moral, what is considered to be a goal to be pursued or is even seen as obligatory, what is regarded to be beautiful, felicitous, great, and what is taken to be the opposites of all these.

But compared to traveling around the world, the taking of courses is a shadowy substitute. If these surrogates are to be significant antidotes to provinciality, it matters how the courses are taught. Enlarging the imagination is

9. If virtuous behavior is like the horse actually drinking, then the acquisition of skills and knowledge is the equivalent of leading it to water. The familiar saying is certainly right to insist that the horse must want to drink, but it overlooks that having it led to water is an equally necessary condition. For certain virtuous behavior, to return to our topic, the right desire, though needed, does not suffice, some knowledge and skill are required as well.

not the same as learning what is the case, though knowing facts is an ingredient in that broader goal. Attending to ends, to what is prized, diverges from the technique-oriented norm of the graduate programs in which most instructors were trained. Moreover, the goal of fostering such understanding may call for a lingering that conflicts with the goal of achieving some conversancy with an entire domain. It is not simple for end-of-twentieth-century urban American students to come to understand the world view of a Don Quixote so as to see him not as a quaint figure in a strange past but as a possible neighbor. Since such examples are easily multiplied, they reveal yet another inevitable tension between breadth and a certain depth of learning. The exhibiting and assimilating of salient features of cultures of different times and places, including the "fictions" of literature or philosophy, require the kind of time and involvement that limits the extent of the material covered. And while "coverage" is emphatically not the goal of conversancy, acquaintance with a certain range of material is needed if a student is to feel at home in the realm studied. A balance is not easy to strike.

By looking at the role of some conversancies, we took examples of the function of expanded knowledge in the cultivation of character traits. We turn now to consider the development of skills as a component, first, of the propensity to reason well and think critically and, subsequently, of the capacity to make moral discriminations, to engage in moral reasoning, and to make commitments.

Skill is certainly needed if one is to reason well, think critically and carefully, and solve problems effectively. This simple fact underlies a veritable industry of books and courses, either entitled "critical thinking" or suggesting that activity in some other way.[10] This genre of syllabus originated in philosophy—a fact made still more obvious when the label "informal logic" is used—although it has attracted teachers and writers of texts from several other fields. However, even today we can detect the descent of these courses from Aristotle's *Rhetoric*, because often, following that ancient model, the role of fallacies—the ways in which thinking can go wrong—is most prominent in their syllabi.

That an account of the pitfalls to be avoided is often the way in which authors stake out the territory of critical thinking, expresses well the difficulty of providing a characterization that is both general and positive. Two quite different recent formulations are helpful. The first, by Kurfiss, informally characterizes the "essential skills" involved in critical thinking, avowedly an incomplete list: (1) identifying the issues requiring the application of thinking skills; (2) determining and gathering the relevant background knowledge; (3)

---

10. Two recent books on the topic are useful and, together, provide ample references. For an excellent list of textbooks and treatises on the topic, see Ruggiero, *Teaching Thinking Across the Curriculum*, [1988]. This volume is primarily oriented toward instruction, while the following takes a somewhat more analytic approach: Kurfiss, *Critical Thinking* [1988].

generating plausible hypotheses; (4) developing procedures to test—confirm or disconfirm—these hypotheses; (5) articulating the results of these tests in the form of an argument; (6) evaluating arguments and revising hypotheses where needed.[11]

A second analysis, by Resnick, looks at such components of critical thinking—to which she refers by the more general term, "higher order thinking"—and then spells out what *kind* of thinking it is. Accordingly, higher order thinking is seen to be (1) nonalgorithmic (with the path of action not fully specifiable in advance); (2) complex (with the path not visible from a single vantage point); (3) yielding multiple solutions (rather than unique ones); (4) involving nuanced judgments and interpretation; (5) calling for the application of multiple criteria (sometimes conflicting with each other); (6) often involving uncertainty (with not everything relevant known); (7) involving self-regulation of thinking (rather than following prescriptions); (8) involving the imposing of meaning (finding structure in apparent disorder); and (9) involving significant effort.[12]

The first list of "essential skills" hardly tells the reader what to do in order to think critically (nor does it set out to do so). Part of the second account characterizes these skills, on the other hand, and can therefore be regarded as an explanation as to why they seem so remote from actual mental activities. We have climbed to a high level of abstraction and from that platform try to describe a vast array of mental processes by means of a single complex formulation. In effect, we are trying to talk at one and the same time about activities ranging from the construction of deductive proofs in mathematics to the interpretation of poetry, from the devising of laboratory tests for hypotheses in chemistry to the reconstruction of an historical event to the justifying of a controversial moral decision. That this should be difficult is not surprising.

And the difficulty of formulating succinctly what critical thinking is, is reflected in controversies about the pedagogy by means of which these higher order skills are to be acquired. While courses in critical thinking, under whatever name, are indeed widespread (and not infrequently required), there is no agreement about their effectiveness. At the conclusion of such a course, some students will certainly do well on a final examination. But it is quite another matter as to how what was so well learned in a critical thinking course also transfers to improved thinking in poetry, politics, history, science, and so on.

The issue, after all, is not the learning of informal logic as a subject matter—however desirable that may be—but learning how to reason well, wherever reasoning is called for. Alas, the prevalence of critical thinking courses is a function of a perceived *need* for a certain result but not of

---

11. Quoted and summarized from Kurfiss, *Critical Thinking* [1988, p. 20].
12. Quoted and summarized from Resnick, *Education and Learning to Think* [1987, p. 3].

knowledge that such courses are *effective*. There is little empirical research that sheds light directly on this crucial topic.[13]

But there *is* considerable skepticism. A variety of studies suggests that much learning concerned with thinking occurs primarily within the context of specific subject areas, "that problem solving, comprehension, and learning are based on knowledge and that people continually try to understand and think about the new in terms of what they already know."[14] More theoretical reflections arrive at a similar conclusion by suggesting that since only the most *general* methods of thinking apply to a range reaching from mathematics to poetry and from history to physics, they are also the *weakest* of those techniques. To become more effective in solving problems that are field, context, and substance bound—as are all problems except those in logic itself—the techniques pertaining to those fields need to be acquired as their substance is being learned.[15]

Courses in critical thinking may have the merit of inducing students to become self-conscious about thinking, but their value for the cultivation of a broad trait remains questionable. Yet even if we were more optimistic about the effectiveness of such a course —and supposed, furthermore, that every undergraduate were actually enrolled in one—that would by no means take care of the goal of having undergraduates become critical thinkers. Two sets of considerations take us far beyond a single course, even while we are considering only the acquisition of skills.

The first reason has already been broached. Whatever the harvest from the successful completion of a course in informal logic, it does not change the fact that in different scholarly fields and different human endeavors, we make use of many and diverse ways of reasoning and solving problems. Since these ways are embedded in those specific fields and endeavors, a single course that attempted to deal with all those "methods" (and not only with the most general rules of informal logic) would have to do so most superficially, touching lightly on an array of techniques. The modes of thinking appropriate and customary in a subject matter can be treated more deeply and extensively only within those subject areas themselves.

Second, it is notorious that acquiring skills calls for practice. Even on the most optimistic assumptions regarding effectiveness, it makes no more sense to suppose that some single course will convert a student into a critical thinker than that a year's worth of studying will transform him or her into a

---

13. For a succinct review of what is known about the topic of transfer, including references to research, see Resnick, *Education and Learning to Think* [1987, pp. 16–19].
14. Glaser, "Education and Thinking" [1984, p. 100].
15. "[T]he dilemma posed is that general methods are weak because they apply to almost any situation and will not alone provide an evaluation of specific task features that enable a problem to be solved. In contrast, skills learned in specific contexts are powerful enough when they are accessed as part of a knowledge schema, but the problem of general transfer remains," Glaser, "Education and Thinking" [1984, p. 102].

pianist. And practice is not simply repetition. Progress is achieved through a cumulativeness that comes about when students are required to use the methods of solving problems in different settings and contexts, with different problems and issues, and over extended stretches of time.

These considerations (and the importance of the issue of better thinking!) must influence the way in which a whole range of subjects is taught to undergraduates. Methodological self-consciousness in teaching is called for. The vast majority of college instructors are fully competent in the sense that they are themselves well versed in the methods of their fields. In their teaching, however, they tend to *use* these methods, to *apply* them, and even demand of students that they show those competencies. But, in another sense, they take these procedures wholly for granted by refraining from articulating what they are and how they work.[16] Concern with critical thinking requires that what is implicit be made explicit, made pedagogically available. It does not follow that methods should be taught instead of subject matter—as if it were possible to do that. The recommendation, rather, is adverbial, and asks for attention to the *way* in which subject matter is taught. It is not enough to have an instructor simply *exhibit* what it is to think well in the field being taught, a deliberate effort must be made to reveal how that is done and to involve students, interactively, in doing it.

Again, such self-consciousness and the provision of opportunities for students to practice take teaching and learning time. And if there is no one-course pill to guarantee the acquisition and cultivation of thinking skills, methodological awareness must pervade most subjects for most of a college career. No doubt, a shift in emphasis reduces the amount of subject matter covered. Professorial anxiety should be somewhat allayed, however, by a recognition that ten years later students will be better served by the acquisition of useful traits of character than by the retention of a somewhat larger number of fragments of a field.

While we will want to make some pedagogic observations about the component of skill in two additional character traits, there is little to say about the first of these, the fostering of creativity or imaginativeness. Because of the existence, since Isocrates, of logic and rhetoric as subject areas for study, one is plausibly misled into thinking that in a course dealing with them students might acquire generic skills of thinking. No equivalent temptation exists with respect to imaginativeness and creativity, and no widespread movement has sprung up offering courses called Imaginative Thinking. Imagination must be fostered in all of the areas in which it can play a role, and, again, what matters is *how* those subjects are taught. An instructor must, to be sure, establish some order in a course—indeed, in any given class hour—if something is to be

---

16. We laugh at Molière's M. Jourdain when he discovers, in embarrassingly public fashion, that he is speaking prose. But note that no one is born with this bit of knowledge. Long ago, some teacher should have told him.

accomplished. But order need not mean mechanical rigidity, any more than intellectual discipline means following bureaucratic rules for the mind. The opportunities for imaginativeness exist in the interstices, and such opportunities are taken where there is stimulation and encouragement.

By contrast, there is neither a dearth of academic subject matter nor a paucity of courses pertaining to the realm of morality. Ethics or moral philosophy—with no distinction here intended between the Greek and Latin formulations—is an ancient and complex field, capable of generating several quite distinct types of introductory courses at one end of the pedagogic continuum and of stimulating a continuous stream of students and thinkers to write doctoral dissertations, monographs, and treatises, at the other. The nonspecialist will have numerous good reasons, moreover, to study moral philosophy and its history, if only because moral thinking has both given expression to and influenced the tradition that has shaped our own thinking. But our concern here is a much more specific issue. If it is a goal of undergraduate education to foster the propensity to make moral discriminations and commitments, we must inquire by what pedagogy the skills associated with this attribute are acquired.

It should not be surprising that the role played by courses in ethics is closely analogous to that played by courses in critical thinking, since, after all, *moral* reasoning is a species of *reasoning*. Courses that stress moral reasoning, in other words, make manifest to students that thinking about moral issues is subject to standards of rigor quite analogous to reasoning in other disciplines, with a corresponding requirement to assess evidence, examine assumptions, and build sequential arguments. Not only may such a course introduce students to the *ways* in which one reasons about issues of morality, but it may make clear to them for the first time that moral beliefs are not simply matters of personal opinion about which it is pointless to argue at all.[17]

But two limitations must also be recognized. As a serious contribution to a student's ability to make moral discriminations, general courses in "problems in ethics" inevitably hover between the generic and the once-over-lightly. They can make students aware of considerations that must enter into adequate moral thinking, but they cannot import life into the classroom. On the other hand, those ethical problems whose treatment requires more than commonsense knowledge, and where special sophistication in reasoning is needed as well, are precisely the problems embedded in various professional practices. Medicine, business, engineering, and law are among the most prominent professions generating moral problems that require considerable expertise for their solution. It is only in the context of such specific spheres, accordingly, that serious contributions can be made to the discrimination of, and thinking about, moral problems of the "real world."

The second limitation is nothing more or less than the already stressed

---

17. This last point is stressed by Bok in his "Can Ethics Be Taught?" [1976, p. 28].

limitation of the conception of character traits as composed of skills alone. Even strong proponents of the teaching of ethics in higher education do not claim that becoming proficient in moral reasoning—generic or specific—will contribute to more moral *behavior* by the successful student. Plato already asserted that one who acquires the art of healing a sick person thereby also acquires the art of making a healthy person ill; a physician and a poisoner are distinguished by how they use their skill.[18] It is time, then, that we return to a further consideration of the ineliminable component of character traits that take these attributes beyond knowledge and skill.

THE CENTRALITY OF AUTONOMY

Earlier we noted in passing that some arbitrariness is introduced when certain character traits are classified either as moral or as intellectual virtues. We will be helped in our effort to determine how important character traits are fostered during the undergraduate years if we explore a certain strain shared by members of both lists of virtues.

We can begin to uncover this connection by recalling a favorite cliché of commencement speeches. "Remember this and that, as you go out into the world," seniors are exhorted, as they are about to depart from campus. In plain English, that metaphor reminds graduates that they are on their own now—above all, that they will have to earn their own living. This economic interpretation certainly gets at the way things are, but so does an intellectual and moral interpretation of the commencement platitude.

Undergraduate institutions no longer stand literally in the place of parents—if they ever did—but they nonetheless engage in certain parental practices. Instructors tell their students what to do and, often in parental manner, prod them to do it. They determine in advance what students should discover, they make assignments, usually with great specificity, they impose deadlines, they coerce by means of examinations, they reward and punish with grades. In sum, like many a child's home, the professorial establishment provides a structure that frees even the best student from the need to make decisions of a certain kind. And while campus dormitory and social life is vastly less regulated than it was a generation ago, it still provides a framework for acceptable behavior that is absent when one goes out into that world.

The undergraduate years, however, are placed between the period of

18. Even a report that stresses the importance of teaching ethical reasoning in higher educa- tion is aware of the two-edgedness of that skill. Courses in ethics can provide students "with the tools for a more articulate and consistent means of justifying their moral judg- ments and of describing the process of their ethical thinking. To be sure, *the verbal behavior may represent nothing more than clever sophistry; bad moral positions can be skillfully defended.* That danger must be run. . . ." From *The Teaching of Ethics in Higher Education* [1980, p. 54, italics added].

dependency of childhood and the much greater, if never complete, independence of adulthood. It is clearly an important function of undergraduate institutions to facilitate that transition. And when this role is recognized, one can see that the development of these central intellectual and moral virtues contribute to that independence by making their possessor increasingly autonomous. As the disposition actually to exercise a variety of abilities grows alongside the acquisition of relevant skills, an externally imposed discipline is progessively replaced by a discipline that is self-imposed.

Imagination, for example, is misconceived if thought of as something one just has, like red hair or the ability to hold a tune. Imaginativeness—an intellectual virtue as important as it is rare—is more than the capacity to envisage possibilities beyond those that have been experienced, more than the viewing in the mind's eye of a film depicting unseen worlds. It signifies an active following one's own vision, rather than the routes and routines created by others. In other words, being imaginative involves autonomousness, often to the degree of requiring courage.

Critical thinking, similarly, calls for thinking for oneself, on one's own. It means not short-circuiting an effortful process by giving way to prejudices, to the pressures of popular or otherwise received opinions. Skills of all kinds are needed, as has already been stressed, but the employment of these capacities consists of acting for oneself, resisting inertia from within and pressures to conform from without. Critical thinking is also a manifestation of personal autonomy and, like imaginativeness, it is the function neither of habit or routine nor of an explicit decision that the imagination or the skill of critical thinking should, on a given occasion, be exercised.

If autonomy can be seen as a central feature of important intellectual virtues, we can certainly expect to find this attribute playing a role on the moral side. Indeed, making moral commitments and taking risks are purposive acts of a self that is potentially or actually overcoming obstacles—internal and external, active and passive. To commit oneself is to assert oneself in a way that differs sharply from doing what one is told to do, since the burden of responsibility shifts to the actor, in conformity to the very meaning of autonomy.

Making moral discriminations and judgments, on the other hand, seems at first glance to be a primarily cognitive activity, like assigning quality ratings at a wine tasting. But because we are speaking of *moral* discriminations and judgments (and because they are *ours*), we are held to account for our views in a special way. We cannot decide to be mere spectators at the game of morality; rather, we are participants—and regarded by others as such—in an activity that is not a game at all, because by virtue of being human we have no choice but to take part. Moral judgments, then, are more like moral commitments than like judgments about wine or weather, and when we make and justify them, we express the autonomy of our selves.

Autonomy is a significant component even in the ability to cooperate, a trait that appears to call for its very opposite. Prisoners crushing stone at the side of a road under the watchful eyes of armed guards, soldiers marching into battle together under the command of their lieutenant, or a crowd surging forward to break into the headquarters of the secret police are not examples of cooperation, however well coordinated such activities may be. The explicit coerciveness of armed guards, the more subtle form of duress exercised by the platoon's commanding officer, or the blind impulse that "carries away" the member of a crowd are all deeply antithetical to what we mean by cooperative activity.

The ability to cooperate with others in the performance of tasks, usually complex, is a multi-faceted one, composed, no doubt, of a disposition of a most general sort, as well as of capabilities that are task specific. It is an important capacity, moreover, which we have every reason to foster in our students. In the present context, however, we are, above all, concerned with pointing out that cooperating presupposes a freely made decision to submit to the discipline that is required in any joint effort. A necessary, though by no means sufficient, condition for cooperation is the autonomy of the cooperating persons.

Some of the character traits that are of particular importance as goals of undergraduate education thus depend in various ways on the autonomousness of their possessor. The exercise of imagination and the propensity to think critically about issues theoretical and practical, the making of moral commitments as well as moral judgments, and even the disposition to cooperate with others—all presuppose a self capable of making itself independent of external constraints in numerous different ways. Accordingly, even though this feature is only a component of a more complex cluster of abilities that must be acquired and fostered, its pervasive significance has important pedagogical implications.

"To become creative, one must practice being creative. To become a risk taker, one must try to take risks."[19] To become autonomous in some particular way one must act by oneself, autonomously. This is one of a number of succinct ways of introducing the central point that must be made. That a capability or a disposition is developed and strengthened through its use was known to the Greek philosophers and constitutes a bit of wisdom that has never actually disappeared from the history of thought, at least in the West. Nevertheless, we seem to need periodic reminding, since there has ever been a reluctance to put this knowledge of how things work into actual practice.

In the world of education, the basic impulse that resists the implementation of this fundamental truth of pedagogy is the desire to have things orderly. To permit the exercise of a skill not yet fully developed or the expression of incomplete and tentative knowledge is to permit error to creep into the world: wrong notes into a Mozart sonata, wrong tenses into a French sen-

---

19. Frank Newman, *Higher Education and the American Resurgence* [1985, p. 62].

tence, wrong chemical compounds into a test tube. To encourage such practices is to be an active accomplice in the making of mistakes.

Not surprisingly, a considerable proportion of the people who become teachers have a passion to get it right—whatever the "it" may be. In itself, this is a laudable characteristic of those to whom we entrust the education of our young. Unhappily, a certain excess of this passion is also found among teachers—a metaphysical fear of error, so to speak—that requires the prevention, rather than simply the correction, of mistakes. This compulsion is metaphysical because it upholds the rectitude of a subject matter *as such*—that Mozart sonata, those French sentences—even though, prior to some articulation, no mind is aware of that subject, with or without error. An unfortunate corollary of this impulse is the stifling of the kind of practicing that plays so important a role in students' acquisition of skills and knowledge, as well as traits of character.

But apprenticeship for autonomy in thinking and acting is not just disruptive of a metaphysical order. Critical questioning, pursuing imaginative, unforeseen alternatives, making decisions that embody moral commitments, not to say risks—these are all activities that disrupt an earthly scene. An element of unpredictability is introduced into our daily world and not just into a platonic heaven. A student population that is actively practicing to be autonomous markedly decreases the control possessed by various authorities of the institution, because it challenges—potentially or actually—an established order.

But social order, usually taking hierarchical form, is also prized, both inside the classroom and in the larger institution that contains it. To the extent that this is so, teachers and administrators are more successful in maintaining harmony where there is conventionality and compliance, rather than questioning, imaginativeness, and experimentation. Clearly, some of the effects of the process of educating are disruptive of some of the attributes that so many institutions aim at maintaining. Whether we speak of a classroom or a university, the very conception of an *educational institution* thus contains an internal tension. Moreover, given the authority or power of those who speak for an institution, the danger is great that the years of college will, in effect, contribute to the squelching of desired character traits, even while they are celebrated as important goals of undergraduate education. To serve those goals, notable and self-conscious efforts must be made if that tension is to be resolved somewhat more in favor of the needs of pedagogy.[20]

And still more is involved in that pedagogy than providing opportunities for students to be in different ways, on their own—more even than *requiring*

---

20. The context of this discussion should make it clear that this is no call for a version of the 1960s anarchism of a Paul Goodman (see his *Growing Up Absurd* or *Compulsory Miseducation*) or Ivan Illich (as found in *Deschooling Society*). Institutions *are* needed—classes, colleges, universities—because *disciplines* are needed and *discipline*. This constitutes a plea for a course that steers between education in a utopian state of nature and in institutions in which bureaucratic rigidities have crept into the very classroom.

that they frequently and variously practice being autonomous.[21] We have earlier recognized that the exercise of moral and intellectual autonomy is effortful, at times even painful. Thus, to encourage someone to give up passivity for a more strenuous path requires more than labeling certain traits as *virtues*, more than showing that the world is a better place to the extent to which its inabitants think critically and make moral commitments. In addition, an educational environment must be created in which students derive *satisfaction* from the occasions when they strike out on their own, so as to continue on a path that progressively develops those dispositions.

No one should harbor any illusions, therefore, about dealing with the development of traits of character in some first-year student general education course, a senior seminar, or by means of some other neat package. We saw that cultivating the skills associated with intellectual and moral virtues called for active practicing on the part of the student; we can now see that this is only part of a larger picture, one that affects an entire institution. The following chapters focus more directly on some of the means that will help to bring about the goals of undergraduate education.

---

21. It is not surprising that Rousseau's political dictum that men must be forced to be free should have its application in education.

CHAPTER 7

DELIVERY

TEACHING

The point of four years of undergraduate education is learning. We also take seriously, perhaps too much so, getting grades and graduating—forms of certification—but their importance would wither did they not signify that there had been learning. Institutions posit curricular goals to get clear about their educational objectives. But those goals are achieved, and the curriculum actually delivered, only to the extent to which students learn.

Though obvious when set down, such assertions serve as a needed antidote to a common misapprehension. Take the case of potters, where things are clearer. These craftspeople engage in all kinds of activities—pounding clay, shaping, glazing, and firing it—but in the end they are defined by the products they fabricate: bowls, cups, and plates; pots, that is. If no pots, then no potting and no potter. In education, we are variously prevented from seeing clearly that there is a similar relationship between activity and outcome. First, the very elaborateness of the process dwarfs its product; it thus becomes easier to overlook that in the absence of an education, there has been no educating. What we had instead was complicated scurrying. Moreover, since an education lacks the palpable presence of a ceramic bowl, one is tempted to presume that it exists without bothering to examine the evidence. Finally, educators do not work with a passive medium; sentient students, unlike clay, can thus be judged regarding their abilities and motives, and made responsible whenever there is a paucity of educational product. All this lets stand a conception of an *educator* without the assurance that educating actually took place.

If the judiciousness and clarity with which educational institutions formulate their goals are an indication of their quality, that measure is incomplete if it does not also consider how those goals are best achieved. In parallel fashion, we will shift our attention—in this and the following chapters—to a discussion of some of the means that serve to accomplish educational objectives of the kind that have here been advanced. As we move from the center outward, we make our start, in this chapter, with teaching as the paradigmatic instrument of learning and continue with a consideration of a number of activities that enable students to make more effective use of the educational possibilities offered to them. The chapter to follow looks at the bearing that a number of features of the wider institutional environment have on the accomplishment of educational goals, while the concluding chapter will take up a number of ways in which these educative activities might be supported.

Teaching does stand at the center of the activities that deliver a curriculum; it is what faculty members do in their capacity as educators. One learns much without teachers—from experience, by watching others, and in the school of hard knocks—but the primary way of learning in an educational institution is by being taught. A statement of current practice makes a good starting point of a discussion of this chief means for the accomplishment of educational objectives. A 1987 study of universities "found lecturing to be the mode of instruction of 89 percent of the physical scientists and mathematicians, 81 percent of the social scientists, and 61 percent of the humanities faculty (but 81 percent of the art historians and 90 percent of the philosophers lectured)."[1] One imagines that similar results would have been obtained in earlier decades, with the missing fractions undoubtedly made up mostly of discussion courses and seminars (including lectures that are merely *called* discussion courses and seminars) and of laboratory sessions.

Until recently, few questions were raised about these modes of teaching in higher education. Why should the job not be done the way it always had been? Granting that some people are more talented lecturers than others and that, independently of knack, *preparing* for those fifty-minute sessions helps, the very professors who are teaching now are thought to be evidence of the method's success in the past. Yet this implicit "if it was good enough for us, it is good enough for them" is flawed, both as to the inference itself and with regard to the premise on which it rests.

Let us begin by assuming that because traditional methods of teaching brought the present professorial generation to the business side of the lectern, it *was* good enough for them. Yet how small is that cadre of teachers, as a sample of all of the undergraduates of their day. For in any year, at any college, only a minute fraction of a twenty-fifth anniversary class reunion (supposing perfect attendance!) would be professors. And if one looked at these fractions over time, one would find that they decrease markedly during the last half-century, by virtue of the surge of college enrollment during the period since World War II. If it was good enough for them, nothing much follows for that large majority with different interests and abilities from the breed that became academics.

The sample is small, and it is biased. We are looking at individuals who are engaged in careers that call for considerable intelligence, independence, and initiative. Do we know whether that success was attained because of

---

1. Katz and Henry, *Turning Professors into Teachers* [1988, p. 161, citing W. Thielens, "The Disciplines and Undergraduate Lecturing, " paper presented at the annual meeting of the American Educational Research Association, Washington, D.C., April 1987.] The section on teaching here is particularly indebted to the many thoughtful discussions on teachiing at the undergraduate level in the Katz-Henry volume.

traditional teaching methods or in spite of them? The most highly motivated and talented will learn without being taught at all, provided the environment offers opportunities for relevant experiences. While anecdotal evidence points to undergraduate teachers who spurred and inspired, it also reveals much contempt for classes remembered as useless or as genuine obstacles to the real learning that one did on one's own or with fellow students.

Perhaps "it wasn't really good enough for us, and it certainly isn't good enough for them" is a more appropriate formulation; but, if so, little of the impetus for such a revision comes from undergraduate teachers reflecting on their own education and their current effectiveness. Indeed, "the notion that there is a pedagogy of higher education is a very recent one and even now it is an idea that would be strange to most professors."[2] Since the concern for *learning*, however, requires serious consideration of the activity of teaching, it will be useful to look at some of the factors that have given birth to a pedagogy of higher education.

That the motivation of students should explicitly become a component in thinking about teaching on the undergraduate level constitutes a significant break with the past. Two different sources, both previously alluded to, bring this quite specific, though central, issue into the picture. The growth in size and variety of the American student body came to pose practical problems for college teachers that they had not faced before. Not that in the good old days of greater elitism student motivation was to be taken for granted. That familiar fiction about college life during the century before World War II, in which many are depicted as studying little, is founded on realities that are also reflected in the notion of the "gentlemanly C." Selectivity in admission did not mean that only the motivated became undergraduates but that a significant proportion of students simply did not need scholarly success in college to ensure success in life. Since for many just having been there and "gotten through" was enough, the professoriate could ignore the unmotivated with impunity. That is no longer so; now colleges admit large numbers of students whose careers depend on what they learn as undergraduates, not to mention profound underlying changes in the world of work and careers.

Concern for motivation in teaching on the college level is given a theoretical basis—and respectability—by the recent scientific work on human development that followed the lead of Piaget's research earlier in the century. Developmental theories and accounts of stages, put forward since Piaget's work, of course differ from each other in various respects. What matters for our present issue, however, is the fact that "it is characteristic of personality

---

2. Katz and Henry, *Turning Professors into Teachers* [1988, p. 1]. Among the causes here not to be explored here are those rooted in the economics of higher education. Sharply escalating costs—either to the parent, the taxpayer, or both—have given rise both to healthy and foolish forms of consumerism.

theory not to segment the person into easily isolable parts."[3] Growth from one phase to another is a complex process that precludes any separation of the cognitive from the conative, as was the practice in classical faculty psychology. While this view of a bifurcated human psyche is still popular among professors who see themselves "in charge" only of a subject matter to be conveyed to an intellect, developmental thinking, to put things with excessive simplicity, does not regard *interest* in learning independent from *ability* to learn and unrelated to a developmental stage.

Motivation deserves singling out, not only because of the long tradition of indifference to it in undergraduate education but because consideration of motivation symbolizes most clearly that effective teaching cannot limit its concern to the subject matter being taught. The impact of the discipline of psychology on pedagogical thinking goes well beyond this topic, however. A 1981 review essay notes that "instructional psychology has become a vigorous part of the mainstream of research on human cognition and development."[4] And while in psychology most of the research on teaching and learning is concerned with much younger ages, the more basic principles being discovered and rediscovered can often be extended to an older, college population. This fact is corroborated by some of the empirical work in the pedagogy of higher education undertaken by college instructors themselves and by researchers in higher education whose work is rooted in observations of such practitioners.

One principle stands at the center of virtually all recent discussions of teaching: a call for "the transformation of student passivity into active learning."[5] Our understanding of "the new pedagogy"[6] will be helped by a grasp of this distinction between passivity and various degrees of activity, together with some sense of the conditions that foster activities that promote learning.

Both students and teachers would have an easier task if learning were simply a matter of passive receptiveness. A medieval tale provides a paradigm. A wondrous device, the *Nürnberger Trichter*, the "Funnel of Nuremberg," has the remarkable ability of infusing knowledge into the head of a student during sleep. Depicted as the heart's desire of lazy pupils everywhere, this contraption achieves by magic what many come close to assuming is possible without it: to effect learning in perfect passivity.

While the myth's appeal to students is obvious (they would learn without

---

3. Katz and Henry, *Turning Professors into Teachers* [1988 p. 2]. The summary to be found there of studies in human development is as masterful as it is brief.
4. Resnick, "Instructional Psychology" [1981, p. 660].
5. Katz and Henry, *Turning Professors into Teachers* [1988, p. 6], in a particularly felicitous formulation of this theme. That there should be ambiguity as to whether principles are being discovered or rediscovered is brought home by the reminder that, more than half a century ago, followers of John Dewey preached that one *learns by doing*! See also Astin, "Student Involvement" [1984]. Astin's conception of involvement calls for analogous activity in learning, while its scope goes well beyond pedagogy. See especially pp. 299ff.
6. The term is taken from *The Liberal Art of Science* [1990, pp. 27–49].

having to study), there is an attraction for teachers as well. A woodcut I remember depicts whole books disappearing into the *Nürnberger Trichter*, the small end of which is lodged in a sleeping boy's head. No sorting, no pedagogic agonies: the teacher collects what is to be taught and just shoves away. A triumph of content-oriented "teaching."

Alas, neither modern techniques of pharmacology nor hypnosis have yet been able to make this fairy tale come true. A prevalent form of lecturing, however, comes close to trying to be a nonmagical equivalent, by making few demands on students beyond wakeful receptivity. Whether the lecture is composed and delivered more artfully or less, many simply place before students the findings of scholars and scientists that the class is to learn. This genre's mark of distinction is its exclusive attention to conclusions; it makes it especially attractive to some teachers because of the maximal efficiency with which it conveys information, and thus promotes coverage—in one sense, at least.

Such an enterprise may well conform to the hoary and cynical definition of the college lecture: words going from the notebook of the professor into the notebook of the student without passing through the heads of either. For there is no magic. The effect of lecturer retailing conclusions and of student passively receiving them is temporary memorizing, at best, to serve the need of some test; there will have been little learning.[7] One moral of this tale is that students will get out of an educational experience what they put into it, but another is the observation that what students will *do* is bounded by conditions created by the teacher.

Attending to any lecture is of course characterized by a certain uneliminable passivity: someone up there is talking; I sit here quietly, listening. Our notion of what it is for a student to be active will be considerably clarified if we note that, in at least two different ways, even lecturing can be modified so as to reduce student passivity significantly, while still leaving the fundamental relationship between lecturer and hearer unchanged. The first of these modifications is substantive, while the second is methodological.

For many reasons a teacher might think it important for students to come to know how conclusions are reached, but powerful pedagogic grounds alone suggest that they be made acquainted with the processes of inquiry that led to the results being put forward.[8] A mind that *follows* a sequence of

---

7. All instructors are familiar with the inevitable query, "Will there be questions on the final exam about material 'covered' before the midterm?" Many teachers are annoyed, because the question suggests that what had been taught need no longer be known some few weeks later. But then, more substantial learning is perhaps not to be expected from teaching methods like the kind of lecture described. Note that in the Oxbridge system, where the examinations that determine a student's standing are placed at the end of the three-year undergraduate stint, tutorials that call for extensive speaking and writing by the student are the central method of teaching, while lectures remain peripheral.

8. For reasons that include those stated here, but also go beyond them, this principle is at the center of the new pedagogy recommended in *The Liberal Art of Science* [1990].

steps—an argument, an account of information regarded as standing in relation of evidence to conclusion, a set of components so depicted as to reveal a
whole, and so forth—is a mind that is *doing* something. Passive taking in
won't do because the lecturer's sentences do not just express items to be
collected but are connected to each other by links that must be apprehended,
understood. What those relationships are and how they are conveyed will
differ as much as do the methods of inquiry in literary criticism, physiological
psychology, American history, or chemical engineering. But what they share is
that they convert findings presented dogmatically—simply to be registered by
the mind and remembered—into the exhibition of a thinking process to be
followed actively, to be understood.

The lecture as report of findings is modified methodologically when it
takes explicit cognizance of the audience to whom the material is to be
conveyed. Many lecturers of course do precisely that, usually quite unself-
consciously. Instead of confining their discourse to an orderly exposition of
the material to be learned, the lecturer envisages hearers who are learners,
regarded as minds working at following, understanding. By having such an
audience in mind, speakers repeat certain points or formulate them in more
than one way, for example, because they consider them difficult for the hearer
to grasp. But besides such rhetorical—and even visual—methods for coaxing
listeners into comprehension and into seeing relationships, listener passivity
can be overcome in still more explicit ways. Thus lecturers formulate questions and pose them in a way that invites an answer, while deliberately building into the ongoing disquisition opportunities for listeners to make the
attempt for themselves. In short, these modifications of the lecture as exposition integrate into a lecture a variety of occasions for reactions by listeners,
ideally converting an archetypical form of one-way communication into what
might be called a protodiscussion. Though limited by their very format, even
lectures can contribute to the task of transforming student passivity into active
learning.[9]

When a lecture is thought of as a protodiscussion—as a communication to
which there might be a response—certain conditions become necessary for it
to be effective. When a lecture aims simply to expound a certain content, the
character and structure of that *content* governs the language and order of the
discourse. But when it aspires to engage in virtual discussion with its hearers,
success presupposes knowing something about those hearers' minds. But one
cannot prod a mind into productive activity without having some knowledge
of where it is. Although this is recognized in expressions such as "talking over
someone's head," a cognitive formulation tells only part of the story. Richer
theories of human development become relevant, as do typologies of styles of
thinking and learning. Such accounts give a general picture of the likely and

---

9. The variety of suggestions in Katz and Henry, *Turning Professors into Teachers* [1988] are
   best pursued by following up on the index entries under "Lecturing."

approximate characteristics of the students in a given class—and with a richness and subtlety likely to be unfamiliar to most faculty members. Above all,
for a teacher such accounts might begin the conversion of a class of content-
receivers into persons.

But it can only begin that task. Those qualifications—*general, likely,
approximate*—must be taken seriously, since no general scheme can describe the differing individuals to be found in any class. More specific information is needed about any given group of students, from sources as diverse as
files forwarded from admissions or advising offices to the use of an Omnibus
Personality Inventory. In any case, the possession of particular knowledge
about students must be regarded as a condition for effective teaching, for
activating minds.[10]

Parenthetically, without this concern for the individual students in a class,
the entire practice of lecturing in much of the undergraduate curriculum is
not easily justified when compared with having students work through a well-
crafted textbook. No doubt, a living person speaking to students is likely to
hold their attention more effectively than a book; no doubt, the ritual of a
class meeting together at specified times has a variety of beneficial consequences. These differences, however, would hardly justify the disparity in cost
if the lecturer did not address individual students in ways in which no book
can, whether that is done in the form of an implicit or explicit dialogue.[11]

Nor are the requirements of individualization fully satisfied by information about students at the beginning of a course. Even the limited goal now
under discussion calls for maintaining two-way communication between instructor and student throughout a course. Knowing at any point what students
have and have not learned should affect the teachers' strategy by enabling
them to address students-as-they-have-become at various junctures in a
course. On an individual level, such knowledge suggests when more specific
instructorial intervention is called for and what kind it needs to be. Testing
can here clearly play an important informational role, a topic to which we
return at the end of this section.

But it also matters that teachers come to know their students in such a way
that the students know that they are known. If a dialogue is conducive to the
transformation of a passive into an active mind, it will be greatly assisted if the
conversation—even if is only virtual—takes place among acquaintances.
Much learning is hard work; most people, not to mention adolescents, are
more inclined to work "for" someone known and respected than merely in
pursuit of a disembodied goal, possibly including a grade. Even within the
limited framework of a lecture, if students are to be brought to active learn-

10. Although the issue of knowledge about students is an important theme throughout their
    book, see particularly chapters 6 and 7 of Katz and Henry, *Turning Professors into Teach-
    ers* [1988].
11. In Plato's *Phaedrus* (274b–278b), Socrates puts down writing as inferior to speaking, pre-
    cisely because of the rigidity of the former and the responsiveness of the latter.

ing, it is vital that the relationship between lecturer and student be more personal than it usually is.

The economics of higher education will assure the continued prevalence of lecturing, whatever its limitations, as a way of inducing learning. While that alone justifies this preoccupation with the topic, it matters still more to suggest that even where students are at their most passive, there are ways of making them into more active learners. But lecturing, though widespread, is not the sole means of undergraduate education; it will be helpful to comment on how other modes of teaching support active learning.

Student activity increases notably when that virtual discussion is made actual. Such exchanges might merely interrupt or conclude otherwise formal lectures, or they may make up most of a course. But students who are talking are not necessarily engaged in a pedagogically relevant discussion. All too often, a perceptive eavesdropper might note that rather than conversing "freely," the participants seem to follow an unwritten script. One prevalent form has students competing in the game, "What is in the instructor's mind?" There is a known (to the teacher) right answer to the question that launches the discussion, making student contributions either just wrong or, to varying degrees, the correct answer. Class "discussion" is a collective attempt to get it right. Or, from such rigid control to well-nigh perfect freedom: the model at the other end of the continuum tacitly presupposes the exhortation, "You tell me what you think, and I'll tell you what I think." Each participant presents a point of view; the rest of the company, instructor included, takes note of it without much elaboration and no analysis or critique.

Yet collective catechizing and communal confessing both miss the pedagogic point. The former may help participants to *remember* this or that proposition but contributes little to their *learning*. The central pedagogic point of a discussion is to have the participants "learn by doing," to use the Deweyan phrase, in that they themselves build intellectual structures, explicitly and not just virtually, under the useful constraint of having to be clear and persuasive to others, with challenge or correction or corroboration and support coming hard on the heels of an exposition. Such an activity of building must, therefore, be disciplined by being rooted in relevant information and observant of the canons of logic. It is, furthermore, subject to rhetorical criteria that derive from the need to be intelligible and convincing to fellow discussants. No doubt, there is value in saying out loud what one thinks, if only because it is a good way to find out what one *does* think. But if other discussants do not contribute by their comments to modifications—changes or refinements, either substantive or stylistic—the discussion will not have made a contribution to active learning.

On the face of it, the activity of writing resembles more the solo expression of a point of view than it does taking part in a discussion in which the participants truly address each other. That writing is nevertheless acknowledged to make superior contributions to active learning deserves a few comments, supplementing the discussion of writing in chapter 2. As a limiting case, a given piece of writing might have no pedagogical efficacy beyond that of a verbal comment—both of them tossed off from "the top of one's head." Fundamentally, however, writing is not like speaking, a difference that begins with the marked dissimilarity with which we acquire these two skills. A self-consciousness that is only rarely attained in speaking under such formal circumstances as making a speech to an attentive audience, testifying on the witness stand, or the like is associated with most writing as a matter of course. On paper, one is much more inclined to "choose one's words," where the notion of choice symbolizes how writing stimulates the mind to a higher level of activity. One might even select those words carefully (that is, those phrases, constructions, sentences, paragraphs), deliberating with oneself about the linguistic moves to make. While oral discourse is completed once the words are spoken—and can be revised only by means of a separate, second discourse that does not itself alter the prior one—self-consciousness in writing permits changes of mind that cumulatively revise the *same* discourse. Whether these modifications are ongoing and minor or whether revisions take the form of entire drafts, self-criticism can remain operative until an explicit decision is made that the discourse now says what the writer wants to say. Writing, then, is truly building and uses a miraculous method of construction that permits the bricks to remain fully manipulable until the fixing mortar—in the form of a decision to conclude—is inserted.

A final point about writing as a way of activating minds brings us back explicitly to the educational context. The complexity of a process that permits ongoing *self*-criticism also makes possible the enlisting of other minds in the building of intellectual structures. Teachers can comment on a piece of student writing—raise questions, make suggestions, reinforce—and so can fellow students. Some understanding is of course to be gained from a grasp of these reactions by other readers. They truly serve as aids to further learning activity, however, only to the degree to which they function in the revision of what had been set down, making commentator into collaborator.[12]

We have looked briefly at certain pedagogic aspects of writing, without considering subject matter. But since writing is always writing about *something*, many a writing project also qualifies as an example, large or small, of what is called *independent study*. That label so clearly implies the absence of passivity that it becomes the obvious pole of the "active learning" end of our pedagogical continuum. But because this honorific title is in practice bestowed on a wide variety of activities, some explication is needed.

---

12. Without meaning to imply that this section will provide an extensive, not to say complete, survey of ways of teaching, it is worth pointing out that laboratory exercises constitute a kind of analogue to writing. The relationship of the former to merely watching a laboratory demonstration—not to mention to just hearing an account of it—is like the relationship of the latter to listening to a lecture. Independent of content, passivity is transformed into active learning.

Finding out the cheapest way to get to Paris, or how to open a jammed window, or whether to open a savings or a checking account are cases of the kind of independent study people undertake most frequently. A lot of life is "independent study," for we often engage in inquiries, mostly limited and short, that gain us some knowledge we didn't have before. If one ignores endless numbers of trivial and repetitive ones (Has the mail come this morning? What will the weather be like in San Francisco when we get there?), others yield more than some single item of information. At times, one even comes to know a considerable bundle of general principles or a full-fledged method for doing something. And if one adds the worlds of work and hobbies and other systematic amateur activities, independent studies assigned by life can come to resemble closely what is confronted in the academy.

But life is an uncaring pedagogue. Large numbers of its assignments are so inconsequential and routine that one can hardly speak of learning. Other demands are so formidable that one is doomed to fail or is pushed into compromise and evasion. The order in which life sets its investigative tasks is not a function of educational policy; only over long stretches of time—and then presuming luck—can one speak of cumulative learning from experience. Whether there is guidance depends on circumstances; there is not even assurance of the opportunity to bring tasks to completion. There is some sense to those stern grandfatherly warnings that life is not like school!

Or at least not how school ought to be. Though the notion of independent study implies that one is learning on one's own, it is nevertheless compatible with a teacherly function—an agency that provides an educational framework less arbitrary than life. The very choice of problems to be solved is of much pedagogical significance. The tasks set must be challenging, on the one hand (how often does independent study consist of routine chores performed for credit·rather than learning?), but not be so demanding as to constitute an insuperable brick wall. School can and must improve on life, moreover, by assuring that learning is cumulative, with the later building on the earlier. Finally, educational institutions must be benign in ways that cannot be counted on in life. Guidance need not undermine self-reliance, for example, nor should the insistence on closure. Instead, such supervision, together with constructive criticism and evaluation, can much increase the pedagogic effectiveness of the experience of independent inquiry.

As one moves from pedagogic approaches in which the minds of students are relatively passive to ones that promote increasing levels of active learning, autonomy increases concomitantly. The serious use of independent work in the latter part of undergraduate study fosters the transition from greater dependence to greater self-reliance, which is precisely one of the purposes of undergraduate education.

At the active end of the continuum, we come close to the way of life outside the walls of the academy, where one tends to learn without being taught at all. But as long as we remain concerned with undergraduate education, we must look, as well, at the complex relationship between the activity of teaching and knowing about that teaching's effectiveness—about the role of testing, that is, of what students have learned, about assessment.

Most examining is undertaken for the dual purpose of motivating students to work at their studies and assisting instructors in determining their grades. Clearly, however, the information contained in test results can also serve to let teachers know what is being accomplished by their efforts. The information thus gained, as was earlier mentioned, can lead to modifications "in course," just as periodic navigational sightings prompt adjustments of a ship's rudder to compensate for effects of currents and winds. Tests, in short, can measure teaching effectiveness, as well as student learning

Gained by means of suitable examinations over a period of time, a grasp of what students have learned in a course is, in principle, a significant datum for the design or refashioning both of syllabus and teaching approaches. But to be useful for such purposes, two conditions must be met, neither of which is easy to achieve. In the first place, information must be sought about the students' knowledge and skills *before* they embarked on the educational experience in question, so that what is measured is not simply what students know and can do, but those changes in knowledge and skills that constitute what was actually learned. Second, considerable clarity must be attained about the goals of a given course, about what it seeks to accomplish. For no expertise is required in the complexities and technicalities of testing to understand that a coherent examination can be constructed or evaluated only where there is clarity about what is to be measured.

Done well, such systematic examining can lead to ongoing pedagogical improvements in all of a course's facets, including its very goals. For in all spheres, the discovery of what is actually accomplished by given sets of means can lead to fruitful rethinking about the ends themselves. And when this kind of information is sought for an educational program, such as a major, or for an institution's efforts in the entire task of undergraduate education, the practice of examining what students have learned has come to be known as assessment. Where it is carried out in conformity with the account here given, moreover, it does not merely measure what has misleadingly been called "learning outcomes"—a term that designates simply what students know at the time they are examined—but what has been referred to as "value-added" or "talent development" assessment.[13]

When the logic of assessment is articulated in this fashion, it has the commonsensical merit that commentators on that movement have frequently noted, since its aim is to ascertain educational effectiveness at all levels, so as to increase it. As such, assessment is as much an integral part of institutional practice as teaching itself, since it "simply" grows out of institutional self-

13. The latter term is Alexander Astin's, who argues for the practice of this form of assessment in his "'Assessment, Value-Added, and Educational Excellence" [1987].

consciousness regarding its goals and the desire to devise the most effective means for achieving them.[14]

Yet this tale of assessment growing out of and serving the needs of pedagogy is not at all the typical story in the many institutions now engaged in assessment activities. For the majority, the demand for assessment has come from outside—often from state legislators and officials who want to know how well the colleges and universities for which they provide funding have been doing their job. But the source of the impulse to assess can have a significant effect on its character. Thus, when the origin of assessment is external to the institution and its activities and when its motives are political and budgetary, rather than pedagogical, a new set of considerations comes into play.

The desire for simplicity and comparability, together with a demand for credibility that is associated with a simplistic conception of objectvity, has a number of effects. It pushes toward the testing of "outcomes" rather than growth, frequently by means of standard examinations that embody the goals of the people who devise them, rather than those of any given institution. Since external pressure is inevitably exercised on a central administration rather than on individual instructors, a plausible response is to have assessment activities carried out by some central campus bureau created for that purpose.

Think of this as the political model of assessment. At its worst, this scheme actually works, and significant decisions are based on this product of the licensing conception of educational institutions. Then, because "what is measured will increase, and what is not measured will decrease," this manifestation of assessment will push the faculty toward converting its teaching into coaching sessions designed to secure good grades for their students on the assessing examinations.[15]

At its best, this political model of assessment is a bureaucratic epiphenomenon, a useless form without content. Where neither budgetary nor political consequences are drawn from such assessment results, the faculty may learn to shrug off the entire operation as mountains of paper piling high in the marble warehouses of state capitals, alongside other voluminous reports legislators exact from the academy. Aside from the waste of money and effort, the biggest harm wrought by this impotent version of the political

14. Two very different examples of such "natural" developments of assessment are to be found at King's College in Wilkes-Barre, Pennsylvania, and at Alverno College in Milwaukee, Wisconsin. For an account of the former, see Hutchings and Marchese, "Watching Assessment" [1990, pp. 32–34] and, for the latter, "Praxis" [1988, pp. 27–29].

15. The comment is Linda Darling-Hammond's, quoted in Hutchings and Marchese, "Watching Assessment" [1990, p. 28]. When, in 1917, Whitehead first published his lecture, "Aims of Education," he expressed a similar fear when he called "the uniform external examination" "deadly" [1967, p. 5].

model is that it preempts the place that might be taken up by an activity of value and importance.

The larger community, consisting of legislators, officials, and taxpayers—not to mention parents of present and future students, as well as the undergraduates themselves—*do* have a vital interest in knowing how well institutions of higher education are doing. But what that public will want to find out is *not* distinguishable from what teachers, individually and collectively, must know if they are to improve their efforts: what differences does undergraduate education bring about for the students who participate in it. Moreover, highly qualified observers of assessment in higher education are convinced that "where [assessment] works, it works because it's integral, not as a separate function off by itself but as a process woven into daily activity,"[16] which is precisely how evaluation must function if it is to be of pedagogical use. Accordingly, the goals of assessment are best served when it is seen as an implication of teaching regarded as delivery.

PARAEDUCATIONAL GOALS

To give a generous bundle of money to the proverbial stranger from Mars for shopping in a well-stocked suburban supermarket is by no means sufficient to enable that creature to purchase what it wants and what suits its constitution. Compared to the visitor, we natives have amassed an immense amount of information about the contents of that store: about the nature and some general effects of many different foods, and about our own tastes—even if we are neither health buffs nor tutored in upscale foods and brands. For many students, the choices offered when they come to college look more like the merchandise seen through the eyes of the Martian than they do to an average local shopper; very few arrive proficient at consuming what now becomes available to them. And yet, the educational opportunities offered to undergraduates *are* opportunities only if those students have the ability to make satisfactory selections.

Moreover, the stakes, during a four-year educational shopping trip, are vastly higher than in visits to the supermarket. On the one hand, the government largely protects us from being poisoned outright; on the other, metabolic processes make trips to the store almost wholly cyclical, so that shoppers can try again where they missed the boat earlier. By contrast, educational choices, once made and acted on, are doubly irreversible: what has been imbibed leaves permanent effects (if not always those originally envisaged), and the forward march of time mostly prevents going back and trying an alternative route. To be effective, therefore, to insure that the possible be-

16. Hutchings and Marchese, "Watching Assessment," [1990, p. 36].

comes actual, undergraduate institutions must provide a kind of paraeducation if students are to benefit fully from proffered educational opportunities.

Linguistic deterioration has made it hard to talk about this topic with the seriousness it deserves. The terms conventionally used to designate these paraeducational activities have become the names of peripheral chores or worse. *Orientation* for first-year students takes place before real college work begins; *advising* exists to serve the bureaucracy at least as much as it does students; and *counseling* is regarded as trying to treat an illness. But orienting, advising, counseling, when stripped of the connotations that have become routine, are serious activities, presupposing neither stupidity nor disease in those who are served—only a certain ignorance and relative immaturity to be expected of youngsters making a transition from secondary school to college, from adolescence to adulthood. We turn, therefore—avoiding a nomenclature that has become frayed in conventional usage—to characterize at least briefly some of the knowledge and insight needed by an adequate consumer of undergraduate education.[17]

Of five paraeducational goals I have somewhat artificially distinguished, two are clearly introductory and therefore need to be tackled at the very beginning of a student's undergraduate career. The others must be pursued interdependently, in an ongoing fashion, through most or all of the undergraduate years. First, it is easy for insiders to underestimate the importance of an introduction to the entire institutional environment for those newly arrived there. Strangers do need a map, intelligible to them, of the bureaucratic paths by means of which possibilities are made actual. Even on this most mundane level, the denizens of higher education must be aware that a first-year student's climb from the previous stage involves a move from a world of prescription and dependency to one in which the increased opportunity for choice demands a greater independent capacity to cope.

This need suggests that students be made familiar with the various divisions of the institution and their functions, coupled with an indication of the know-how needed to deal with them. Above all, it must not be left to individual initiative or chance for freshman to become solidly acquainted with institution-wide resources that support student learning. The most prominent of these tends to be the library, whose singular name masks an internal

---

17. The remarks that follow assume as subject of this paraeducational activity a "normal" student in need of advice, guidance, and counsel, but not of therapy. However, two comments are in order, especially in view of the fact that no amount of defining will make the distinction between these two modes of assistance sharp and clear. First, *in loco parentis* or not, an American undergraduate institution is expected to do as well or better than parents in making available a certain range of therapeutic services to students in need of them. Second, such services must be rendered by persons professionally trained and qualified. A discussion of these issues would take us beyond the scope of this book, except for the observation that whoever engages in the paraeducational activity that *is* our topic here must be able to recognize when actual therapy is needed and have the judgment to make the requisite referral.

complexity and often a physical plurality as well. Faculty members mostly take it for granted that students will avail themselves, as needed, of the varied kinds of aid that libraries can offer. But, for students, even the intention to utilize different collections, bibliographies, or search techniques depends on their knowing that these exist and are relevant to a given task, as well as on familiarity with the path that leads to them. And the probability that such intentions are actually formed increases where following up on them is envisaged as worthwhile and without hassle. In short, the process by which newly arrived students are made familiar with the library (and similar resources such as access to computers) must not be thought of as a bureaucratic duty that is discharged when a lecturer has addressed a student audience or when students have been provided with a booklet of information. This introduction must be viewed as an aspect of education, where success is measured by what is learned.

Second, a different kind of preparatory mission must introduce students to what might be called the *way* of higher education. If only by virtue of the pluralistic character of education in America, students come to college with a large range of abilities and training in broadly applicable skills and attitudes important for development and cultivation throughout the undergraduate years. Of course, first-year students will vary in their abilities to read reflectively, think analytically, engage in discussion that combines openness to the views of others with a recognition that the merit of all views is dependent on supporting evidence, and in the proficiency with which they can put on paper thoughts derived from these activities so as to convey them clearly to readers. More significantly here, it cannot even be taken for granted that all secondary schools have acquainted their students with this style of intellectual discourse, one that allows for inconclusiveness as an outcome of inquiry and debate, leaving questions without answers and disagreements without resolution. Accordingly, a signal, and not merely a symbolic one, must be given to the newly arrived, to the effect that most of them will encounter a significant break between the ways of the educational phase recently concluded and those of the educational venture now beginning. First-year student seminars are an effective method for meeting this goal and can initiate students into higher education by being a concentrated *example* of it—a focused study of a quite specific topic in a small class, working in seminar, that is participatory fashion, under the supervision of an experienced faculty member.[18] This course would not be *about* thinking and learning, discussing and writing, but would *consist* of thinking, learning, discussing, and writing in circumstances in which feedback would be well-nigh continuous. One must not be deluded

18. Success in such an introduction is probably dependent on having seminars abstain from fulfilling various other purposes, which, in different times and places, they have been used to serve. For a history and overview of the practice of freshman seminars, see Gordon, "Origins and Purposes of the Freshman Seminar" [1989].

into the belief that writing proficiency or critical thinking, for example, might be "acquired" in such a seminar for all future purposes. But the value of insisting, at the outset, on intensive practice of these capacities not only has immediate pedagogic value, but the kind of exemplary power that makes it an appropriate introduction to things to come, to the way of higher education.[19]

The third component of the paraeducational activity intended to convert students into competent consumers of undergraduate education is widely, if inadequately, acknowledged. Students need assistance beyond that given by the prose of catalogues regarding the educational choices available and appropriate for them.[20] (A structure of requirements tends to reduce the number of alternatives but just about never eliminates the need for making choices.) There is more to do here than meets the eye, especially early in a college career, since the language of course titles and of academic fields is in effect a technical language that is acquired only fragmentarily, at best, without protracted residency in the world of higher education. But in the absence of explications of what courses and fields are about, choices regarding them are made blindly or with one eye half open.

Yet even improved accounts of what undergraduate instruction offers are drastically incomplete bases for decisions, unless two further paraeducational functions are fulfilled. For insiders of the academic world, the labels placed on many courses and most disciplines come to refer to domains that are intelligible on their own, not needing further knowledge of relationships. But for novices—and perhaps even for self-critically inclined sophisticates— courses and disciplines become comprehensible only when they are seen as components of a larger intellectual sphere, on the one hand, and, perhaps more pressingly, as related to the world of professions and work, on the other.

It is no mean feat to develop a serious display, as the fourth component of the paraeducational task, of the several maps that would be needed to exhibit these relationships. On the intellectual side, comprehension of how the disciplines are related to each other anticipates an understanding that can come only from actual study of the fields. As regards the map that shows how pursuits within the academy are related to careers out there in the world, its draftsperson must not only be well informed about the worlds of study and

19. If in some classes of secondary schools students who put together a piece from two encyclopedias are encouraged to believe that they are engaged in research, the kind of freshman seminar described can take up the difference between research and plagiarism "in course" and thus be vastly more intelligible to students than are abstract descriptions.

20. Tools designed to perform many tasks are seldom the best for some particular one of them. Course bulletins are used as much to recruit future students as to inform current ones, with course descriptions additionally subject to bureaucratically determined length and form. Thus, even if catalogues were always available to all students and if students were inclined to read them with care, they could not be counted on to convey the information needed for adequate decisions.

work but must know how to sort out deeper from conventional connections between what needs to be learned and the demands of the workplace.

Nor must the metaphor of the map convey thoughts of an unchanging terrain. Both teacher and student must resist the temptation to ossify pictures that are merely snapshots of an ongoing process. Change must be regarded as normal, while stasis is exceptional. On the biographical side, many students change their major while in college, many will shift careers during a lifetime, and virtually all will have numerous and different jobs. At the same time, one can predict with equal certainty that evolving knowledge, technological developments, and changes in social organization will cause shifts in the relationships between undergraduate education and the world of work. Accordingly, for students to make sound educational choices, the needed information about relationships of undergraduate study to broader worlds must be conveyed and understood with considerable sophistication.

But when we think about the subjects of this paraeducational activity, we are impelled to introduce a fifth condition for an adequate use of the offerings of institutions of undergraduate education. To know what one wants not only presupposes knowledge of what there is to be had but also knowledge of oneself—one's interests and predilections and what abilities one has to pursue them. Only an exceptional youngster will come to college in full command of the requisite insights. Lack of experience and opportunity alone are barriers, not to mention the deeper complexities that pertain to the still-developing nature of students' personalities. Fruitful decisions are dependent on clarity of mind about the relationship between one's own true goals and capacities and what exists and is possible in the world, present and to come.

Our discussion, to this point, has focused primarily on the cognitive aspects of being an adequate consumer of undergraduate education, one could become that simply by acquiring information. But, first, the needed information is certainly not of a piece: self-knowledge is not like knowledge about the Civil War; and, second, when we remind ourselves that we are speaking about help with *decisions*, small and large, it becomes very clear that we are working with a very broad conception of paraeducation.

The two-sided transaction of helping and being helped is dependent on a complex, pervasive relationship that is, above all, characterized by trust. Several of the paraeducational functions that have been outlined can and should, of course, be carried out in formal and informal groups. The entire undertaking cannot, however, be accomplished without an individual relationship of person to person at its center. If acquaintance is a necessary ingredient, so are such personality traits as tact and a genuine interest in helping, and, beyond personal characteristics, a know-how that is seldom god-given but must be learned.[21] Actual relationships will differ as greatly as students and their needs

---

21. A compendium of useful knowledge and skills can be found in Kramer and Gardner, *Advising by Faculty* [1983].

differ from each other. But success in helping with students' decisions importantly depends on the potentiality of a sustained association in which confidence and trust are developed.

This matter of trust, however, is as much an institutional issue as it is an individual one. The very method of selection of faculty members and other participants in these paraeducational activities expresses an institutional attitude, not to mention whether and how these participants are trained and rewarded. An ever-present danger about which institutions must be vigilant is the substitution of form for content. The introduction of coercive elements into the paraeducational process, for example, can have this counterproductive effect. Required signatures, required attendance at lectures, required meetings with advisors, and the like, easily become bureaucratic surrogates for substantive relationships. Still worse, the application of duress reinforces an attitude already prevalent—if only because students bring it to college from prior experience—that all these paraeducational activities are at best remedial and therefore needed only when a defect has been perceived and the need to correct it acknowledged.

But for the most part, the work that must be done to convert students into acceptable consumers of undergraduate education is neither corrective nor curative. Nothing thus cries out to insist that these functions be performed. Indeed, there is no obvious necessity that students be proficient consumers of education. In most cases, they themselves become aware of mistakes and wasted opportunities only much later, if at all. And if one leaves out bureaucratic errors, only a few of the most flagrant educational missteps students make are ever brought to the attention of members of the educational institution. This lack of manifest urgency—the absence of squeaks in institutional wheels—makes it all too easy to limit these paraeducational activities to the ones that seem needed if the bureaucracy is to function smoothly. Reflection on the goals of undergraduate education, however, will yield an understanding of the importance of these means.

CHAPTER 8

BEYOND THE CLASSROOM

THE RELEVANCE OF THE NONCURRICULAR

This book is concerned with the goals of undergraduate education, not with everything that might be discussed about four years of undergraduate life. Why, then, should there be a chapter about goings-on beyond the undergraduate curriculum? One viewpoint justifies a simple answer: learning "academic" subjects is not all that students should be doing in college; those four years must contribute to the preparation for life in all of its facets. A student should learn to write and to calculate in college but also make friends who might later further a career. History is important, but so is learning to take part in group activities; knowledge of societies beyond our own is required for getting along in the modern world, but so is that desire to outdo others that is sharpened by participation in competitive sports. The job of college is to develop the whole person.

Yet, there is no need to appeal to the ideology of education of the whole person in order to justify roaming beyond the classroom. The mere fact that the whole person is *there* raises broader questions. The four undergraduate years, each consuming about three-fourths of the calendar year, engage most of each participant's capacities and touch on the larger part of every person's needs. Being a college student is relevant to most aspects of a human life in ways in which shopping at a supermarket, camping in a national park, or performing a summer job as a mailcarrier are not.[1]

The presence of students around the clock requires undergraduate institutions or their accessories to perform a variety of functions: students must eat and sleep somewhere; they must have opportunities for sociability; there must be possibilities for recreational activity—entertainment for diversion and respite from study, as well as physical activity for the sake of well-being and health. Many will want religious ministration. The constant co-presence of possibly large numbers of students, however, also gives rise to less cheerful needs. Aside from the necessity of assuring safety and a modicum of order, undergraduate institutions must deal with such social pathologies as the use

---

1. Full-time undergraduate study as a residential student continues to be assumed. However, many things to be brought out here are also relevant for part-time and commuting students.

of alcohol and drugs and with what one might label the anthropological pathologies of enmity among different cultural and racial groups on campus.

Business and auxiliary functions are often ignored in discussions of education, although most of them impinge on most students, including commuters who spend little discretionary time on campus. A brief and incomplete survey, in alphabetical order, suggests the magnitude of this presence. Most students will have had dealings with an office of admissions and most depend for some of their needs on the institution's bookstore; just about none can avoid the office of the bursar. At various times, most students need to make use of the computer and copying centers (or their surrogates); many must satisfy the requirements of the office of financial aid. Most will use campus food services with frequency; fewer will become clients of the health center. The need for part-time work will bring some students into contact with the office of personnel or human resources; virtually no one can (or should) avoid the institution's library or libraries. A placement office assists seniors seeking work upon graduating; everyone falls within the jurisdiction of the office of public safety; no one escapes the ministrations of the registrar.

Student housing and student life, recreational activities, auxiliary, and business functions: a few paragraphs conjure up a formidable array of enterprises, offices, organizations, and buildings. The people who run all this are likely to be equal in number to those who participate in the academic activities discussed earlier. All of these units have their own goals (the housing office houses, the registrar registers); thus, how they conduct their business impinges significantly on the lives of students.

How this world beyond the classroom bears on the achievement of educational goals will be considered under two headings, without supposing the distinction to be firm. We will first survey ways in which student activities can foster some of the goals of undergraduate education. Second, we will take a brief look at the functioning of the institutional bureaucracy and the apparatus of student life as a "hidden curriculum"—as processes that *teach*, whether their lessons are intended or not. Comments on two controversial topics pertaining to student life—fraternities and sororities and "big time" intercollegiate athletics—will conclude the chapter.

But before talking about fostering educational goals, it is worth making explicit an elementary observation. The maintenance of a certain level of physical and psychological well-being is a necessary precondition for education. College work requires time and concentration. Having the former swallowed up by the mechanics of living or the latter disrupted by frequent intrusions or anxiety makes performing the tasks set by the educational enterprise much more difficult. The issues are more basic than comfort or coddling (the missions—and price tags—of different institutions determine levels of luxuriousness). Privacy must be an option: for many, if not for everyone, its lack undermines the concentration needed for successful academic work. Physical safety must be coupled with a *belief* in physical safety, so that fear and anxiety do not occupy minds that might be busy with more constructive thinking. Where cafeteria lines are endless and eating a meal consumes vast amounts of time, adolescents are not merely being inconvenienced, their educations are being hampered. The same is true if doing laundry is akin to climbing Mt. Everest or if the pursuit of physical exercise requires squandering time and manipulative ingenuity. Examples could be multiplied, but the point is clear: if proper attention is to be devoted to education, simple existence must not be a continuous mental and physical struggle.

STUDENT ACTIVITIES AND THE GOALS OF UNDERGRADUATE EDUCATION

Undergraduate institutions arrange or facilitate a large array of "extracurricular" activities on their campuses and help students gain access to others, possibly at distant places. Both the *ways* in which students are engaged in these activities and the *substance* of such ventures are educationally pertinent and will be taken up in turn.

We stressed earlier how important the undergraduate years are as a transition from greater dependency to increased autonomy, as well as the need for practicing such independence. Campus activities—student government and organizations devoted to special purposes—as well as volunteer roles in off-campus social, governmental, or political organizations, provide the opportunities. But the educational effectiveness of such ventures will depend importantly on some of the attributes of the participation.

Many activities of students are valuable without having educational significance. Students who help paint the social hall of a local church or address invitations to potential donors may be contributing to the survival of an estimable institution. A summer job as a ranger in a national park may teach a good deal both about the ways of nature and of vacationers. Yet neither project is an exemplary supplement to education in the sense here intended. Those contributions to the welfare of the church, while possibly strengthening the student's propensity to serve,[2] lack the complexity needed to be significant steps toward greater autonomy. On the other side, much may be learned from that park service job, but it is educational in the way in which life is—postcurricular, so to speak, rather than extracurricular. The ideal extracurricular educational enterprise falls somewhere between these two poles.

The relevant kinds of activities, to begin with, are tasks that aim at the achievement of goals, or, at least, include such goal-oriented tasks as compo-

---

2. Service must by no means be dismissed as irrelevant to an adolescent's development, for surely, "service is a way for students to become responsible, engaged adults," Boyer, *College* [1987, p. 216].

nents. Further, there should be room for what we call judgment as to how that end is specified and discretion in the choice of means, selected from among possibilities that are ascertained by the student engaged in the project. While the complexity of tasks and the depth of reflection and research needed to carry them out vary immensely, these differences distinguish between the performance of a chore and the conduct of a project of pedagogic value.

Second, what makes such a project extracurricular and sets it apart from a mere exercise or laboratory dry run is its place in the real world. That world contains impurities and cantankerousness; it sports other people with contrary opinions; it contains rules and regulations, rational and arbitrary; and it is inevitably beset by financial constraints that require ends to be compromised and making do with less than the best means. As distinguished from the classroom, more is at stake than a grade.

Third, if extracurricularity consists in such an infusion of reality into a task to be performed, it also matters that this reality not be so stark as to make the risks of the undertaking excessively high and burdensome. Life often teaches, but it can also crush; in more controlled situations, one can benefit from the former propensity without courting the danger of the latter. Students are apprentices, not yet fully formed practitioners. Only those projects, then, are appropriate where failure does not have disastrous consequences or tasks can be and are supervised in ways that save students from failures that do harm. Participation in student government, for example, is unlikely to have irrevocably damaging consequences—though perhaps it needs accounting surveillance in order to keep student practitioners out of jail. On the other hand, a student working with sick patients in a hospital must have guidance that assures the prevention of harm that can stem from error.

Participation in many an extracurricular activity calls for collaboration with others to accomplish the desired goals. This desideratum is worth singling out, both because it is valuable and because it is difficult to simulate in more formal pedagogic settings, even when an effort is made to go against the individualist grain of our educational practices. Although accomplishment achieved in competition against others is central in the ideology that dominates our public rhetoric, real life tends more to conform to a secondary ideology that lauds cooperation and the achievements of teams. Whether a group collaborates to put on a play or works to further a social cause, individuals are required to fit their own initiatives into the broader one of a corporate entity. They are thus provided with experiences that resemble the ways of work in our era.

If these are some of the formal characteristics that help to make extracurricular projects supportive of educational goals, we turn now to some general observations about their pedagogical value when content is considered. One fruitful relationship is obvious, though not easy to implement on a large scale: the coordination of course work with other activities on campus and beyond. Especially, though not only, in professional education, a worthwhile symbiosis can be set up between theory and practice through internships, volunteer activities, work-study schemes, and cooperative work programs. The closer the mesh between academic and extracurricular careers—both as to the nature of the projects and their levels of complexity and independence—the more educationally beneficial such a collaboration is.

Not all links need be individual and direct: student organizations devoted to the informal cultivation of different academic subjects constitute another and quite different support for the pedagogy of the classroom. A history club, a student biology organization, a business club, and the like, can pursue pertinent themes with considerable freedom, without regard to the demands of a curriculum. Faculty guests and visitors from elsewhere speaking to a club's membership and participating in its discussions tend to "humanize" a field of knowledge or a profession. They do so by displaying it as embodied in practitioners—present as persons, rather than grade-dispensing authorities—willing to engage in informal exchanges with students. Such organizations provide opportunities for individual initiative and exploration and in a setting that also promotes sociability and friendship.

Observers of the passing scene on any campus will note that such organizations flourish and wane (at times disappearing altogether) with changing student generations and departmental faculties. While some such fluctuations of fortune are unavoidable, the value of extracurricular activities of this kind should induce the implementation of policies that would make flourishing more likely and decrease the probability that the activity level of such voluntary associations will drop below a certain threshold.[3]

Extracurricular support of substantive goals of undergraduate education need not be related to disciplines actually studied but can be found among activities that are classified as entertainment. Much of campus life is devoted to diversion from academic work and, for most students, from part-time employment as well. But what is taken to be fun is not ordained by nature. Within a framework set by human physiology, what any individual takes to be entertaining or recreational is learned, the product of a complex interaction of personal traits and individual upbringing, of the practices of one's peers, and of the customs and institutions of one's culture. Thus, when students arrive on campus, they will bring along with them predilections previously acquired. But, given the stage of their development, their tastes and habits will not at all be fully formed, what they take to be recreational is still subject to modification and growth.

The customs and institutions of the surrounding culture are powerful and inevitably dominate the repertory of activities to be found on a campus. Insistent student demand for the decade's leading entertainments—rock concerts, video games, popular films, or whatever—make some choices virtually

3. This simple exhortation raises significant organizational issues that are touched on in the concluding chapter.

unavoidable. Still, by providing a certain cultural leadership, an institution can encourage the extracurricular establishment to support the goals of undergraduate education in important ways.

The passivity with which so large a proportion of people confront the arts—briefly discussed in chapter 3—is partly responsible for the fact that many students arrive at college with little interest in "high" art and even less knowledge. The environment from which many of them come to college, including primary and secondary schools, is likely to have provided little nurturing of such an interest and will thus have done little to engender the belief that experiencing works of art might be enjoyable. Having a taste for something, so that to experience it is pleasurable, is mostly not an elemental fact about a person. Aside from a small number of simple sensations—such as sweetness—which are pleasurable in virtue of the physiological and psychological constitution with which human beings are born, the taste for most of what is found pleasurable is acquired by a process that stretches over time. That it should be possible at all to acquire a certain taste may, of course, be based upon inborn characteristics; that a taste for some set of experiences actually comes to be, however, is importantly dependent on repetition, whether of eating olives, drinking wine, or listening to Mozart.

For the acquisition of some tastes, moreover, *mere* repetition is insufficient, even assuming a requisite native affinity. The repeated tasting of olives may well do the trick—if anything will. The enjoyment of listening to Mozart, on the other hand, also depends in part on an ability to make complex auditory discriminations that must somehow be learned. At the least, this calls for paying attention—what we call listening, rather than just hearing—for a degree of focusing that is more than passive savoring of an experience. Repetition can thus become cumulative, with sound progressively becoming music, so to speak, and tolerance becoming enjoyment.

For this process to go forward, opportunities for the appropriate seeing and hearing are obviously needed. But, on analogy with the horse led to water, it is equally important that a novice be motivated to *use* the opportunities available and to continue with the process of taste acquisition until the experiences of looking and listening become fully self-rewarding. The undergraduate years are the right time for students to acquire and develop tastes for the more complex products of culture and undergraduate institutions are the right setting. That is the case not simply because institutions of higher education can make suitable opportunities available but because they can do so in a way that encourages their exploitation.

Clearly, this cannot be accomplished if an institution merely responds to expressions of antecedent student interest, analogous to their meeting demands for rock concerts or discotheques. They must, instead, be propagandists vis-à-vis their students for the musical, visual, and dramatic arts (including film) by seeing to it that such works are presented in an inviting way. Not neutrality but advocacy is needed—not in the form of sermons preached but by means of encouragement and support of activities that must be displayed as both serious and recreational.

There is no single way of creating supportive environments for cultural activities; indeed, no single means *could* create the needed atmosphere. Residential units devoted to one or another of the arts can be most effective, although their "clientele" will of necessity remain limited. Conventional—but necessary—ways are the clubs and organizations devoted to the pursuit of different arts, including the forging of links between campus and cultural activities away from campus. At the same time, colleges and universities must act as impresarios, mounting exhibits and presenting performances created on campus, as well as importing others from outside, and sponsoring festivities and celebrations.

Undeniably the success of such ventures depends upon a certain level of physical support—facilities, equipment, money. Such underpinnings are necessary but far from sufficient. A spanking new theater devoted to mediocre performances of the last decade's musicals contributes little to the goals of undergraduate education. Quality (not scale) matters but so, above all, does a thoughtfulness that reflects the didactic purposes of the institution. Finally, while it is important for campus artistic activities to attract a broader lay public—in this way also demonstrating that participation in cultural life is a rewarding recreational activity—an institution must, above all, involve its students and faculty in these activities, harnessing both their knowledge and enthusiasm. An institution of higher education, in short, must not limit its role to the benign toleration of the artistic enterprise of faculty members and students who happen to find themselves there but must take it to be a part of its educative function to assume a leadership role.

THE HIDDEN CURRICULUM

In the discussion of some of the specific ways in which campus life beyond the classroom can foster the goals of undergraduate education, the pedagogic implications of tone were never far from the surface. Maria Montessori wrote, "in our schools the environment itself teaches the children,"[4] but she went beyond this to express her pride in the fact that the environment was so designed as to make significant contributions to the educational goals of her schools. But the Montessori environment can teach only because, willy-nilly, *all* environments have the potentiality to teach, whether their "lessons" are wanted or not. From suggestions that institutional tone matters, we move, then, to a consideration of the pedagogic efficacy of certain institutional traits, aptly named the hidden curriculum.

4. Quoted in Passmore, *The Philosophy of Teaching* [1980, p. 24] from Maria Montessori, *The Child in the Family.*

One formulation, again drawn from the elementary level of education, has it that

> the hidden curriculum involves all the institutional arrangements from which students learn in school. These arrangements include the ways in which school rules are made and enforced, the ways in which teachers and administrators use their power and their ability to praise or sanction, and the ways in which the sheer size of large, impersonal schools affects students' learning."[5]

Although so broad a conception invites a discussion of an endless number of features of an institution as complex as a college or a university, we will here confine ourselves to a central issue, though one that manifests itself in several institutional zones.[6]

In most settings, the thesis that the academic enterprise for undergraduates is an important endeavor is likely to be uncontroversial. Not only is the significance of a college education a central tenet of our ideology, but as a society we also put our money where our mouth is. Huge numbers of dollars are devoted to it and large numbers of person-years. Statistics abound about the national need for *educated* workers and about the correlative increase in the lifetime income of those who continue on for four more years of study after high school. You, who are now reading this book, are presumably doing so because you take undergraduate education to be important.

And yet there is a gap, not sanctioned by the laws of logic, between the general "everybody believes" and the specific "each and every person believes." For our purposes, it matters in particular that many students enrolled as undergraduates actually do not believe in the importance of college, in either of two senses. First, some merely believe in this article of our creed in the way in which some persons believe that smoking is harmful to their health, while consuming one cigarette after another—perhaps even paying lip service to the Surgeon General's warning between puffs. The presence in college of these functional disbelievers is, in all likelihood, a product of parental duress, of the pressure of peers, or the absence of acceptable alternatives.

The second group appears to believe more seriously in the importance of college, and that belief is sufficient to explain their presence there; but a closer inspection of what is actually believed suggests a reformulation. It turns out that *having been* to college is thought to be important, perhaps even

---

5. Fenton, "The Implications of Kohlberg's Research for Civic Education" [1977, p. 118].
6. Because we are taking up issues about the hidden curriculum in a chapter about domains beyond the classroom does not mean that the more specifically academic sphere is exempt from the tension between what is professed and what is actually conveyed to students. Where a language requirement, as we discussed earlier, consists merely of a demand for servitude in class, but does not ask the student to become proficient in the language studied, the hidden curriculum belies the claim that foreign languages are important.

having acquired some knowledge. But *going* there—and *doing the acquiring*—get their significance solely as unavoidable means to those ends. This student population, probably a quite sizable one, thus fails in another sense to take the enterprise of undergraduate education to be as significant as appears.

These paragraphs have been concerned with the motivation of students or, better, with some beliefs and attitudes that underlie the motivation that functions in the day-to-day work of classes and study. To restate, for many students the entire enterprise of undergraduate education is not sufficiently important for them to be able to achieve the level of initiative, conscientiousness, and concentration necessary to derive the greatest educational benefit from their undergraduate years.

Whatever the source of such an attitude when brought from outside college, it should most certainly not be reinforced *within* those ivy-covered walls. And yet, that is just what happens with some frequency. We will take a brief look, in turn, at two nonacademic areas of educational institutions where the tendency exists for the hidden curriculum to teach lessons that are at cross-purposes with the goals of undergraduate education: the administrative bureaucracy and student affairs.

To registrars, to take one example, are assigned the crucial jobs of managing student flow into classrooms, logging the outcome these movements, maintaining these records accurately, and making them accessible when needed. If the currency of registrars are the credits so peculiar to educational institutions, that of bursars, to cite a second example, is the familiar coin of the realm. Their chief mission is the collection of students' tuition and of a myriad of fees, the crediting of various types of financial aid, and the receipting and recording of these transactions in such a way that there is a correct relationship between the flow of money and the flow of students into classes. Both functions are complex and replete with detail, both are labor intensive, both call for extensive interactions between staff and students. The magnitude, moreover, of these and other characteristics of the work of these departments grows disproportionally with the size of the institutions they serve.

Only if higher education were organized in ways radically different from ours could we have institutions without registrars or bursars. While their places in the larger organizations then set their broad goals, the remaining leeway allows a distinction between a managerial conception of the tasks to be accomplished and an institutional one. The former of these focuses narrowly on the assignments to be carried out, stressing such qualities as accuracy, completeness, delineation of spheres of responsibility, and the like. Rules and procedures are then devised to maximize the probability of attaining these traits and developing a smooth registrar's or bursar's operation.

Clearly, the second viewpoint cannot leave out these crucial characteristics; but, in addition, it can take into consideration, explicitly and conscientiously, how these processes serve an educational function in which the needs of students are met. Rules and procedures designed for the achievement of accuracy, and so forth, may thus need to be modified in order to give students additional options or reduce registration time taken from their studies, and the like. Regulations devised to reduce the blameworthiness of the registrar's or bursar's office on occasions in which judgment needs to be exercised may need to be modified to make the system more sensitive to the educational goals of students. If the former conception might be called bureaucracy friendly, the latter might be called student friendly or, better, education friendly.[7]

The operation of the neighborhood bank makes a useful analogy. Tellers must handle accurately the deposits, withdrawals, checks, bills, and coins that pass through their hands, so that at all times the bank's accounts show everything that belongs there and only that. And in a teller-friendly environment, processes can be so designed that the responsibility for errors, when they occur, is more likely assignable to customers and to institutions external to the bank than to the tellers themselves. But while customer-friendly operations must also make accuracy a crucial goal, their procedures (and the attitudes that are encouraged) also ensure that customers are treated courteously, flexibly, and speedily and in ways that are likely to correct some of the errors *they* might make in their part of the banking operation.

The analogy breaks down, however, when the *reasons* for instituting the latter approach are taken up. In a competitive world, if you want customers, you have to serve them well; little more needs to be said. But even if the operations of registrars and bursars had a more direct effect than they do on the competitive potential of institutions of a college, the importance of education-friendly administrative services would still lie elsewhere. The implementation of a bureaucracy-friendly policy constitutes a hidden curriculum that belies what all educational institutions profess explicitly. When solving educational problems seems less important than getting the right slips onto the right piles at the right time, students who are already dubious about the importance of their own undergraduate study are confirmed in that skepticism by agents of those very institutions. A lesson, taught by action, communicates clearly that being students is at best secondary to the smooth functioning of a division that exists allegedly to serve them.

One should not be put off by that last verb and ask, voice rising, why free American adults should *serve* an endless stream of adolescents, whose own behavior may often be far from exemplary? (These comments must in no way be read as condoning rudeness by students toward staff members, any more than of staff rudeness toward students—though it would be interesting to

---

7. We will here concern ourselves only with education friendliness as it affects students. Clearly, however, the way in which the managerial bureaucracy conducts its business will impinge on the faculty as well.

have some empirical information as to the relative number of incidents of each of these.) *Service* is called for, not *servility*; and the objects of the service are not individuals *tout court* but students *insofar as they are students*. Education-friendly administrative operations in this way contribute to the clarity of the institution's focus on the central reason for its existence and, incidentally, by treating students as adults, contribute to their reaching a state of greater autonomy.

We can be brief about the issue of a hidden curriculum in the area of student affairs, since the central issue remains much the same, even though the characteristics with which we will be concerned are quite different. Lack of friendliness toward students is seldom the problem with most of the personnel concerned with extracurricular and residential life. The principles of selection—above all of self-selection—tend to encourage the recruiting of outgoing, gregarious, nonhierarchical individuals into these careers—allowing, of course, for exceptions to any such generalization. Hostility is not a widespread problem, and the ethos of the profession is indeed that of serving students.

Instead, to overstate the case somewhat, problems may stem precisely from a certain kind of friendliness, from a selective empathy with the students served. Those staff members are not themselves students; their relationships to students are shaped, rather, by the different functions they perform among the numerous areas subsumed under the rubric of student life. And they are also shaped by the fact that, however varied these specialties, together they constitute a profession with its own standards, procedures, and purposes.[8] Undoubtedly, a higher level of rigor and purposiveness has resulted from these developments; yet this trend—given also the phenomenal growth of student affairs establishments—has also created a distinct student service subculture of its own. In that it often presents itself as rescuing students from the unpleasant rigors of schooling, that culture is not only quite distinct from the world of undergraduate *education* but can actually be quite antagonistic to it.

Within the same institution, two altogether different curricula can thus present themselves competitively to students: the explicit, official curriculum of the educational institution and a hidden one that regards this faculty enterprise as mere duty and offers itself as a more attractive alternative. Students who come to college with doubts and hesitations about the importance of their participation in undergraduate education are particularly vulnerable to the appeal of that veiled curriculum; but they are not the only ones harmed by it. If that man from Mars were transported into any one of many student residences, it is unlikely that he would believe himself to be in territory devoted to higher education. Their very design is often an obstacle to the kind

8. See, as example and evidence, the 647-page volume, Delworth *et al.*, *Student Services* [1989], with the subtitle, *A Handbook for the Profession.*

of conversation that fruitfully continues discussions begun in the classroom, not to mention collaborative working on projects. In short, the way in which many such buildings were constructed prevents students from finding spaces for any of the out-of-the-classroom academic activities they might want to engage in, not to mention room for more formally scheduled discussions or classes.

But if one retreats to thinking of such structures simply as dormitories and not as functioning parts of educational institutions, one might nevertheless have reason for disappointment. Those dormitories—from a Latin word meaning sleeping place—are often so noisy that they fail to serve even their most elementary function. More generally, many of them are woefully inadequate as personal, private, and quiet refuges from public bustle, whether for study or daydreaming. No amount of conviction about the importance of a college education can make one immune to the noise and chaos that surrounds one in many a student residence.

This observation might be widely shared without leading to a concession that inconsiderate behavior by students should be held to be part of a hidden curriculum. Of course, it can be left to cultural historians to come up with explanations for the fact that the end of the twentieth century is an era of noisy popular music ubiquitously purveyed by powerful stereo contraptions, not to mention one of widespread adolescent use of drugs and alcohol. But it is nevertheless appropriate to ask, in a discussion of institutions of higher education, why such *fin de siècle* phenomena are there permitted to impinge on the lives of students. To do nothing is to convey something: not to curb disruptive student behavior in residential halls expresses a policy that regards those regions beyond the classroom—where such conduct is routinely repressed—to lie outside the realm of academic life altogether.

By confining the educational to certain *places*, the unspoken lesson also narrows that sphere to just those *times* that are spent there. Moreover, once again collegiate life is tacitly bifurcated into the components of duty and constraint on one side, and of freedom and spontaneity on the other. While the functions of classroom and dormitory room are of course different— making it absurd to insist in the second on behavior that is appropriate in the first—pitting the one against the other undermines the significance attached to undergraduate education and seriously handicaps students in the accomplishment of its goals.

A crucial condition for the achievement of a measure of harmony between an institution's hidden curriculum and the educational views it professes is probably found in its table of organization, in the way in which authority is distributed, and in the actual persons who are in positions of institutional leadership. This is the path that will, at any rate, be pursued in our final chapter. Structural manipulations, however, are of little avail, unless the existence of such problems is recognized (or their possibility, where, happily, they have not arisen), and the institution resolves to tackle them. This must begin with the formulation of a code of conduct and continue with its enforcement. To say that institutions of higher education no longer stand *in loco parentis* vis-à-vis its students is a way of signaling that they are not to be regarded as extensions of the family. They are not jungles, however; they remain educational institutions whose role and function go far beyond the classroom. Institutions cannot avoid standing for *something*. Surely they will want to shun the irony that has a world professionally devoted to thought and reflection fail to make explicit choices about its own tenets and precepts.[9]

FRATERNITIES AND INTERCOLLEGIATE ATHLETICS

Before considering some basic issues of institutional support for the goals of undergraduate education, I want to remark briefly on two powerful provinces of the realm beyond the classroom that have for many years been subject to considerable controversy—precisely because they are frequently regarded to be in conflict with fundamental goals of undergraduate education. The institution of fraternities and sororities is one of these areas and the undertaking of "big-time" intercollegiate athletics is the other. Besides being controversial, these two establishments share an additional characteristic: both are of interest to vocal off-campus advocates and therefore test with especial potency the strength of an institution's convictions about its tenets and precepts. The role played by the Greek system and the grounds for contentiousness about it, however, are so different from the functioning and controversies about big-league spectator sports that these two topics are best taken up one at a time.

Fraternities and sororities are accommodations for living and a set of extracurricular activities rolled into one. On many campuses, particularly of liberal arts colleges, numerous students are housed by this Greek system, with many of them also devoting substantial amounts of discretionary time to the activities of their houses. Most, if not all, fraternities and sororities occupy houses in which their members live and eat. While accommodations vary a great deal, virtually all have space set aside for social and other communal activities, as well as rooms in which one or a small number of members sleep and study. Aside from the business of running the house itself, fraternities and sororities engage in a variety of social and recreational affairs—from parties to sports to picnics to formal dances—and organize varying amounts of volunteer philanthropic and service work, from raising money for worthy causes to serving as mentors to teenaged boys and girls. To varying degrees, Greeks will engage in ritual behavior associated with their particular brotherhood or sisterhood. Finally, on most campuses, all fraternities and sororities

---

9. See Boyer, *College* [1987, pp. 204ff] for a persuasive statement on the importance of institutional standards of conduct.

belong to an overarching council that plays a regulative function and may sponsor activities for all Greeks on campus.

If this were not only a correct but also a complete, if general, description of the doings of fraternities and sororities, it would be difficult to see why they have so long been subject to so much controversy. To fill in the picture, we turn to the sins of which the Greeks have been accused—all too often justifiably—somewhat arbitrarily distinguished into three kinds. The first category consists of unacceptable social practices: discriminatory membership policies; racism, anti-Semitism, and sexism. Second, under the heading of reprehensible conduct belong the kinds of actions that become unpleasant stories in the daily press: disruptive rushing behavior; dangerous and sadistic hazing; incidents of flagrant alcohol abuse; offensive behavior toward women that may not even stop short of rape. To the third rubric belong the undesirable attitudes that Greeks are often accused of fostering: the kind of conventionalism and anti–intellectualism that make them resist the broadening influences of a college education.

Much of this conduct is not wanted on campuses; some of it is patently unacceptable. If fraternities and sororities did not exist on a given campus, that unsavory list would surely dissuade one from now importing them. Where they do exist, however, the interests of students, augmented by alumni and the national society with which most fraternities and sororities are affiliated, are often sufficiently powerful to convert controversy into difficult struggle. Where discriminatory membership practices are the issue, for example, the national affiliation of a fraternity or a sorority may be decisive, since a local chapter may lack the power to conform to campus policies that insist on nondiscrimination. While banishment from campus and disaffiliation from the national organization have therefore both been the outcome of campus struggles about these policies, the difficulty of enforcing them with respect to the organizations that remain does not go away.

Some types of the reprehensible conduct earlier cited are peculiar to Greeks: since hazing is, so are its excesses, for instance. Others, where they exist, may be more extreme or more organized versions of what is to be found elsewhere on campus. The struggle, here, is about the regulation of student behavior, where success can never simply be the result of campus policing but must importantly be a product of the ethos of a campus, of the kind of comportment for which an institution stands. Thus, the strife over student behavior must in the end be seen as a contest between sets of quite fundamental principles, the degree to which fraternities and sororities will, on any given campus, actually foster attitudes in disharmony with the academic enterprise depends on the character of the local Greek establishment but even more on the strength with which academic values pervade an institution. Success in any struggle cannot be made dependent on the promulgation of rules aimed at controlling behavior (however necessary that is) but requires the strengthening and deepening of the academic ethos of an institution.

The picture can be one of considerable agony: combat about behavior, clashes of ideologies, efforts to curb Greek sinfulness in all categories. It is not surprising that even in the face of vocal, at times disruptive, opposition, some institutions find their solution to the problem of Greeks in eliminating them from campus altogether. That decision constitutes an assertion of the institution's corporate insistence that campus practices and behavior must fall within a certain range of appropriateness. It is an expression, as well, of a willingness to withstand considerable flack.

Yet what gives strength to the arm that wields the sword that cuts the Gordian knot may well be the desperation that follows the failure to unravel it. For a less radical solution to the problem of fraternities and sororities calls for a continuing imposition of the institution's ethos on a most powerful part. This requires, in turn, the considerable leadership, organization, and just plain know-how that can succeed in controlling the practices and behavior of the Greeks and can make inroads on the attitudes they purvey.[10] And while, on the one hand, it may be unreasonable to set higher standards for Greeks than for other groups on campus, one must, on the other hand, avoid the grave danger of the self-deception that quietly lowers the threshold of the acceptable to the *status quo*.

The banishment of the Greeks has a clarity not possessed by efforts to modify their conduct and attitudes. And yet, an institution reaps certain rewards wherever those latter efforts are successful.[11] Fraternities and sororities can disrupt, but they can also make significant contributions to the goals of undergraduate education. Houses require collaborative activity and self-government and offer numerous opportunities for the practice of decision making and leadership. The associations of which we are speaking are capable of providing frameworks that enable students to be active and involved; they constitute communities of a kind that few, if any, campus organizations can sustain. Where the academic ethos of a campus has the strength to inform the practices, behavior, and attitudes of the Greeks, there are gains that offset the labors of continuous vigilance.[12]

---

10. The degree to which the national units with which campus Greek organizations are affiliated make a reform of local practices at all possible has varied considerably over the years and from organization to organization. There have been and may continue to be cases where *nothing* a campus administration can do that will lead to acceptable practices, leaving no alternative to banishment.

11. Two brief accounts of such alternative routes were described in Seitzinger and Ellis, "Does Greek Life Belong?" [1989], with Colby College replacing the Greeks with a new system of residential life and Lafayette College engaged in reforming the Greek system.

12. A student of Greeks summarizes: "[The Greek system] has a history and clear sense of mission with specific goals and rituals. It communicates that mission to prospective members with ease. It has an effective method of attracting, orienting, and matriculating new members. It provides members with a chance of meaningful achievement and leadership in various roles under the guidance and mentorship of more advanced members. Finally, Greek alumni keep in close touch after they leave the system through a well-organized network. . . . A good Greek system has all the necessary elements of a perfect developmen-

Fraternities and sororities are capable of contributing to the central goals of undergraduate education, but no such claim can be made for big-time spectator athletics. On the other hand, if students and alumni make the banishment of Greeks from campus difficult, that expulsion is child's play compared to a move to withdraw from football or basketball played in nationally visible leagues. Finally, efforts to control the seriously harmful effects on the academic enterprise of participation in such "major-league" sports have constituted a charade that has endured for decades. If considerably more radical steps are not taken, that uncomic opera will continue indefinitely, and American higher education will retain its unique position of being corrupted by its role as a significant part of the country's entertainment industry.

Mens sana in corpore sano has nothing to do with our topic. Even strong proponents of the educational value of intercollegiate athletic competition do not think of themselves as talking about Division I football or basketball.[13] Although the visible protagonists are undergraduates, neither of the two discernible benefits to the participating universities pertain to their academic goals. First, athletic visibility sells the university's name, providing it with astonishing amounts of publicity. Moreover, thanks to a certain sleight-of-mind, success in the sports arena is often regarded as a sign of the quality of the institution's primary missions. One is entitled to raise skeptical eyebrows for areas not related to the athletic enterprise itself: on the quality of the students that choose to enroll, on the faculty attracted, on the donations made to the institution—that is, those not related to athletics. But even if such doubts were anchored in careful empirical research, it would not dispel a dominant myth of our era, that visibility is a good in itself and that, in any case, it has beneficial effects even if they cannot just then be discerned.[14]

The second benefit to the institution is financial—or is said to be, since there is nothing clear-cut about this issue either. To begin with, relative to the number of participants, not that many institutions actually do make money.[15]

---

tal environment, especially for students in the early years of college." At the same time, this advocate of traditional academic values challenges "the guardians of the academy . . . [to] find ways to re-orient the goals of student organizations, such as the Greek system, without damaging the power of the processes these organizations already have in place." From Strange, "Greek Affiliation and Goals of the Academy" [1986, p. 522].

13. The purpose and scope of this section does not justify an attempt at a precise definition of "big-time intercollegiate athletics." We are talking about "revenue sports," where Division I football and basketball should simply be seen as good examples.

14. While school spirit may certainly be increased by big-time athletics, the same result is also achieved in far lesser leagues. In either case reasonably victorious teams are a condition.

15. Richard Lapchick, as director of Northeastern University's Center for the Study of Sport in Society, a most knowledgeable student of intercollegiate sports, recently asserted that "only thirty or forty athletic departments in the country make a profit," Marchese, "After the Cheers" [1990, p. 4]. A substantial study and discussion, just published, provides an extensive and devastating analysis of the finances of intercollegiate athletics. Indeed, this volume provides detailed information about much that is discussed in the summary state-

And if one counts only those amounts not directly or indirectly reallocated to the enterprise of intercollegiate athletics itself, the financial benefit to the academic missions of the university is substantially reduced, even for those institutions that do well. But however large the sum of those profits, it is significantly offset by the deficits in budgets devoted to *aiming* at this pot of gold without attaining it. Looking at an imaginary account of *all* the relevant sums spent by the "industry," that financial benefit to the academic enterprise is at best problematic, if it does not evaporate altogether.[16]

But if one can here raise questions about financial benefits to the academy, there are no doubts about the contributions of revenue sports to the larger economy. From makers of uniforms to manufacturers of band instruments, from printers of programs and tickets to bus services and parking garages, from radio and TV stations to advertising agencies to newspapers and magazines—so might one begin a very long list of enterprises (with their many employees) who participate in the food chain of big-league athletics. Then, of course, there are the "primary" parties (other than the athletes themselves), who are on the university's payroll: coaches, trainers, recruiters, press officers, and so forth, and the maintenance crews and payroll clerks, and so forth, that support them. Add these armies to the legions who buy the tickets, watch the networks, and read the newspapers, and all lingering illusions will disappear that the academy might one morning decide to go out of this entertainment business.

Not, however, because there is a shortage of reasons! Again, a division of sins into three categories will be useful. Into the first, we will place all those transgressions that beset athletic establishments of all kinds, professional and amateur, associated with a university or not. Just two examples will suffice, both all too well represented in the chronicles of collegiate athletics. One is the illicit use of drugs by athletes, with particular reference to such "occupational" ones as steroids, as well, of course as "recreational" drugs. "Say it ain't so, Joe" provides the classical reference to the other: point shaving, accepting bribes, and gambling by participants in the sport.

---

ment here and supports a similar conclusion as is here reached. See Sperber, *College Sports Inc.* [1990].

16. A careful study would undoubtedly show those deficits to be greater than they seem, even to some of the administrations of the institutions in question. Seldom will it be possible simply to add up all and only those dollars that are revenues from, and expenditures to support, intercollegiate athletics. Scholarship funds may be in one budget; some or all costs for recruiting athletes are possibly budgeted in the Office of Admissions (with the cost of the recruiters' automobiles perhaps assigned to the motor pool); tutoring help for athletes may be part of some instructional budget, while heating, cooling, lighting, and maintaining the space used by intercollegiate athletics are buried in still another budget. The list can be lengthened, with the understanding that in many cases, even knowing *which* budget supports some given athletics-related function does not mean that one can readily determine amounts. The ways of academic budgeting contribute to such confusions, but so does the impulse to self-deception about the costs of intercollegiate athletics.

The further categories of wrongdoing arise specifically from the fact that we are speaking of athletic establishments located in *universities* and of athletes who are *students*. This circumstance has led to the creation of a large and ever-growing set of rules, each of which can be and is violated in a variety of ways and with different degrees of gravity. This second and immensely broad category affects every phase of the enterprise. Many regulations cover the recruitment of athletes; the number of ways in which they are breached is larger—most but not all of them by means of illicit expenditures of money. Eligibility to participate in intercollegiate competition is the crucial concept designed to ensure that those athletes actually are and remain viable students. But here, too, rules exist to be violated, as well as obeyed, to the point of lying, cheating, and forging student transcripts, thus providing examples of infractions that are secular crimes as well. To make the demands of the athletic operation compatible with being a student, periods of practice are circumscribed; to keep the student-athlete status an amateur one, strict limits are set to the rewards that may be given to students, even if they are stars. More rules to bend and break; more people to be motivated and habituated to the bending and breaking of them.

In a sense, the third set of sins is yet weightier, even though they can be committed without anyone at the university breaking a rule. A few examples will suffice. Because meeting certain educational standards is a condition for recruitment to collegiate athletics, being eligible is an all-important goal for talented high school athletes. Through this opening, universities have contributed to the corruption of entire secondary schools, where much teaching has come to aim at testing, where the needed scores on tests are achieved with the help of cheating, and where transcripts are doctored when everything else fails.[17] Once the athlete is an undergraduate, his or (less frequently) her eligibility may be supported by similar devices, together with "gut" courses and "gut" majors. That many athletes are thus not educated while they are in college is, however, scarcely discussed, since the fact that so many do not even graduate is so measurably stark.[18] Much of what might be cited under this heading adds up to unconscionable institutional exploitation of individuals, many of them African Americans.

Most of these problems were identified as long ago as the turn of the century, with a carefully researched 1929 Carnegie Foundation report constituting a landmark indictment.[19] Sporadic reforms were proposed throughout

17. "Estimates are that 25 to 30 percent of high school senior football and basketball players are functionally illiterate," Marchese, "After the Cheers" [1990, p. 5]. More than a few of these make it to college teams.
18. "According to [an NCAA report], 68 of the 97 major basketball programs (70 percent), and 53 of the 103 major football programs (51 percent) graduated between 0 and 40 percent of their athletes," Marchese, "After the Cheers" [1990, p. 4].
19. For a brief overview, see "Section I: Historical Background" of Lapchick and Slaughter, *The Rules of the Game* [1989, pp. 3–28].

the years but began to accelerate in magnitude and universality only in the era of television, mostly under the aegis of the National Collegiate Athletic Association (NCAA). Now, rules are numerous and constantly increased and refined; commissions are formed with regularity to propose still more reforms, joined by numerous concerned observers of many different backgrounds. But the very nature and volume of these reforms, instituted and proposed, are evidence of their futility.

Many of the regulations are Band-Aids that do not even hide wounds, not to mention staunch bleeding. Exhortations coming from every side that university presidents should take more active roles in supervising intercollegiate athletics (together with provosts, deans, and other academic administrators) want that tail to wag the dog more vigorously yet, by proposing to pull these officers still further away from their central obligations. A suggestion that shows how the creation of a $50 million annual superfund could significantly improve the graduation rate of athletes shows even more vividly how far behind the eight ball we are.[20]

The apotheosis of the *reductio ad absurdum* of reform proposals is contained in the chapter on policy recommendations of *The Rules of the Game*.[21] That summary makes a total of 134 nonredundant recommendations, many complex, addressing presidents, athletic departments, coaches and recruiters, various academic units, high schools and middle schools, and public media on every aspect of the lives of student athletes and the practice of intercollegiate athletics. If the immense effort were actually made and these 134 proposals were broadly implemented, scandal might be reduced to the average level of less conspicuous institutions of our society. Utopian reforms are needed to achieve normality.[22]

Big-time intercollegiate athletics undermine the educational goals of academic institutions and yet we cannot expect either to eliminate them or to render their impact benign through piecemeal reform. Still, there *is* a solution, put forward, and from lofty platforms, as early as 1905 and as recently as 1988. "Let the football team become frankly professional. Cast off all the deception. . . . Let the teams struggle . . . with no masquerade of amateurism or academic ideas." Thus wrote the former president of Stanford, David Starr Jordan, soon after the beginning of this century.[23] As part of the current debate, Robert H. Atwell, president of the American Council on Education, proposed as a significant alternative to the *status quo*, a "move to acknowl-

20. Marchese, "After the Cheers" [1990, p. 6].
21. Lapchick and Slaughter [1989, pp. 193–212].
22. Eight and a half columns of tiny print, in *Chronicle of Higher Education* are devoted to "Summaries of 119 Proposed Changes to Be Voted On at [the 85th Annual] NCAA Convention" [1990]. Fundamental principles are put forward by the Knight Foundation Commission on Intercollegiate Athletics. See "Knight Commission Tells Presidents to Use Their Power to Reform the 'Fundamental Premises' of College Sports" [1991]. *Le plus ça change, le plus c'est la même chose.*
23. Quoted in Ernest Boyer, *College* [1987, p. 183].

edged professionalism in college football and basketball, pay the athletes a market wage, and remove the requirement that they be students."[24]

Again a Gordian knot would thus be cut. The spectators are left to their spectacles and the economy retains its profitable activity, while the academy puts a distance between itself and what it sponsors. While these new minor leagues would need to be appropriately regulated, much of intercollegiate athletics would be essentially decriminalized. Alumni and the public would scream during the period of transition, since nostalgia leads many to cherish the idea that those players are students. But because there is much public awareness of the problems of big-time collegiate athletics,[25] the resentment is likely to be tempered. In any case, if the teams play well, sports enthusiasts will go to see them; more often than not it will still be the only game in town.

24. Atwell, "Putting College Sports in Perspective" [1988, p. 9].
25. A 1989 Gallup poll reported that 74 percent of the public believes college sport to be out of control. From Marchese, "After the Cheers" [1990, p. 4].

CHAPTER 9

SUPPORT

INSTITUTIONAL POLICIES

Faculty members, above all in their role as teachers, are the principal, if not sole, agents of undergraduate education. Hence, much of what is accomplished is a function of the knowledge, skill, energy, imagination, and devotion of those persons. But unlike the Sophists of the fifth century B.C. (who can be considered to have been the first in the West to make higher education their "business"), those instructors cannot provide that education as individuals working alone. As their name proclaims, they act as members of faculties—of colleges and universities. And even when small, such institutions are complex, for a considerable number of faculty are needed to collaborate, together with supporting and complementary activities, calling for people and offices and services, buildings and facilities and equipment—administered, of course, and funded.

To take up everything that would support a faculty's educative activity would make its own book on how to build a college. Much of that will be assumed. This chapter is limited to a few important policies and organizational principles as examples of supportive practices and will conclude with ways of giving direct help to the faculty engaged in the enterprise of undergraduate education.

Leadership is taken for granted as well. It is certainly needed, if only because academic institutions, like the natural world, obey laws of motion—those of Aristotelian physics, alongside the laws of Newton. A body in motion stays that way, declares Newton, until an externally impressed force changes its direction or velocity, or stops it altogether. Thus, an academic department will go about its usual business until an impetus from outside requires it to change. But often Aristotle's more pessimistic views apply. According to them, *rest* is natural; nothing moves at all unless some force makes things move. A push must come from outside; there is activity only as long as this external pressure persists. Changes in practice, not to mention the generation of new ones, will not just "arise" from the discussions of some committee. Initiation results, rather, from executive action that articulates goals, uses authority to overcome inertia, and goes on to sustain the activity intended to accomplish them.

One pervasive condition is background for any consideration of policies intended to foster undergraduate education. In practice, the institutions within which faculty members function as undergraduate teachers are never devoted to that purpose exclusively. Frequently, research, graduate, and (postbaccalaureate) professional education are prominent parts of the institutional mission. But even where the official purpose is confined to undergraduate education, at least two additional goals play an inevitable role. First, the fact that institutions are located in specific cities and towns leads them to have relations with, and obligations to, the communities in which they are embedded. Members of academic institutions, including faculty, are thus naturally drawn into various kinds of community service, especially educational, that rightfully impose their own demands on individuals and on the institution.

A second goal is a product of the very way in which faculty members are educated and develop. One prepares for becoming a faculty member by engaging in advanced training in a subject matter, a regimen that aims both at competency and at induction into a profession. This professional identity, reinforced by institutional demands that are at least tacit, requires that faculty members remain current in their disciplines, even if some of their teaching lies outside these. Accordingly, research and scholarship—or something very like them—are a part of an institution's mission, even where it is not explicitly said to be a duty and regardless of the proportion of the faculty that actively engages in these pursuits.

Because the setting for undergraduate education is thus inevitably a multipurpose institution composed of a heterogeneous collectivity of people, Adam Smith's invisible hand cannot be relied upon to create optimal conditions for the education of undergraduates. The need for a corporate assumption of responsibility was broached earlier, particularly with respect to curricular matters. But when a larger range of institutional processes are looked upon from the perspective of the students who "receive" the proffered education, the conception of corporate responsibility for educationally relevant practices needs to be expanded. Instead of making lists, we will take a closer look at the practice of course scheduling by way of example and take up some of the implications of a changed perspective for this lowly institutional arrangement.

Begin with the list of courses that are taught. Some are required courses or basic to the fields represented. If these offerings are at least nominally the product of corporate decision making, many another course is present solely because some faculty member wants to teach it. The result, as earlier noted, can be a bewildering array of options, from which it becomes well-nigh impossible for students to make a sensible selection. But only if the faculty as a body assumes the role of educator of undergraduates can such an abundance be shaped and pruned, so that even at more advanced levels closer attention is paid to providing courses that students need.

The exercise of such authority does not need to violate *Lehrfreiheit* (freedom in teaching), a central component of academic freedom. The development of certain advanced courses by a pedagogically minded committee is not different in kind from the accepted practice of having departments specify the content of introductory courses. Educational decisions about topics to be covered, level of detail, and degree of technical proficiency of the methods introduced do not dictate an instructor's substantive commitments, even if there is an occasional lack of clarity about the distinction. Academic freedom, a necessary condition for the vitality of any academic institution, is compatible with paying closer and collective attention to students' needs. Nor would *Lehrfreiheit* be diminished if that variety of undergraduate courses were reduced. Institutions will, in any case, want to be sure that their instructors do teach courses in which they have great interest, not only for the intellectual welfare of the faculty, but for the sake of the students taught, since the quality of teaching is surely closely related to the enthusiasm of the teacher.

In addition to exercising more corporate control on *what* is scheduled, more attention should be given to the impact on students' educational careers of the *way* courses are scheduled. Scheduling usually begins with the preferences of faculty members, modified by departmental efforts to avoid internal competition and circumscribed by the availability of rooms. Some eccentricities of scheduling are limited by market mechanisms, since departments must to some degree justify their size by the number of students they teach. This is not enough, however, to eliminate the frustration of students whose educational choices are significantly dictated by the vagaries of what is taught when. Moreover, the magnitude of the problem is masked by the fact that, somehow, students enroll and get through, with no one aware of how many course selections were second and third choices.

No method of scheduling can eliminate all conflicts for students, not to mention accommodate itself to their nonacademic needs and preferences. But much more becomes possible once a conceptual shift makes the needs of students the primary principle of scheduling, one that is *then* modified by faculty preferences, room availability, and the like.[1] To adopt such a perspective is to introduce investigations and discussions about ways of scheduling that might be optimal from the students' point of view. At present there is no provision for such discussions among prevalent institutional practices. Scheduling decisions so made will much increase the likelihood that courses that are *offered* by the faculty become more *available* to the students for whom they are intended.

A final issue about scheduling arises from current reflections about teaching. In the vast majority of colleges and universities courses are scheduled into time slots that envisage a normal course to consist of three fifty-minute

---

1. What classrooms *are* available is by no means a pure fact that must merely be ascertained. Many rooms are "owned," for good reasons and frivolous, by various academic units and are usually excluded from the pool into which classes are routinely scheduled. In the dynamics of campus politics, the "special interest" owners of rooms tend to have loud voices, not matched in volume by voices that represent the needs of undergraduates.

sessions a week, or their equivalent. Prescribing such a temporal grid has the advantage of bringing some order to a complex flow of students and activities. The disadvantage, on the other hand, is its relative inflexibility and relative inability to accommodate to ways of teaching that are different from those that have been honored, if not proven, by time.

Serious thinking about teaching in higher education has only recently begun, and much more will surely be found out about how, in different regions of the curriculum, students can more effectively be brought to learn. There is a need, therefore, to be alert to the institutional ramifications of such findings, so that rigidities originating in one area do not prevent, in another, the application of what has been learned. But a few broad scheduling implications of these pedagogical reflections are likely to remain fairly stable. The importance of interactions, formal and informal, of teachers and students is stressed everywhere as potentially a means to more effective learning. If so, the average number of "contact hours" is likely to need increasing. But instead of mechanically adding a fourth lecture to the three that are now *de rigeur*, the time gained must be suitable for working with small groups of students, for off-campus activities, and the like. Such increases in the time the instructors would devote to interchanges with students in any given course would, however, be offset by the reduction of course preparations resulting from a decrease in the variety of courses offered. Students would spend more time with a given instructor and instructors would get to know some students considerably better—complementary changes on which improvements of teaching and learning can founded.

These mundane issues of scheduling are usually thought of as nuts-and-bolts concerns to be dealt with by lower-level managers; academic administrators or important faculty groups seldom give serious consideration to them. Yet, when it is asked, as happens with some frequency, how faculty members might be induced to take teaching more seriously, a partial answer must surely be, "when the institution itself takes teaching more seriously." Such seriousness, however, needs to be manifested less in the fervor with which the importance of teaching is acclaimed than in the ways in which the very structure of an institution nurtures that activity. If the policies of a college or university made it more obvious that its business was teaching—good teaching, effective teaching—that function would be clearer to faculty members.

ORGANIZATIONAL ISSUES

"Sociology is destiny" might here be the motto, since the way people are organized for collective action strongly influences the character of their decisions. In response to the complexities typical of decision making in the academy, two paths need to be pursued in putting forward examples of organizational issues particularly relevant to the goals of undergraduate education. First, faculty members are not simply the employees of managers, but themselves possess broad authority over educational and, at times, other institutional policies. Thus, how faculty members are grouped when they exercise their authority affects the recommendations and decisions produced. Second, colleges and universities are nevertheless administered by officers hired to serve as managers and leaders. How administrative reporting lines are worked out therefore makes a difference to the character of an institution.

Turning to the ways in which faculty members are organized, one is immediately confronted by the fact that in all but a handful of institutions, the most prominent faculty unit is the academic department. Moreover, even where institutions are not engaged in graduate or advanced professional education, this subject-centered departmental structure is patterned after the organization of institutions that are. The source of that design, in turn, is primarily located in the needs of scholarship and research, modified by history and tradition. (This serves as a useful reminder that at least tacitly, undergraduate institutions pursue additional goals as well.) Not surprisingly, therefore, the departmental structure is in some respects in harmony with the goals of undergraduate education, while it is dysfunctional in others. Such a judgment might leave it an open question whether one would today adopt this organizational scheme, were the academic world to be created *de novo*; given the academic world as it exists, however, prudence surely limits sharply the options available to any particular institution.

Two related reasons suggest that undergraduate institutions would be well advised to stay close to the departmental structure, both rooted in a concern for the kind of persons wanted as teachers of undergraduates. Whatever the breadth of an institution's mission, it is emphatically desirable that its faculty have qualities of mind identical with, or analogous to, those to be fostered in our students: a capacity to delve beneath the surface, a questioning attitude (including the ability to question oneself), independence of mind, intellectual meticulousness, an adventurous spirit, and more. It may be utopian to expect *every* college teacher to possess *all* of these traits, but it is imperative that these attributes be sufficiently well represented in a faculty so as to dominate the spirit of any that engages in undergraduate education.

Success, here, is of course dependent on success in the faculty's selection. But it would be naive to think that once the right people are brought aboard an institution's job is done. Without policies that support and reinforce the prized activities and attitudes, some of the well-selected faculty members would leave for more congenial environments, while the spark of others would surely dim in time. Research and scholarship, informed exchanges and debates, and intellectual colleagueship are the central ingredients of any support and reinforcement. For such activities, a common subject matter is virtually a necessary focus, and the organization that brings together people who share knowledge of a subject is the department.

But success in the recruitment of faculty members is crucially dependent on subject matter departments in the first place. On one side, the searching institution must make use of experts capable of judging the talents and accomplishments of other specialists, even if theirs is not the only voice to be heard in the process of selection. On the other side, given that young candidates are just emerging from departmental settings that gave them their advanced education, many of the most able think their development as scholar-teachers requires a similar environment for stimulus and support.

If these are reasons for retaining a traditional departmental structure, quite different units are needed for various purposes of undergraduate education. Evidence can be found everywhere, since colleges and universities abound in faculty committees that cross departmental lines. Yet often, the work of these nondepartmental groupings falls short of expectations—precisely because too little cognizance is taken of the fact that the new group is superimposed on a prior and powerful departmental structure.

Given the strength of departments, the mere creation of committees is not enough to take care of the needs of writing across the curriculum, language proficiency, courses in science for nonspecialists, or for any function that cannot be assigned to a department. The fact that such committees may need space or facilities "belonging" to departments, and that they require the time and energies of departmental faculty members, necessitates that they also be foci of power—if not the equal of departments, at least strong enough to have their respect. When faculty members form a unit to perform these special educational tasks, they must regard themselves as occupying a home away from their departmental home and not just a flimsy shack.

No single measure will solve all problems for these nondepartmental units. A room of one's own is as vital here as control of territory seems to be for all living things. A nontrivial budget is essential: there is no such thing as status without fiscal power. To secure needed teaching forces, administrative fiat (Latin for "let it be done!") must assess specific departmental contributions of faculty time. At times it helps to have an academic administrator lead such a committee and provide some administrative "protection," in partial compensation for the group's less-than-departmental status.

The basic requirement still remains the availability of faculty members competent and interested in the needed curriculum. Infiltration that places advocates on departmental search and promotion committees is a beginning. But real potency is attained only when faculty positions are allocated to these nondepartmental groups, though constrained so as to prevent a program from inadvertently turning into a department.[2] Not all of these measures are applicable to all cases, and there are other means of strengthening nondepartmental programs. The central issue is the need to embody significant institu-

2. One method is to allocate half-time faculty slots to curricular programs, so that they can proceed to recruit jointly with various departments (which contribute the other halves), for faculty with requisitely broad interests who will have shared teaching duties.

tional functions *structurally* and to provide the resulting units with the capacity they need to operate. Since many specifically undergraduate responsibilities tend to fall into the interstices of an institution, especially in larger and more complex ones, thoughtful organizational support must replace wishful thinking as their foundation.

It has here been assumed that members of curricular committees are chosen for relevant abilities and interests. Yet, resort to this principle of functional selection cannot be taken for granted. Function has a way of yielding to politics, partly because in their self-governing respects, faculties tend to behave like political entities. At times, representation by interest groups is perfectly appropriate. Whatever committee advises on an institution's fringe benefits, for example, must include representatives from all affected constituencies. But when the propensity to assure such broad representation spills over into areas where it does not apply, the result can be committees that include members who lack the necessary knowledge and concern at the cost of others with some indispensable expertise. Such distortion is easily magnified when a dominating personality brings irrelevant concerns or worse to the committee table and thus undermines the effectiveness with which an important task can be carried out.

Some specific lessons follow from these general considerations. When a committee or task force is created, one must begin by determining whether its charge is primarily of one kind or another. If its purposes are of significant concern to various interest groups on campus, the committee's success will be measured by the (subjective) satisfaction of those groups. Such satisfactions, on the other hand, are essentially irrelevant to the tasks that other committees seek to accomplish, including most educational ones; their success is measured by criteria that belong to the metier with which they are concerned—language instruction, student recruitment, campus beautification, or whatever. Granting that committee goals seldom fall neatly into one or another of these categories, clear thinking will nonetheless have an effect on the outcome. A well-established strategy serves the first type of purpose: election by various constituencies of those who are to represent their interests. The convenience of this procedure, however, and the favorable aura it gains from its acknowledged fairness—where fairness is pertinent—must not tempt one into having committees of the second variety determined by the ballot box. There it is essential that interested and knowledgeable persons be identified, so that a group's membership is chosen from that circle.[3]

Inattention to such mundane considerations can account for the gap, often puzzling and frustrating, between the desires and capabilities of members of

---

3. Where the purposes of a committee are truly of both kinds, procedures can be adopted that take this real-world complexity into consideration. A nominating committee, for example, can be asked to identify candidates who are suitable, while the final selection from among them is left to election by constituencies.

an academic institution, and what is actually accomplished. In a similar way, how an institution's administration is organized can make a significant difference to its achievements. The genteel manners of the academy and a style that distances itself from the ways of corporate hierarchies veil from outsiders that some people are other people's bosses and may confuse even the participants themselves. Nevertheless, there are relationships of superior to subordinate, and clarity about this relationship makes for a more effective pursuit of educational goals. Accordingly, we turn to some comments, first, about the selection of administrators in the academy and, second, about the relevance of reporting lines to these goals.

When a corporate vice-president appoints the head of a division, he or she uses internal and external resources to generate and investigate candidates, and then makes an appointment—with or without consultation—when the right person, in his or her opinion, has been found. If a good choice is made, a favorable judgment of the vice-president's own performance will result; conversely, a poor selection will reflect negatively on his or her standing. All this holds for the academy, except that complex Rube Goldberg contraptions can significantly weaken and delay the connection between cause and effect. The job, then, is to ensure that those elaborate devices are linkages, rather than breaches.

In the customary consultative process, the tension, again, is between politics and function. While the claims of the former cannot be ignored, neither must it be overlooked that the end of the process is the appointment of the best possible person for the job. Once more, success depends on a search committee's composition, on its members' knowledge, concerns, motives. "A-people hire A-people," a wise saying has it, "while B-people hire C-people," with the corollary that "relevant people recommend relevant people, while an inappropriate committee recommends inappropriate candidates." The best committee does not relieve an administrator from the responsibility of directing it. Search committees are not autonomous links in a chain, with a "charge" at one end and a recommended slate at the other. Rather, they are consultants, a role that cannot be adequately performed without extensive discussions in which the person consulting them explicates goals and conditions.

The probability can thus be increased that appropriate candidates will be recommended. Nevertheless, the process can go awry, leaving in its wake the unhappy alternatives of having an entire slate rejected or an inferior appointment made. This is the time to remember that the administrator, not the consultants, retains the responsibility for the proper functioning of a domain. The easy path is easy only for the moment. The politics of a search process seldom matter the day after the chosen one starts on the job, and they never mitigate the consequences of a poor appointment.

The characteristics of the appointed administrator depend much on who does the appointing; subsequent performance, similarly, is strongly influenced by the nature of the office to which that person reports. Declarations to the effect that everyone works for the goals of the institution are undermined by such prosaic particulars as who sets salaries, provides resources, and has the dominating voice about advancement. Even where administrative style eschews formulations of explicit principles and goals as directives for subordinates, these underlying relationships of power bear directly on the effectiveness with which action supports institutional rhetoric. Does the library truly serve the needs of students and faculty? Does the registrar smoothen students' paths to the classes in which they seek to enroll? Does the professional staff concerned with extracurricular activities and athletics support or undermine the academic goals of the institution? Does the personnel that tracks the accounts of extramurally funded researchers facilitate the work of those faculty members or hamper it?

An organizational scheme becomes the framework within which goals are formulated for particular administrators; it determines what questions are raised formally and informally, which actions evoke praise or criticism. The kinds of issues that are discussed by an admissions officer with the person to whom he or she reports depend on whether the admissions director reports to the chief academic officer, the chief budget officer, or the administrator in charge of student life. This relationship similarly determines which aspects of an operation are scrutinized by a supervisor (and which ignored), which shortcomings are reproved (and which others excused), and many more. Over time, the ethos of an admissions office will to a significant degree be a product of its place in an institution's organization.

At a fraction of liberal arts colleges the personality of the institution as a whole may still suffuse the operation of the parts. For the rest, the marked growth of the size and complexity of colleges and universities, in the last four decades, has undoubtedly increased the impact of reporting lines on their character. In addition, this burgeoning was accompanied by an increasing professionalization of virtually all of the functions of academic institutions, a fact that underlines the importance of reporting lines for the achievement of institutional goals.

The conflict between faculty members' allegiance to their field-defined professions and their obeisance to the needs and purposes of their particular institutions has been widely noted. Now, the establishment of professions concerned with such activities as admissions, the supervision of student activities and residential life, registration, research administration—not to mention the earlier professionalization of library services—has introduced analogous tensions into academic institutions. On the one hand, colleges and universities are to a degree delivered from the idiosyncratic amateurishness that in earlier days was often found in these "peripheral" areas. They benefit, instead, from an expertise that transcends the know-how of any given individual. But, on the other hand, this professionalization brings new centrifugal forces into particular institutions. A defining mark of a profession, after all, is the fact that it shapes the character of its goals and that it sets the standards for the activities intended to bring them about. The formulation of institutional ends, accordingly, as well as the ways in which they are pursued, are significantly influenced by forces that come from outside it.

Administrative supervision must be a unifying force, although that presupposes some clarity about institutional goals and the reflection of this clarity in reporting lines. Specifically, if primacy is to be given to the educational goals as they have here been understood, the heads of such nonacademic units as admissions, registrar's office, and student life—not to mention the library and computer center—must be supervised by academic administrators. By these means, the needs of the academic enterprise can be effectively conveyed to all of a campus's components, thereby counteracting the centrifugal forces of different professions.

But in order to make something of these opportunities, it is important to ensure that this supervision is not a mere formality. Even assuming, for example, that the president of a smaller institution (or the chief academic officer of a larger one) has his or her academic heart in the right place, it is not enough for the heads of all the major institutional divisions to report to that office. Setting an institutional tone is a vital function of leadership at the pyramid's apex, but supervising the activities of administrators is a time-consuming activity that goes well beyond the general and the symbolic to the specific and routine. If Aristotle was right to hold that Plato's attempt to extend family bonds to the whole city would achieve but a "watery affection," so the stretching of the supervisory mantle over many people and domains secures a watery surveillance at best. Where academic oversight is an illusion only, centrifugal forces are at work in actuality.

To all this, conventional wisdom might worriedly respond that there are huge differences between the functions of faculty members and administrators, such that many of the former are most unsuited for the roles of the latter. Although this observation is perfectly sound, it must not pull us into the technocratic frame of mind where means are everything. Managerial bumbling does not make institutions happy, but it is far less damaging than management for its own sake. Assume, for the sake of the argument, that a mistake was made in the appointment of an administrator. Experience in the ways institutions work suggests that recovery from the damage done by managerial ineptitude—of failure in the realm of means—is likely to be faster and more complete than a return to health from a period during which the institution's goals were distorted. Managerial efficiency, in short, can never replace the administrative embodiment of the educational mission of an institution.[4]

---

4. I believe that future historians will show, to take an example from the larger political world, that the effects of the inadequacies of the Carter administration were wiped out more expeditiously than those of the weaknesses of the Reagan presidency. It is not just that the latter had twice as many years to get things wrong but, rather, that the scars left by the former stemmed essentially from Carter's inability to fit means to the ends he sought for our country, while those caused by Reagan resulted from his warping of our national goals.

HELP

Because undergraduate education is pursued in colleges and universities that have other purposes as well, support for this central activity, it has been insisted, must be adequately incorporated into an institution's organization. The following sketch of a model institution-within-an-institution—to be called an Academy for Learning and Teaching—will serve as an example of how this might be accomplished.[5]

It matters that a single organizational unit concern itself with a variety of issues pertaining to undergraduate education and teaching: intellectual, economic, and sociological. It matters that it do so in an ongoing fashion and not merely during periodic flurries of educational reform. The purpose, then, of an Academy for Learning and Teaching is to serve as a locus for continuing reflection on, improvement of, and innovation in learning and teaching, and thus to foster *thinking* about problems of curriculum and teaching and to disseminate the product of these reflections to the community. It aims to provide *support* for individuals and groups seeking to make special efforts to improve undergraduate education. One effect of these functions should be the enhancement of the *status and recognition* accorded to teaching and to the enterprise of educating undergraduates.

What's needed, to start with, is a place: a library/seminar room, a number of private offices, a space for secretarial assistants cum word processors, with some room for reception, as well as for copying and coffee machines: the essentials. A central location is best (as it would be for almost everything else on campus). The people in the place are five or more senior fellows, depending on the size of the institution. These distinguished members of the faculty, drawn from a variety of disciplines, are released from some of their normal duties in order to serve (perhaps for staggered, renewable, three-year terms) as the academy's governing board. They recommend to the chief academic officer not only their successors, but also the director—again a senior faculty member who devotes a significant portion (but not all) of his or her time to this task, serving for a term of, perhaps, five years. This director is the board's executive officer, an arrangement that should give to the academy considerable independence from the institution's administration. An assistant or associate director, modest secretarial staff, plus student interns round out the academy's establishment.

5. As provost of the University of Pittsburgh, I had appointed a number of task groups on issues pertaining to undergraduate education, including one that was asked to focus on the status and recognition of teaching, and another on ways in which learning and teaching might be improved at the university. What follows makes particular use of the report from the latter group, chaired by Professor Lauren B. Resnick, co-director of the University's Learning Research and Development Center. The report recommended the establishment of such an academy and gave it that name. I resigned as provost before my subsequent development of these recommendations (of which a version appears here) could be implemented.

From purposes and structure, we turn to what this academy *does*, remembering that even though any account of activities must focus on one at a time, the academy's potency depends, in part, on its devotion to all of them at once. For two reasons, the role of the academy as think tank is central.[6] That function recognizes that teaching and curriculum pose deep intellectual problems, made harder in a period of rapid changes in the state of our knowledge, the structure of our economy, and the demography of our society. Second, such institutional acknowledgment of the intellectual significance of pedagogic reflections helps to confer on that enterprise the *sine qua non* of academic respectability. The academy conducts seminars, sponsors talks, engages in pedagogic experimentation, with its senior fellows active and providing leadership, but drawing in other members of the faculty and importing visitors from elsewhere. These activities offer opportunities for sparking discussions among teachers steeped in their fields with experts on learning and cognitive psychology. Opportunities are thus also created for thinking about issues and problems that are specific to an institution at a particular time in its history but free of the practical and political framework that constrains the deliberations of a curricular committee formed to solve a specific educational problem. Selected academy papers and discussions are disseminated in some form to the entire campus.

A parallel function of the academy is to serve as an internal foundation, by supporting individual faculty members and groups in curricular development and in special efforts to improve student learning. Faculty fellowships—in the form of released time, summer support, or other assistance—are awarded by the senior fellows to competing faculty proposals, thus creating an ongoing stimulus to experimentation and improvement in undergraduate education. Whenever a broader institutional effort is in progress to tackle a certain set of curricular problems, such support can, for a period of time, be harnessed to those goals. Help to faculty members aiming to introduce multicultural material into conventional courses might thus be provided by the academy—not simply in the form of faculty fellowships, but through the sponsorship of workshops and seminars, for example.

While the primary purpose of the academy is to generate and stimulate new thought about teaching and undergraduate education at its own institution, it should also be able to provide more mundane assistance to faculty members seeking to improve some aspect of their teaching. It should give help with the use of new technologies (and old!) and serve as a resource for instructors interested in exploring unfamiliar methods of teaching. For example, it might devote some space to computer stations for pedagogic experimentation and innovation. Similarly, where students, graduate or undergradu-

6. Campus think tanks are called for in Joseph Katz et al., *Vitality in General Education*, [1988, pp. 49–52]. The idea is a product of several discussions I had with Katz, in particular while serving as a member of the task group devoted to the project of the above book.

ate, are used in teaching, their preparation for that task can be undertaken or guided by the academy.

On many campuses, awards for outstanding teaching are given annually to selected faculty members. While presidents or chief academic officers will want to present such awards themselves—as a symbol of the importance of good teaching to the institution—the task of selecting the award winners might well be left to the Academy for Learning and Teaching. Finally, the academy must have an important role in the evaluation of undergraduate programs on campuses where educational offerings are periodically subjected to scrutiny. A faculty-conducted agency—neutral with respect to subject matter but committed to pedagogical effectiveness—is a most useful voice in a process that tends to be laden with fiscal politics.

That last "finally" is, of course, arbitrary. A viable academy might perform fewer functions or more; the optimal cluster is a product of local conditions. But one principle must hold academy imperialism in check. The intellectual enterprise of thinking seriously and rigorously about serious educational issues must be its center. The addition of other functions, as outlined, will strengthen the academy by bringing it from the periphery toward the center of an academic institution. On the other hand, one must be alert not to choke, by an assignment of too many chores, the free and open spirit needed to maintain the milieu of a think tank, or compromise its independence from administrative domination.

If adequately funded[7] and ably led, an organization of the kind described should do much for the status of teaching and campus educational functions. Its centrality and visibility should help to bring prestige to those activities. Its ability to provide funds for pedagogic projects will contribute to the respect in which such work is held. Above all, the participation by respected faculty members and visitors in ongoing discussions about pedagogical topics will raise the intellectual standing of these concerns. Giving institutional embodiment to these supportive efforts is one way in which a campus can be fashioned into a more hospitable environment for the dedicated pursuit of undergraduate education.

But the creation of such an environment is still only background—necessary background—for what cannot be done without: providing encouragement and support for the role of *individual* faculty members as teachers and educators of undergraduates. While the "reward structure" (ugly term) for faculty is a large and widely discussed topic, the assertion of some broad principles will be a fitting conclusion to this discussion.

We should be clear, in the first instance, that faculty members can tell

---

7. To establish an academy such as this, "new" money will most certainly need to be allocated. To the degree to which some of its proposed activities are already funded in other campus units, reallocations can augment this academy budget. Finally, an academy of the kind described should be in a good position to raise outside funds for some of its projects.

when the authority's concern is genuine and when exhortations are merely lip service. To have the entire institution and its leadership take teaching and students seriously, in word and deed, *is* necessary background. In the absence of this condition, only extravagant—and utopian—monetary rewards might overcome the indifference of those who lack interest on their own account.

Second, while that institutional concern must begin to function at the time a faculty member is interviewed and hired, even the most conscientious judges can, at that time, assess only certain *potentialities* for teaching, just as they are largely limited to determining a *talent* for research. With respect to both aptitudes, even assuming the best possible choices to have been made,[8] there is much to nurture and encourage in subsequent years, and much to judge at later times.

Let us turn, third, to the most crucial of these judgments: the decision regarding promotion with tenure. At many institutions, it is widely believed that at promotion time it is research that matters, while supposed attention to teaching performance is merely talk. Although that view is often correct, neither of the two reasons often put forward make very convincing justifications. An institution can quite reasonably ask that its candidates for tenure be proficient both in research and in teaching—at a level not only commensurate with its aspirations, but its fiscal capacity. The claim that a candidate's scholarly work is so outstanding that it must override all negative assessments of teaching is far more often made by advocates of a candidate than is warranted by the evidence.

Arguments about the primacy of research over teaching as promotion criteria are further abetted by a perceived difference between our ability to evaluate them. "Perceived," if only because we're not as skilled at assessing research as we take ourselves to be. Were we as concerned with the quality and importance of scholarly work as we are with productivity and numbers of publications, we might be just as puzzled in appraising the research of many a candidate as we are about that person's effectiveness as a teacher. To this must be added that many more ways of evaluating the teaching and educational proficiency of faculty members have been devised than are generally in use. How teaching effectiveness can be evaluated as a component of assessment is yet to be fully explored. More humility on one side, in any case, and greater diligence on the other would reduce the gap in the confidence we have in making those two kinds of judgments.

There are models, moreover, from which one can learn. Law schools, especially the best, as well as outstanding business schools, take teaching very seriously indeed. Such institutions do believe that they can ask their faculty to be scholars *and* educators, and they make their tenure decisions accordingly. Admittedly, the greater maturity and purposiveness of professional students

---

8. Equal stress must be placed on "best" and "possible," just as it remains an independent question precisely how good Candide's best of all possible worlds really was.

facilitate the evaluation of teaching. But so does a prevailing concern (as in "prevailing weather") about teaching that puts instructors and administrators into a much better position to know what kind of educators their associates are: the effectiveness of different ways of evaluating teaching is related to the environment in which they are used. Where pedagogical issues and concern about students are a part of the ongoing conversation, it is vastly easier to know how one's colleagues are doing as teachers. Lunch conversations about syllabi and exchanges over coffee about pedagogic tricks that worked or didn't work make good background for more formal assessments of teaching.

Fourth, even granting that certain conditions affecting academic salaries cannot be changed by any individual institution, often more can be done than is believed to improve salaries in order to reward excellence in teaching. Since the demand for research stars is greater than the supply, their high cost (by an academic, not corporate, scale) in salary and other support is a function of the market. Where the institution benefits from having a star and where that makes no discernible difference must be determined locally. If one implemented some careful thinking with respect to this and related salary issues by augmenting the salaries of outstanding educators on a campus, greater credibility would be conferred on an institution's profession of the importance of undergraduate education. To be sure, this discussion assumes a system by which salaries are set and raised on the basis of merit and, further, that even where actual salary figures are confidential, it becomes known that excellence as an educator is rewarded.[9]

Finally, in the academic world, even more than in some others, time is money or, at least, is welcomed as a form of remuneration. We release exceptional scholars from some teaching or give them term-long leaves, so that they can go about their research. Similarly, we can grant time off in both of these ways for excellence in the role of educator. The time gained is available for the scholarship that might have been neglected in the face of teaching demands, or it might be used for activities that will redound to the faculty member's future role as teacher. In either case, the implementation of such a policy gives economic support to the educational function of an academic institution.[10]

To provide an undergraduate education of quality to a large and heterogeneous population is a difficult and complex business. Hard thinking is required for the establishment of educational goals in any specific institution and within any specific subject area. How such goals are pursued rests, in turn, on the competence with which a curriculum is "delivered" to those for

9. Mr. Dooley advised that when the collection plate is passed among Sunday worshipers, it is wise to toss one's coin from some distance. The resulting clang and commotion would let everyone know of the donor's generosity. But, perhaps, academic administrators will not need this exhortation to self-advertisement.

10. Boyer's recent *Scholarship Reconsidered* [1990] argues for a redefinition of scholarship so as to include aspects of teaching.

whom it is intended, an interrelated set of activities that depend much on a favorable institutional environment and support. From lofty considerations of general educational principles we are led to the details of a local curriculum, to tough decisions about the allocation of funds, and to institutional arrangements and devices that seem far removed from the classroom. Words will not do as substitutes for any link of this chain; rhetoric and exhortation cannot replace decisions, actions, or support. If education is not what educators do but what happens in the minds of students, all of the chain must hold.

POSTSCRIPT ON COHERENCE AND COMMUNITY

Writers frequently express two aspirations for undergraduate education and deeply regret that they are mostly not attained: coherence of the curriculum studied and a sense of community among those spending four undergraduate years together. Although the nostalgia that often suffuses such discussions implies that we should look to the past for a model of what might have been lost, skepticism about the outcome of such a historical inquiry and a concern for brevity suggests, instead, that we briefly explore these themes within a contemporary framework.

Advocates of a coherent curriculum want students to have an education that hangs together. A strong sense of such cohesion can derive from the fact that most of the curriculum's parts are in some significant way related to one another or are subsumed under an overarching principle that unifies its components. The educational payoff of a coherent curriculum is that students come to understand the connections or theme that convert a diversity of curricular parts into a whole. It is the job of texts and teachers to make such relationships visible, but they must be there to be pointed out in the first place.

The parts of a two-year course sequence of the history of Western Europe, from the decline of Rome to the end of the Third Reich, for example, are significantly connected to each other, with many relationships certain to be brought out in the course of instruction. On the other hand, the components of a group of courses aimed at teaching how to design a bridge differ considerably from each other, while their overarching, unifying purpose nevertheless remains manifest. But without making unpalatable assumptions, we cannot extrapolate from the coherence of such partial curricula— including that of a well-designed major—to the entire undergraduate curriculum. For if the components of the whole curriculum are to be significantly interconnected, the glue of a powerful synthetic philosophy would be required—like that of Thomas Aquinas, Hegel, or Marx—to determine what belongs to the curriculum and why. Where a curriculum's coherence is to depend on an overarching, unifying principle, the most likely candidate is an a priori conception of what every educated person must know. In either case, some doctrine must shape the curriculum in such a way that the relationships among its parts are to be found within the curriculum. Teachers must do some pointing, either by showing how things cohere in a Thomistic, Hegelian, or Marxist world view, or by elucidating why it matters

155

that every educated person master those particular curricular components. To learn is in part to see those connections.[1]

But because such systematic curricular coherence depends upon doctrinal presuppositions, it is attainable only in certain highly sectarian contexts and can hardly serve as a general goal. Accordingly, those who regret the absence of systematic connectedness in the curriculum—perhaps without being fully aware that it exacts the price of doctrinal assumptions—might do well to attend to another way in which one might speak of curricular coherence. For after all, we can turn around and observe that in a piecemeal way virtually all of the components of any given curriculum are related to all the others in a myriad of different ways—some of them significant, many quite trivial. This truism, that an indefinitely large number of relationships are there to be discerned as linking topics and subjects studied, serves as the basis of a pluralistic conception of coherence that assigns quite different roles to students and teachers.

Given the pervasiveness of relationships, abstract and concrete, there is no escaping from the tasks of discerning connections, making links, and selecting useful affinities from among the many inconsequential ones. Indeed, these activities are a part of what makes learning cumulative, where the stuff of a curriculum studied in school functions as a sample of the stuff that life serves up as we experience it. For we are constantly required to assimilate (passively) and deal with (actively) new information, new experiences, new tasks, and new obligations. Our ability to stay afloat among those oncoming waves is importantly dependent on a perspicacity that sees relationships between what has already been learned and the novel, and on a capacity to assimilate by building on already existing foundations.

Coherence, here, is essentially a power of the mind to be developed and honed, rather than a set of principles to be learned: an ability to look, sort, and connect. Yet just as imaginativeness is not significantly promoted by a course devoted to that goal, so there are no pedagogic shortcuts to fostering the ability to make connections. Interdisciplinary courses are often regarded as paradigms of connectedness and may therefore be too exclusively relied upon as builders of the power of coherence. But interdisciplinarity derives from a most specific context, for it constitutes an academic effort to put together what academic fields have rent asunder. It is, therefore, a more impressive example of coherence for professors than for students, since the latter are neither as familiar nor as concerned with the disciplinary boundary lines on which it depends, as are their teachers.

---

1. When modest portions of the curriculum are considered, coherence can be achieved by means of small clusters of courses some institutions offer on a variety of topics, such as historical periods (the ancient world), geographic regions (the Pacific rim), or such themes as ethnicity or modernity. Where the grouping is taken seriously (and the instructors of the different component courses talk to each other), such unifying topics generate a coherent curricular package analogous to the major.

Interdisciplinary courses, accordingly, exhibit but one type of connectedness among many; both the opportunity and the need to develop the capacity to make connections are ubiquitous in the curriculum. The way material is presented, the discussions that are encouraged, the exercises that are assigned must then all contribute to the development of the power and habit to connect and juxtapose and must hone the ability to distinguish between unimportant and significant relationships. Only if coherence as a capability is an educational goal in the entire curriculum is that power likely to gain the strength that will carry it beyond the study of the classroom and beyond the years of formal education.

A third conception of curricular coherence might simply be called biographical. We observed earlier that from a student's perspective the curricular offerings of a college even of modest size tend to be bafflingly large and varied. If, then, what is actually studied is determined largely by unexplicated rules and dogmatically presented advice, taking courses is like picking up seashells while walking along the beach: here a little white one, there a bigger grey one. Biographical coherence, by contrast, is created when what comes next makes sense to the person to whom it comes. That the succession of courses traversed by different students may all differ from each other does not prevent any one of them from possessing a kind of individual logic that makes that specific sequence intelligible to the student following it. The burden of bringing about such biographical coherence rests on the different paraeducational activities that were described earlier.

Indisputably, biographical coherence contains a significant component that is subjective, since it depends on how a menu of courses *appears* to a student and on the way in which it is related to his or her *particular* interests and goals. But the value of this form of coherence is not thereby diminished; on the contrary, a student's motivation to work hard at studying will depend significantly on an understanding of the manner in which those studies further his or her longer-range concerns, purposes, and preferences. Subjectivity, moreover, plays an important role in community, the second topic of this postscript. Indeed, when this matter is discussed, speakers often alternate freely between expressing the desirability (or regretting the absence) of a campus community and extolling the presence (or lamenting the lack) of a *sense* of community, a phrase that refers to the way people feel.

Clearly, the presence of objective features of community would not bring satisfaction if its members did not feel themselves to be a part of such a body. In the strongest sense, being such a part involves not only the sharing of beliefs and goals but such potent commonalities as property held collectively and conduct that conforms to common principles and rules. Most monasteries, as well as some other religious settlements, are such communities, and so are certain other groups joined together for political or ideological reasons. While alienation is possible even where objective features prevail, they make a *sense* of community most likely, reinforced by a size that is sufficiently modest to have the interactions of common business make most members of the community acquainted with most of their fellows.

But when we look at colleges and universities, we see that communities with objective structures that depend on homogeneity of interests and beliefs and a willingness to submit to a highly regulated life are options only for a very few denominational institutions.[2] The objective commonalities central to the academic enterprise as such—most notably the pursuit of learning by both students and faculty—constitutes at best a most heterogeneous commonality, to coin an oxymoron. This discovery is quickly made when one moves from vacuous generality toward greater specificity of what is learned and how, not to mention when one looks at the sharp differences in the degrees of commitment to that quest. As an objective bond this shared trait is thus too weak to generate much of a sense of community—another case of watery affection.

Various measures can be and are taken to bolster these links. Some are fun and games, the collegiate version of ancient Rome's bread and circuses. Others—consisting of convocations, special campus-wide lectures, and a variety of academic ceremonies and rituals—involve campus citizens more directly in activities relevant to the creation of an *academic* community. While most of these activities help, their efficacy is limited, if only because they are episodic rather than ongoing. They tend to contribute—importantly—to a community-friendly institutional tone rather than to bring about the kind of community sought.

A far more potent step toward the formation of an intellectual community is the sharing of some portion of the curriculum by the entire student body. The decision as to *what* every student should read and learn is much less important, from this vantage point, than the determination *that* all students should have a common curricular experience—provided the works read or topics taken up have the capacity to stimulate discussion among students and have the kind of fundamentality that makes them relevant to a diversity of subjects and topics subsequently studied. Where there is a significant amount of shared curricular material, and it is in some way characteristic of a particular institution, relevant interactions are likely to increase and be reinforced by a sense of distinctiveness.

But, however valuable such a catalyst for discourse may be, unless a substantial portion of the curriculum is shared during most or all of the undergraduate years, it cannot be expected to overcome powerful centrifugal forces. The size alone of many institutions and the heterogeneity of most prevent the development of bonds that would give a significant majority the

---

2. It is sometimes suggested that the campus of a past now departed did constitute an objective community in this sense. This claim seems more firmly grounded in history than the belief that what was then studied was a systematically cohering curriculum. See, for example, *Campus Life* [1990], pp. 3–5.

sense of belonging to a single community, not to mention a community linked by virtue of its academic interests.

Nevertheless, a campus need not be splintered into fragments so small and diverse that individuals, alone or with two or three friends, go about their business there like shoppers in a crowded shopping mall. Departments and programs, curriculum-related societies, and extracurricular activities bring people together who share interests and commitments at a level of specificity that can serve as an objective basis of community. Since the number of people who are associated with these units is often sufficiently small to make possible at least casual acquaintance of most with most, all campuses have the potential to achieve a plurality of units, each of which is pervaded by a sense of community.

Such potentialities, however, must be actualized; the creation of communities must be consciously posited as a goal. Only when different settings are looked upon as opportunities, will there be an impetus to provide the necessary context, support, and inducements to the leadership needed to shape and sustain a plurality of communities, in which common interest leads to collaborative and cooperative activities that foster interactions and acquaintanceship. Just because at times communities spring into being spontaneously, it cannot be assumed that a sociological law assures such an outcome whenever the requisite ingredients are juxtaposed. Upon inspection, it will undoubtedly turn out that on those occasions the needed supportive catalysts were present by chance, whereas more usually they must be provided.

Stress has been placed on the importance of communities based on goals relevant to the academic nature of the institutition, so that students benefit from the distinctive character of colleges and universities during their undergraduate years. That principle deserves emphasis but not elevation into dogma. All constructive associations are of value if they foster comradeship in a world in which it is easy to be lonely. Nor are campuses enclaves hermetically walled off from a changing world, a fact that is particularly exemplified by current efforts of higher education to serve minorities hitherto largely excluded. One corollary of the recruitment of African American students to predominantly white campuses is often commented upon with disapproval: African American students "keeping to themselves" and voluntarily promoting a segregation that laws have attempted to eliminate. On many a campus a community of African Americans has thus been formed, with many students living, eating, and spending much of their leisure time together.

The causes of this separatism are surely complex, though they undoubtedly include the fact that communities are formed not only when a group of individuals share a goal but also when they are bound by a view of their surroundings as alien or hostile. However discouraging it may be that in the waning years of the twentieth century communities based on race are still common—and at times needed for some of their members' emotional survival—it is not appropriate or helpful to direct strident sermons or coercive measures against them. For it is also true that at this late date we have barely begun to bring our population of African Americans into higher education. The achievement of such incorporation is a national necessity. But it must be recognized that the long road still ahead will inevitably consist of several stages, with the current period that began with the civil rights movement of the sixties merely an early phase. And since even where a student's primary community is grounded in the commonality of race it is not likely to be his or her sole association, the broadening experience may be an important step in the direction of a different future.

More generally, individual students will participate in a number of communities in the course of their undergraduate careers, with some considerably more central to their lives than others. Thus, except on a limited number of small campuses, most students' sense of belonging will be multiple as well. Rather than regret the absence of what may in any case not be attainable, it would seem wise to aim at shaping a campus that contains a plurality of vital communities, thriving under an institutional umbrella that sets the tone for all of them and secures their disparate flourishing by virtue of an atmosphere of civility.

REFERENCES

ACTFL Provisional Proficiency Guidelines, reprinted in *Foreign Language Proficiency in the Classroom and Beyond*, edited by Charles J. James, in conjunction with the American Council on the Teaching of Foreign Languages. Lincolnwood, IL: National Textbook Company, 1985, Appendix A, pp. 165–172.

APPLEBEE, ARTHUR N., LANGER, JUDITH A., AND MULLIS, INA V.S. *Learning to Be Literate in America: Reading, Writing, and Reasoning.* Princeton, NJ: National Assessment of Educational Progress, ETS, 1987.

ASTIN, ALEXANDER W. *Four Critical Years: Effects of College on Beliefs, Attitudes, and Knowledge.* San Francisco: Jossey-Bass, 1977.

ASTIN, ALEXANDER W. "Student Involvement: A Developmental Theory for Higher Education." *Journal of College Student Personnel 25*, July 1984, pp. 297–308.

ASTIN, ALEXANDER W. "Assessment, Value-Added, and Educational Excellence." In *Student Outcomes Assessment: What Institutions Stand to Gain,* edited by Diane F. Halpern. San Francisco: Jossey-Bass, 1987, pp. 89–107.

ATWELL, ROBERT H. "Putting College Sports in Perspective: Solutions for the Long Term." *AAHE Bulletin 40*, Feb. 1988, pp. 7–10.

BARROWS, THOMAS S., Project Director. *College Students' Knowledge and Beliefs: A Survey of Global Understanding, The Final Report of the Global Understanding Project,* Educational Testing Service. New Rochelle, NY: Change Magazine Press, 1981.

BERLAK, HAROLD. "Literacy in a Democracy: Our Responsibility as Educators and Citizens." In *Social Issues and Education: Challenge and Responsibility*, edited by Alex Molnar. Alexandria, VA: Association for Supervision and Curriculum Development, 1987.

BLACKWELL, DAVID, AND HENKIN, LEON. *Mathematics: Report of the Project 2061 Phase I Mathematics Panel.* Washington, DC: American Association for the Advancement of Science, 1989.

BLOOM, ALLAN. *The Closing of the American Mind.* New York: Simon & Schuster, 1987.

BOK, DEREK C. "Can Ethics Be Taught?" *Change 8*, Oct. 1976, pp. 26–30.

BOK, DEREK C. "On the Purposes of Undergraduate Education." *Dædalus 103*, Fall 1974, pp. 159–172.

BOWEN, H. R. *Investment in Learning: The Individual and Social Value of American Higher Education.* San Francisco: Jossey-Bass, 1977.

BOYER, ERNEST L. *College: The Undergraduate Experience in America.* New York: Harper & Row, 1987.

BOYER, ERNEST L. *Scholarship Reconsidered: Priorities of the Professoriate.* Princeton, NJ: The Carnegie Foundation for the Advancement of Teaching, 1990.

Campus Life: In Search of Community. Princeton, NJ: Carnegie Foundation for the Advancement of Teaching, 1990.

CHENEY, LYNNE V. *50 Hours: A Core Curriculum for College Students*. Washington, DC: National Endowment for the Humanities, 1989.

The Compact Edition of the Oxford English Dictionary. New York: Oxford University Press, 1971,

"Dana Award Winner's Innovations in Educating Minority Students in Math and Science Attract Nationwide Interest." *The Charles A. Dana Foundation Report 3*, Spring 1988, pp. 1–5.

DELWORTH, URSULA, HANSON, GARY R., AND ASSOCIATES. *Student Services: A Handbook for the Profession*, Second Edition. San Francisco: Jossey-Bass, 1989.

DOSSEY, JOHN A., MULLIS, INA V.S., LINDQUIST, MARY M., AND CHAMBERS, DONALD L. *The Mathematics Report Card: Are We Measuring Up?*. Princeton, NJ: National Assessment of Educational Progress, ETS, 1988.

EURICH, NELL P. *Corporate Classrooms: The Learning Business*. Princeton, NJ: Carnegie Foundation for the Advancement of Teaching, 1985.

FENTON, EDWIN. "The Implications of Lawrence Kohlberg's Research for Civic Education." In *Education for Responsible Citizenship: The Report of the National Task Force on Citizen Education*, B. Frank Brown, Director. New York: McGraw-Hill, 1977.

FLESCH, RUDOLF. *Why Johnny Can't Read—And What You Can Do About It*. New York: Harpers, 1955.

"Further Debate on Core Curricula. . . ." *Chronicle of Higher Education*, Jan. 24, 1990, p. A17.

GAMSON, ZELDA F., AND ASSOCIATES. *Liberating Education*. San Francisco: Jossey-Bass, 1984.

General Education in a Free Society: Report of the Harvard Committee. Cambridge: Harvard University Press, 1966 (first published in 1946).

GILLIGAN, CAROL. *In a Different Voice*. Cambridge: Harvard University Press, 1982.

GLASER, ROBERT. "Education and Thinking: The Role of Knowledge." *American Psychologist 39*, Feb. 1984, pp. 93–104.

GORDON, VIRGINIA P. "Origins and Purposes of the Freshman Seminar." In Upcraft, M. Lee, Gardner, John N. and Associates (Eds.), *The Freshman Year Experience: Helping Students Survive and Succeed in College*. San Francisco: Jossey-Bass, 1989, pp. 183–197.

GRAFF, GERALD. "What Should We Be Teaching When There's No 'We.' " *The Yale Journal of Criticism 1*, Spring 1988, pp. 189–211.

Great Books of the Western World, Robert Maynard Hutchins, Editor-in-Chief. Chicago: Encyclopedia Brittanica, Inc., in cooperation with the University of Chicago, 1952.

HAIRSTON, MAXINE. "The Winds of Change: Thomas Kuhn and the Revolution in the Teaching of Writing." *College Composition and Communication 33*, Feb. 1982, pp. 76–88.

The Harvard Classics, edited by Charles W. Eliot. New York: P. F. Collier & Son, 1909–1910.

HEERMANN, BARRY. *Teaching and Learning with Computers: A Guide for College Faculty and Administrators*. San Francisco: Jossey-Bass, 1988.

HIRSCH, E. D., JR. *Cultural Literacy: What Every American Needs to Know*. New York: Vintage Books, 1988.

HUTCHINGS, PAT AND MARCHESE, TED. "Watching Assessment: Questions, Stories, Prospects," *Change 22,* Sept/Oct 1990, pp. 12–38.

HYMAN, H. H., WRIGHT, C. R., AND REED, J. S. *The Enduring Effects of Education*. Chicago: University of Chicago Press, 1975.

Integrity in the College Curriculum: A Report to the Academic Community. Washington, DC: Association of American Colleges, 1985.

JOHNSTON, JOSEPH S., JR., ET AL. *Those Who Can: Undergraduate Programs to Prepare Arts and Sciences Majors for Teaching*. Washington, DC: Association of American Colleges, 1989.

KATZ, JOSEPH, AND HENRY, MILDRED. *Turning Professors into Teachers: A New Approach to Faculty Development and Student Learning*. New York: American Council on Education and Macmillan, 1988.

KATZ, JOSEPH, ET AL. *A New Vitality in General Education: Planning, Teaching, and Supporting Effective Liberal Learning by the Task Group on General Education*. Washington, DC: Association of American Colleges, 1988.

"Knight Commission Tells Presidents to Use Their Power to Reform the 'Fundamental Premises' of College Sports," *Chronicle for Higher Education,* 37, March 27, 1991, pp. A1, A33–A36.

KOHLBERG, LAWRENCE. "Moral Stages and Moralization: The Cognitive-Developmental Approach." In *Moral Development and Behavior*, edited by Thomas Lickona. New York: Holt, Rinehart and Winston, 1976, pp. 31–53.

KOZOL, JONATHAN. *Illiterate America*. New York: Anchor Press, Doubleday, 1985.

KRAMER, HOWARD C., AND GARDNER, ROBERT E. *Advising by Faculty*, Revised Edition. Washington, DC: National Education Association, 1983.

KURFISS, JOANNE G. *Critical Thinking: Theory. Research, Practice, and Possibilities*. ASHE-ERIC Higher Education Report No. 2. Washington, DC: Association for the Study of Higher Education, 1988.

Language Study for the 1980s: Reports of the MLA-ACLS Language Task Forces, edited by R. I. Brod. New York: Modern Language Association of America, 1980.

LAPCHICK, RICHARD E., AND SLAUGHTER, JOHN BROOKS. *The Rules of the Game: Ethics in College Sport*. New York: American Council on Education and Macmillan, 1989.

LEVINE, ARTHUR. *Handbook on Undergraduate Curriculum*. San Francisco: Jossey-Bass, 1978.

The Liberal Art of Science: Agenda for Action. The Report of the Project on Liberal Education and the Sciences. Washington, DC: American Association for the Advancement of Science, 1990.

Liberal Learning and the Arts and Sciences Major. Vol. 1, *The Challenge of Connecting Learning*. Vol. 2, *Reports from the Fields*. Washington, D.C.: Association of American Colleges, 1991.

LIPKING, LAWRENCE. "Competitive Reading." *The New Republic 201*, Oct. 2, 1989, pp. 28–53.

MARCHESE, TED. "After the Cheers: Is Higher Education Serving Its Student Athletes," an interview with Richard E. Lapchick. *AAHE Bulletin 42*, Feb. 1990, pp. 3–8.

McLUHAN, MARSHALL. *The Medium Is the Massage*. New York: Random House, 1967.

MILLER, JON D. "The Five Percent Problem." *American Scientist 76*, March/April 1988, p. 116.

MIROLLO, JAMES V. "Happy Birthday, Humanities A." *Columbia*, April 1987, pp. 32–38.

NEWMAN, FRANK. *Higher Education and the American Resurgence*. Princeton, NJ: Carnegie Foundation for the Advancement of Teaching, 1985.

PASSMORE, JOHN. *The Philosophy of Teaching*. London: Duckworth, 1980.

"Praxis," *Liberal Education 74*, May/June 1988, pp. 27–36.

PURKEY, WILLIAM WATSON. *Self Concept and School Achievement*. Englewood Cliffs, NJ: Prentice-Hall, 1970.

RAVITCH, DIANE, AND FINN, CHESTER E. JR. *What Do Our 17-Year-Olds Know?: A Report on the First National Assessment of History and Literature*. New York: Harper & Row, 1987.

RESNICK, DANIEL P., AND RESNICK, LAUREN B. "The Nature of Literacy: An Historical Exploration." *Harvard Educational Review 47*, August 1977, pp. 370–385.

RESNICK, LAUREN B. "Instructional Psychology." *Annual Review of Psychology 32*, 1981, pp. 659–704.

RESNICK, LAUREN B. *Education and Learning to Think*. Washington, DC: National Academy Press, 1987.

RUGGIERO, VINCENT RYAN. *Teaching Thinking Across the Curriculum*. New York: Harper & Row, 1988.

Science for All Americans: A Project 2061 Report on Literacy Goals in Science, Mathematics, and Technology. Washington DC: American Association for the Advancement of Science, 1989.

SEARLE, JOHN. "The Storm Over the University." *The New York Review of Books 37*, Dec. 6, 1990, pp. 34–42.

SEITZINGER, JANICE ARMO, AND ELLIS, DAVID. "Does Greek Life Belong? Two Roads to Community." *Educational Record 70*, Summer/Fall 1989, pp. 48–53.

SHAUGHNESSY, MINA. *Errors and Expectations*. New York: Oxford University Press, 1977.

SPERBER, MURRAY. *College Sports Inc.: The Athletic Department vs The University*. New York: Henry Holt, 1990.

STARK, JOAN S., LOWTHER, MALCOLM A., AND HAGERTY, BONNIE M. K. *Responsive Professional Education: Balancing Outcomes and Opportunities* ASHE-ERIC Higher Education Report No. 3. Washington, DC: Association for the Study of Higher Education, 1986.

STRANGE, CARNEY. "Greek Affiliation and Goals of the Academy: A Commentary." *Journal of College Student Personnel 27*, 1986, pp. 519–523.

"Summaries of 119 Proposed Changes to Be Voted On at NCAA Convention." *The Chronicle of Higher Education 27*, Nov. 21, 1990, pp. A29-A31.

The Teaching of Ethics in Higher Education: A Report by the Hastings Center. Hastings-on-Hudson, NY: Institute of Society, Ethics, and the Life Sciences, 1980.

WALVOORD, BARBARA FASSLER, AND SMITH, HOKE L. "Coaching the Process of Writing." In

Teaching Writing in All Disciplines, edited by C. Williams Griffin. San Francisco: Jossey-Bass, 1982.

WHITEHEAD, ALFRED NORTH. *The Aims of Education and Other Essays.* New York: Free Press, 1967.

The World's Greatest Literature: The Masterpieces of the World's Greatest Authors in History, Biography, Philosophy, Economics, Politics; Epic and Dramatic Literature, History of English Literature, Oriental Literature (Sacred and Profane), Orations, Essays. Sixty-one Crown Octavo Volumes. New York and London: The Co-operative Publication Society, 1900.

ZEMSKY, ROBERT. *Structure and Coherence: Measuring the Undergraduate Curriculum.* Washington, DC: Association of American Colleges, 1989.

INDEX

ISBN 0-89774-807-7

90000

9 780897 748070